Anatomy of a Massacre

Journal of the American Revolution Books highlight the latest research on new or lesser-known topics of the revolutionary era. The *Journal of the American Revolution* is an online resource and annual volume that provides educational, peer-reviewed articles by professional historians and experts in American Revolution studies.

Other Titles in the Series

The Burning of His Majesty's Schooner Gaspee:
An Attack on Crown Rule Before the American Revolution
by Steven Park

General Peter Muhlenberg: A Virginia Officer of the Continental Line
by Michael Cecere

Grand Forage 1778: The Battleground Around New York City
by Todd W. Braisted

The Invasion of Virginia 1781
by Michael Cecere

John Adams vs. Thomas Paine: Rival Plans for the New Republic
by Jett B. Connor

The Road to Concord: How Four Stolen Cannon Ignited the Revolutionary War
by J. L. Bell

Washington's War, 1779
by Benjamin Lee Huggins

A JOURNAL OF THE AMERICAN REVOLUTION BOOK

ANATOMY
OF A
MASSACRE

THE DESTRUCTION OF GNADENHUTTEN, 1782

ERIC STERNER

WESTHOLME
Yardley

Westholme Publishing, LLC
904 Edgewood Road
Yardley, Pennsylvania 19067
Visit our Web site at www.westholmepublishing.com

ISBN: 978-1-59416-351-7
Also available as an eBook.

Printed in the United States of America.

CONTENTS

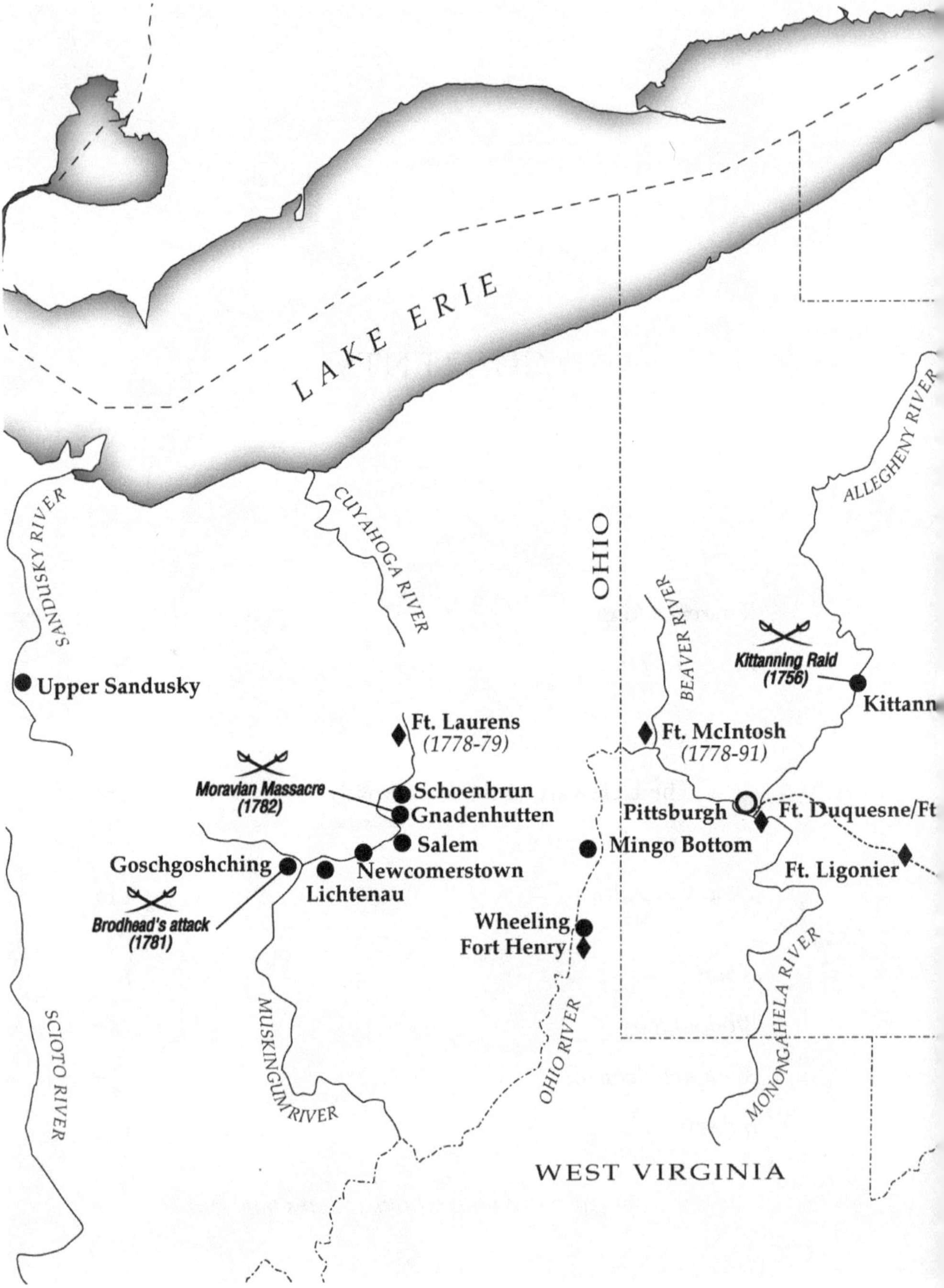

LAKE ERIE
OHIO
WEST VIRGINIA
SANDUSKY RIVER
CUYAHOGA RIVER
BEAVER RIVER
ALLEGHENY RIVER
SCIOTO RIVER
MUSKINGUM RIVER
OHIO RIVER
MONONGAHELA RIVER
Upper Sandusky
Ft. Laurens
(1778-79)
Moravian Massacre
(1782)
Schoenbrun
Gnadenhutten
Salem
Goschgoshching
Newcomerstown
Lichtenau
Brodhead's attack
(1781)
Ft. McIntosh
(1778-91)
Kittanning Raid
(1756)
Kittann
Pittsburgh
Ft. Duquesne/Ft
Mingo Bottom
Ft. Ligonier
Wheeling
Fort Henry

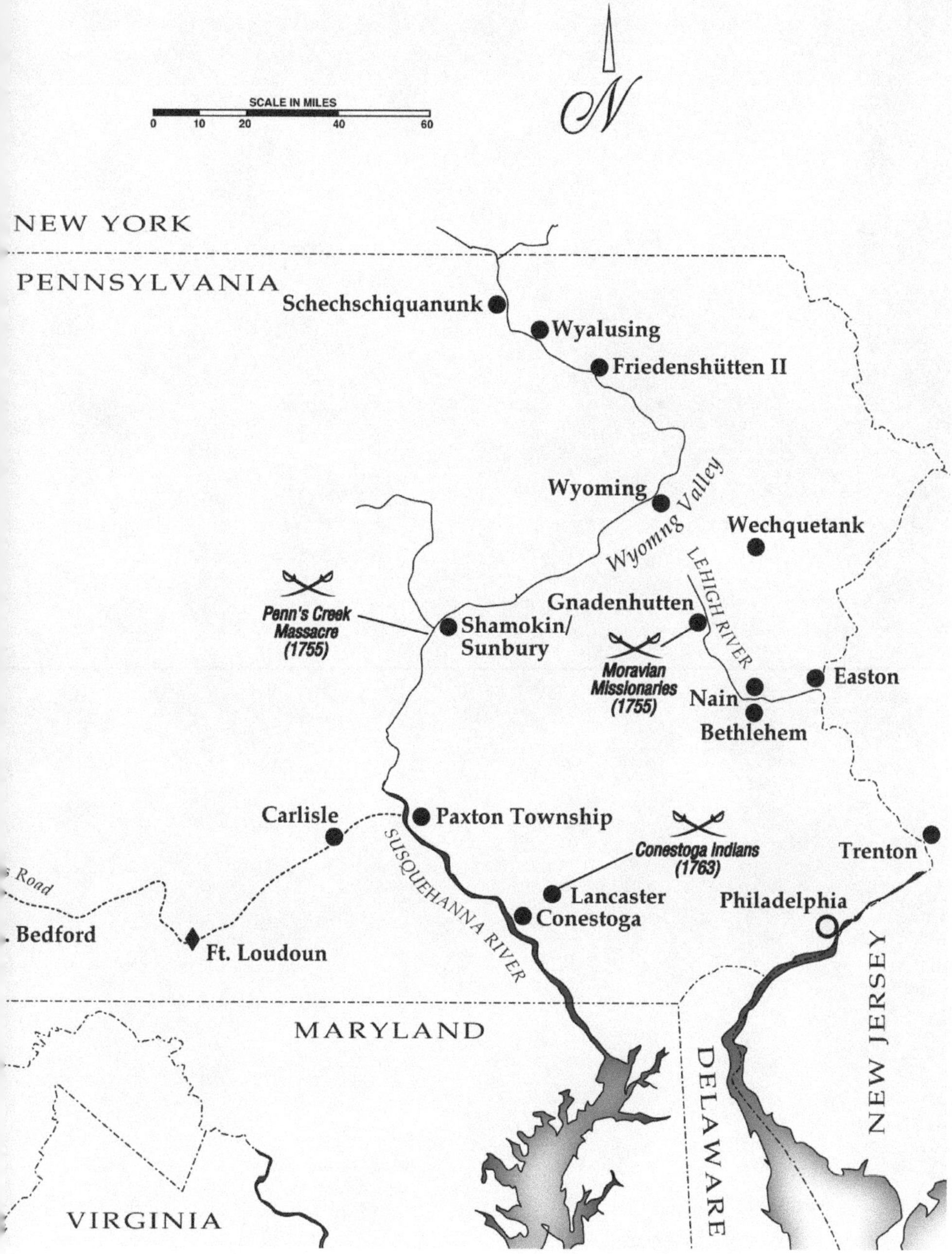
SCALE IN MILES
0
10
20
40
60
N
NEW YORK
PENNSYLVANIA
Schechschiquanunk
Wyalusing
Friedenshütten II
Wyoming
Wyoming Valley
Wechquetank
LEHIGH RIVER
Penn's Creek Massacre (1755)
Shamokin/ Sunbury
Gnadenhutten
Moravian Missionaries (1755)
Nain
Easton
Bethlehem
Carlisle
Paxton Township
SUSQUEHANNA RIVER
Conestoga Indians (1763)
Trenton
Road
Lancaster
Philadelphia
Conestoga
Bedford
Ft. Loudoun
NEW JERSEY
MARYLAND
DELAWARE
VIRGINIA

INTRODUCTION

NOVEMBER 24, 1755, UNFOLDED LIKE ANY OTHER DAY AT THE village of Gnadenhutten (pronounced Zha-NAY-den-hut-en) on Pennsylvania's Lehigh River. Gnadenhutten was a small settlement of Mohegan and Lenni Lenape, or Delaware, Indians who had adopted the Christian faith preached by missionaries from the Church of the United Brethren, themselves known as Moravians due to their geographic origins in the Austro-Hungarian Empire.[1] The river split the town in two, with the newer section east of the Lehigh and the older section on the west bank, near the Mahoning River.[2] Fading light that autumn afternoon marked the day's passing and many residents in the older part of town gathered for supper in a communal building known as the House of Pilgrims. On the east bank, a messenger from the church in Bethlehem, Brother David Zeisberger, was just setting out to visit the older side of town.

As people finished their meals, cleaned up, or ruminated about the passing day, dogs sounded the alarm at outsiders entering town. One missionary, Joachim Senseman, rose from the table and went out the back door to check on the barking and close up the Congregation House.[3] The barking set off a de facto signal for a band of Indians to attack. Throwing open doors to the House of Pilgrims, the raiders immediately fired, killing Martin Nitschmann and wounding a young boy, Joseph Sturgis.[4] The raiders pushed into the building, killing five more in the initial chaos and seizing Nitschmann's wife, Susanna.[5] In the back, Brother George Partsch leapt through a window, but his wife, Maria, did not follow. Brother Worbas, who was quarantined in a small building attached to the House of Pilgrims due to illness, found his way out of a window and also escaped, though the Indians were watching his front door.[6] The remaining missionaries and their families managed to retreat to the attic through a trap door, which they barricaded.

The moment's respite only sealed their fates. The war party, fearing nothing from the missionaries, attempted to break into the attic, firing occasionally into it from below. They failed, retreated, and instead barred the doors from the outside, then set fire to the building.[7] With the flames spreading, the senior pastor, Gottlieb Anders, rushed to an attic window and appealed for help, but the warriors only mocked him.[8] His wife, Joanna, cradled their baby daughter and prayed, knowing the end was approaching.

Despite his wounds, Sturgis pushed through an attic window to the burning roof. Burned by the flame and bleeding, he jumped and fled into the woods. Then it was Maria Partsch's turn. She followed Sturgis, jumped, and made it out safely.[9] New to town, she became lost and hid in the woods.[10] Seeing the route Sturgis and Maria Partsch had taken, George Fabricius followed. Warned perhaps by the earlier escapes, the Indians quickly shot him, seized him, drove tomahawk blows into his body, and then scalped him while the others burned alive. Fabricius had recently graduated from a European university and was studying Delaware dialects.[11] In moments, the rest of the village, houses, stables, and a barn laden with supplies for the winter followed the communal building into the conflagration. Livestock "bellowing in the stables" added their dying screams.

Crossing the river, Zeisberger encountered George Partsch and Joachim Senseman, who related part of the tale. Senseman had the misfortune of watching the House of Pilgrims burn with his wife in it. Maria Partsch reported Anna's final words were "Tis all well, dear Saviour—I expected nothing else."[12] Together, they recrossed to new town with flames spreading behind them. Although the raiding party remained in old town for much of the following day, looting and making a "feast" by the milk house, it did not cross the Lehigh in any force, giving residents there, and some from the old town, time to escape.[13]

Altogether, eleven people perished: Anna Catharine Senseman, Gottlieb and Joanna Anders with their daughter, John Gattermeyer, George Fabricius, George Schweigert, Martin Presser, John Lesly, and Martin Nitschmann. Martin's wife Susanna was captured, married off to a "brutish" Indian, and died six months later, making her the last casualty.[14]

News reached the seat of the Moravian Church at Bethlehem, Pennsylvania, after midnight, even though the glow of a burning Gnadenhutten was visible over the mountains and had already raised concern. Chaos quickly descended when hunting parties absent from Gnadenhutten returned to Bethlehem along with Zeisberger. The Christian Indians, already armed, begged the missionaries to let them pursue the raiders and retaliate. Moravian authorities at Bethlehem, however, remained true to their faith and encouraged their new converts to lay down their weapons. With that, the Christian Indians melted back into the forest.[15]

Other refugees from Gnadenhutten filtered into Bethlehem throughout the night and the next day. One, an Englishman named John Joseph Bull, who also went by the Indian name Schebosh, remained at Gnadenhutten to search for other townspeople who might have hidden during the night. Two missionaries, Martin Mack and Bernard Grube, who had been up all night with their wives on the road to Bethlehem from the vicinity of Gnadenhutten, turned around and went back to the smoldering ruins to join Schebosh in his search.[16] Among other things, they found George Fabricius's charred body protected by his faithful dog.[17]

Ironically, groups of white frontiersmen suspecting the Moravians of serving French and Iroquois interests were already gathered in Bethlehem, contemplating what to do with the Christian missionaries and Indians they viewed with suspicion in the midst of the French and Indian War. The flames at Gnadenhutten did more to dispel their concerns than all the prior protestations of the Moravian missionaries.[18] Still, none would rise to the occasion and help the Bethlehem-based community venture out to retrieve and bury the bodies. Eventually, members of the Gnadenhutten congregation returned to the village on their own while local soldiers set a guard on the town to protect those stores the raiding Indians had not destroyed.[19] They built a fort after the United Brethren abandoned the site. The identity of the attackers was never firmly established, but they were likely surrogates for the Iroquois Confederation, which had its own concerns about the missionaries and their growing Indian congregations.

On March 8, 1782, on another river, in another Gnadenhutten, another massacre struck another Christian community. Unlike the murders on the Lehigh, in which Indians killed white missionaries, American frontier settlers killed ninety-six unarmed Indians in cold blood six months after Cornwallis surrendered at Yorktown. That story has become a simple morality tale on the frontier, with the Americans cast as the racist, land-greedy expansionists and the Indians as their peaceful, innocent victims. That interpretation is too simplistic.

While the Moravian Indians, so-called after their missionaries, were generally peaceful, and a vast majority of frontier settlers were racist and land hungry, it is not as though the settlers simply decided one day to assemble and march on Indian villages to slaughter anyone they found. Instead, the collision between murderer and victim marked the culmination of conflicting forces that had buffeted the frontier for decades and which the American Revolution brought to a head.

Historian Colin Calloway notes, "Indian country was a mosaic of tribal homelands and hunting territories, where individual nations guarding their own interests created a complicated landscape of multiple foreign policies, competing agendas, and shifting strategies."[20] More than this, within each Indian nation, there were multiple clans and leaders, all of whose agendas might shift from year to year. The same can be said for France and Great Britain, whose relationships with the Native Americans changed over time. Then there are the

Americans. Each of the thirteen colonies had its own goals, as did different factions within the colony. Things did not improve during the Revolution, when the differences between each colony, the militia, frontier settlers, the Continental Congress, its Indian agents, and Continental army officials were readily apparent.

For years, that fluid situation had enabled individuals, even entire communities, to function and flourish in what historian Richard White called "the middle ground" where people living on the frontier could adjust to one another's presence and interpretation of events through a creative process of misunderstanding and distortion that created a new miasma of values.[21] In some ways, maintaining peace meant looking the other way relative to a more distant party's perspective on self-interest. Clarity was the enemy of compromise. The onset of the American Revolution pushed many unresolved frontier issues to the fore. Simply, the middle ground collapsed, factions polarized, and people had to choose sides. Those who could not, or would not, found themselves beset from all directions.

Moravian missionaries had to navigate these turbulent political, social, cultural, and economic waters. By design, the Christianity they practiced isolated them and their converts from broader white and Indian society. Yet, the missionaries and their Indian congregations could not escape either the expanding settler presence on the frontier or western Indian tribes increasingly resistant to the advance of white society. This placed them squarely on the fault line of cultural conflict, trusted by neither side. Several congregations fled the conflict zone between whites and the Native Americans in the early 1770s, but they settled in the Muskingum River Valley, soon to become the front line of conflict between western tribes and whites again. Their exodus from Pennsylvania had not solved the problem; it only moved it to the west.

This book attempts to explain the massacre in 1782 as the result of those shifting fault lines when the American Revolution reached the Muskingum River. Chapter 1 examines the Moravian experience, largely through the eyes of two key missionaries, David Zeisberger and John Heckewelder. It identifies those characteristics that separated the missions from white and Indian society, making them targets of both, and explains what brought the Moravian communities to the Muskingum River.

The second chapter explores the Native American experience from the perspective of the Lenape/Delaware nation, among whom the Moravians found allies, and highlights the strategic dilemma facing Native Americans in the Ohio Country. The collapse of French power west of the Appalachian Mountains at the end of the French and Indian War upended traditional political structures and led the Delaware to question their future, creating a spiritual void. Prophets stepped in with the answers, calling upon all Indians to renew their strength by rejecting white society. Defeat in Pontiac's War, however, suggested nativism would not secure a future for the Delaware, who began to reassess their strategy.

At about the same time, Moravian missionaries made their first forays into the Ohio Country, where they found a receptive audience and protection among the Delaware. In the early days of the American Revolution, peace seemed possible for the Delaware since both British and Continental authorities sought to maintain the neutrality of the Ohio Indians. As the war dragged on, that changed. Both the Americans and the British sought to enlist the Delaware in their causes. This contributed to a split in the tribe, as some moved farther west to align themselves with the British and others remained behind either allying themselves with the Americans or hoping to remain neutral. When the final break came, the Moravian communities were fully isolated and increasingly vulnerable.

Chapter 3 explains the white experience on the frontier as it contributed to the massacre. It offers some background on the French and Indian War and Pontiac's War, which largely set the pattern for interaction between settlers and Indians during the Revolution. The frontier was weakly governed. British, and then American, authorities were unable to protect frontier settlers from Indian raiding parties. Consequently, they developed a self-reliance and a disdain for power centers along the Atlantic coast. Frontier settlers also developed a fierce and indiscriminate racial hatred of Indians, partly in reaction to brutal Indian raids against isolated frontier settlements and homesteads. By 1779, the battle lines were drawn, which is where chapter 3 picks up the narrative thread as American authorities sought to serve their new country's interests along the Ohio River.

Chapter 4 lays out the maneuvering in the months immediately before the massacre as positions hardened among various frontier groups. When the war led some individuals and communities to choose sides, they sought to force others to make the same choice. The Moravian congregations resisted; their missionary leaders refused. Instead, the Moravians tried desperately to remain neutral by appeasing both sides. Breaking off relations with either the British and Ohio/Great Lakes Indians to the west or the Americans to the east was impossible. Gnadenhutten and other Moravian villages lay on an important trail that ran between both sides. Collectively, the villages became a crossroads of the war. Indian war parties bound for white settlements would stop at the Moravian villages, where the missionaries and their congregations were obliged to feed them. Circumstantial evidence suggested to the Americans that Indian converts had also joined the raids. At the same time, some missionaries passed on intelligence of the Indian raiding parties to Congressional agents at Pittsburgh, enabling them to better prepare for the raids. The western Indians knew that. Whereas some might see duplicity in Moravian behavior, it was actually a desperate attempt to remain neutral and true to their faith.

Ultimately, the larger, more powerful actors on the frontier could not tolerate Moravian neutrality. The western Indians moved first, forcibly relocating the Moravians from their villages to the Sandusky River in northwest Ohio in the fall of 1781. Having promised the Moravians a land of milk and honey, they delivered starvation and privation. When Moravian foraging parties returned to their old homes to salvage crops and feed themselves, the Americans attacked, resulting in one of the worst massacres of the American Revolution.

Unraveling the simple morality play the massacre has become is the focus of this book. It will explain the complexity behind the barbarity in Gnadenhutten and enhance our understanding of a sometimes-noted, but little understood, episode in the American Revolution. The Moravian Indians at Gnadenhutten were victims of that war and not just of the bloody hands that beat them to death in 1782.

A Note to the Reader

I have not corrected grammar, spelling, or punctuation errors in cited material in order to accurately reflect the source material. When possible, I refer to individual Indians by their Indian names. Whites and Indians frequently gave one another names, so an individual usually had several and responded to all of them. I tend to prefer Moravian place names. In referring to groups, I used those names that flowed best for a reader. Thus, the Lenni Lenape are referred to as the Delaware (which is how Delaware leaders referred to their nation in communicating with whites). I use "Indian" and "Native American" interchangeably to describe the indigenous people of North America, largely because they will be more familiar to modern readers. These fail to capture the complexity of the groups living on the frontier, in which whites and Indians might mix as members of the same group. Before the Revolution, "English or British" refers to subjects of the British crown, but I use the phrase "American" to refer to those in rebellion during the war and "British" to refer to those in service to the crown. One of the trickiest problems was how to refer to the Moravian communities, which comprised a polyglot of nationalities during most of the relevant period. Yet, on the frontier, they were generally known as Moravians. Indians who had converted to the church of the United Brethren were similarly known as Moravian Indians, although they might have been born Delaware, Mohican, Shawnee, Mohawk, etc. and retained ties to the nations of their birth. "Moravian Indian" is thus an oversimplification. Converts often saw themselves as members of their original tribe and the Moravian community, as might their original tribes and whites. The dominant identity could change over time depending on circumstances. Period documentation does not account well for this duality, although people at the time recognized it. The missionaries on whom we have to rely for much of the material were loath to admit that it existed, since it implied a less-than-complete acceptance of their teachings. So, when I use the term "Moravian Indian[s]" I mean those Native Americans who lived within the Christian communities at the relevant time.

One

Missionaries and Missions

TWO NAMES DOMINATE THE STORY OF THE MORAVIAN MISSIONS in America: David Zeisberger (1721-1808) and John Heckewelder (1743-1823). Both men were accomplished linguists—which made them critical interpreters—and produced the first dictionaries, grammar books, and histories of the many tribes amongst whom they preached across modern Pennsylvania, New York, and Ohio. Heckewelder wrote an extensive history of the Moravian missions, while Zeisberger kept copious diaries. Their experiences and perspectives influenced subsequent histories of the American Revolution on the frontier. That makes appreciating the two men and their reasons for being in the Western Hemisphere essential. Ironically, understanding Zeisberger and Heckewelder takes us to a fifteenth-century Czech priest and theologian, Jan Hus.

Hus was an early reformer in the Catholic Church. He was eventually tried for heresy, condemned, and burned at the stake in 1415, but not before his teaching had spread into the countryside around Prague. Because the Hapsburg dynasty fashioned itself as a pillar of the Catholic Church, Hussites kept a low profile or went underground to practice their faith. One sect settled about eighty miles from Prague in the 1450s and eventually took the name Unitas Fratrum, or "the Unity of the Brethren."[1]

The Thirty Years War exacerbated the situation and the United Brethren frayed. John Amos Comenius, the last bishop of the Bohemian Brethren eventually fled for Poland in 1628. The remaining Brethren scattered or remained behind in Bohemia and Moravia in secret.[2] When fleeing, Comenius prayed that a "hidden seed" might remain, preserving the faith that had struggled in the region since Hus's execution.[3]

Comenius preached, taught, and wrote about a simpler, more tranquil version of Christianity that did not emphasize formality, ceremony, hierarchy, or, for that matter, poverty. While in Poland, he brought greater attention to the value of education, which he argued was the road "to knowledge, to character, to fellowship with God, to eternal life." He stressed teaching in the local tongue, rather than Latin, cleanliness, moderation, learning by experience, and understanding rather than rote recitation, all useful concepts for navigating the multicultural American frontier. As important, he produced a practical grammar textbook as a methodology for learning languages.[4]

Back in Bohemia and Moravia, Comenius's "hidden seed" did not die. Rather, it planted deep roots. Congregants in the old Unitas Fratrum hid their Bibles, hymn books, and study guides while meeting in secret. Occasionally, ministers living elsewhere visited to spread the latest teaching and practices, maintaining a rough continuity and connections among the "hidden seed" and the church outside Moravia and Bohemia.[5]

Thus, the United Brethren associated improvement of the mind with closeness to God and stressed the importance of language in their schools. The church also established the practice of dispersing congregations, remaining faithful in the face of religious persecution, and communicating among dispersed members regardless of borders. The United Brethren would not be associated with a nation-state, as many churches in Europe were. These characteristics influenced the evangelical model Zeisberger and Heckewelder practiced on the American frontier.

In May 1700, Nicholas Lewis, Count of Zinzendorf and Pottendorf in Saxony, was born in Dresden. Lutheranism dominated his upbringing. Zinzendorf wrote later in life, "Already in my childhood I loved the Saviour, and had abundant communion with Him. In my fourth year, I began to seek God earnestly, and determined to become a true servant of Jesus Christ."[6] Zinzendorf received an extensive education and traveled widely, as befitted a man of his standing, which helped immunize him from the kind of harsh sectarianism many embraced in the early 1700s.

Through a series of connections, Zinzendorf met a young man who had taken the name Christian David (1690-1751).[7] David, a Moravian by descent, made multiple journeys into Moravia as a kind of evangelist, proselytizing among the United Brethren there and eventually seeking to bring them out. (Christian David himself did not practice the catechism of the United Brethren but had a special affinity for the members of the church.)[8] When the two met, David told Zinzendorf that United Brethren hidden in Moravia wanted to emigrate. Zinzendorf offered up his territory. In 1722, Christian David brought the first of several groups into Saxony. One included members of a German colony established in Moravia.[9] They spoke, wrote, read, sang, and prayed in German, making Saxony particularly appealing. They settled in a forest near Berthelsdorf, calling their new town Herrnhut.[10]

On April 11, 1721, Rosina Zeisberger gave birth to a son named David in the Moravian town of Zauchtenthal.[11] The Zeisbergers were well off and their forebears belonged to the Church of the Bohemian Brethren.[12] When David was five, his father and mother bundled him and his baby sister in hiking clothes, hoisted their backpacks, and joined a small party bound for Saxony and the new community at Herrnhut. They arrived in July 1726.[13]

The village had grown and prospered since its founding. Still, not everything was tranquil. Zinzendorf's own responsibilities to the state, his notions of a Christian community, and the multiple sects moving into the area created religious and social conflict.[14] In 1727, Zinzendorf imposed the "Manorial Injunctions and Prohibitions" throughout his territory and offered a series of voluntary "Statutes" defining his idea of a religious society.[15] Then he moved to Herrnhut and studied the United Brethren's teachings.[16] Eventually, he resolved "though I have to sacrifice my earthly possessions, my honours and my life, as long as I live I will do my utmost to see to it that this little flock of the Lord [the United Brethren] shall be preserved for Him until He come."[17] The count's relationship with the Moravians changed from tolerant and welcoming landlord to fervent champion.

Zinzendorf's rules established a pattern the Brethren eventually applied in the Western Hemisphere. All adult males would vote to establish twelve "elders" for the community, who in turn functioned as the legislative and executive branch. Elders controlled access to Herrnhut and had the authority to enforce occupational rules. They oversaw personal arrangements as well; dispensing permission to marry and requiring children of a certain age to be raised in group homes. Zinzendorf and the elders also imposed a strong work ethic and relatively strict economic rules, requiring honest labor and protectionism while prohibiting competition and usury.[18]

Herrnhut's rules produced economic success, but at the cost of leisure and entertainment. Life was strict and disciplined. According to a later church history, "for pleasure the Brethren had neither time nor taste. They worked, on the average, sixteen hours a day, allowed five hours for sleep, and spent the remaining three at meals and meetings."[19] Traveling entertainers were unwelcome.

The Zinzendorf-Herrnhut formula created a true sense of religious community. One brother wrote, "they forgot themselves, and all their longings were directed heaven-ward."[20] Another history declared, "there was great joy at Herrnhut on account of the experience of the Saviour's grace."[21] To be sure, the Moravian immigrants to Herrnhut had their theological disagreements but were largely successful in resolving them. In fact, they began to dispatch missionaries abroad to connect with other disciplines and congregations that followed, or found sympathy with, the teachings of the Unitas Fratrum.[22]

The outside world noticed the communal identity emerging at Herrnhut. Local Lutheran authorities sought to fold the Moravian Church into their disciplines with some success, but complaints still reached the Saxon Court and Austrian authorities.[23] The government finally acted in August 1733, when it prohibited new immigration from Bohemia and Moravia and Zinzendorf resigned his state position.[24] The count attempted to maneuver his way through German politics but eventually lost and was banished in 1736. Zinzendorf instead found value in missionary work, declaring, "I could not have gone to Herrnhut within the next ten years, for we have now to form a Pilgrim-Church, and to make known the Saviour to the world. Henceforward, that place will be our home, where there is most to be done for Christ."[25]

As the church turned outward, suspicion followed Moravian missionaries everywhere they went. For example, Henry Rimius, a former councilor to the king of Prussia who had settled in London, famously composed "A Candid Narrative of the Rise and Progress of the Herrnhuters" in 1753.[26] Ostensibly addressed to the archbishop of Canterbury, with an eye toward spreading opposition to United Brethren in England, Rimius wrote a diatribe against the Brethren, accusing them of picking and choosing those passages of the Bible that suited them, making their teachings simultaneously simple to understand for converts and unintelligible to skeptics, and concluding that his observations would demonstrate that "the Politics of that Society, shewing the Danger that may arise to a State from its favourite Tenets." According to Rimius, it was "the indispensable Duty of a Christian, to undeceive the World whenever it lies in his Power." He concluded "that no Government that harbours them, can be secure whilst their Leaders go on at the Rate they have done hitherto; especially when it is considered, that their Conduct abroad plainly proves, they make no Scruple, under the Cloke of Religion and Liberty of Conscience, to attempt any Thing that suits their Designs."[27] That pattern of suspicion from outsiders followed the United Brethren to America.

In 1736, the Herrnhuters dispatched a small group of families to James Ogelthorpe's new colony of Georgia under the leadership of Augustus Gottlieb Spangeberg. The Zeisbergers followed in a second group, leaving their fourteen-year-old son, David, behind with his sister and younger brother.[28]

Young Zeisberger's time at Herrnhut also came to an end. He followed Zinzendorf to Heerendyk, Holland, taking a job as an errand boy for local merchants and attending a school that specialized in corporal punishment and a curriculum far inferior to Herrnhut's.[29] Accusations of thievery led the young man and a friend to flee to London, seek an audience with Ogelthorpe, and eventually secure passage to Savannah. There, he reunited with his parents in 1738, improved his theological education under a local minister, and learned the frontier skills he would draw on for the rest of his life.[30]

In 1739, war threatened to break out between England and Spain, putting the politically aloof Moravians in an awkward position.[31] Before long, tensions with the locals led the Brethren to move to Pennsylvania, eventually founding a new community on the Lehigh River, roughly seventy miles north-northwest of Philadelphia. Zinzendorf visited the settlement in 1741 to celebrate Christmas and named it Bethlehem.[32] At the time, it was little more than a large log house with a gabled attic and attached stable.[33]

Bethlehem became a "base" from which the externally focused church could conduct its missionary work, dispatching missionaries throughout New York and New England.[34] The process did not go well. Whites and Native Americans often resented the spread of Moravian influence, which undermined existing social, economic, and political relations. Shekomeko, a Mahican-dominated Indian village on the border between New York and Connecticut predated the Moravians. When the United Brethren dispatched Christian Henry Rauch to the area, he found it dominated by Indians who lived "day to day in a state of intoxication" and the subject of frequent ire from their white neighbors, who no doubt had provided the alcohol.[35] Initially, the Mahicans listened, but then they laughed at Rauch. His response was to visit them daily in their huts "representing to them the total depravity of their hearts, and their blindness to spiritual things, extolling the grace of God revealed in Christ Jesus, and the full atonement by him, as the only way by which they might be saved from perdition."[36] Not only did the Indians resent Rauch, whites started to object and sought to counter Rauch's teachings among the Indians by getting them drunk and telling them that the missionary intended to deceive them and carry some off as slaves. White efforts to undermine the Moravian mission were often successful and Rauch reported one Indian chased him with a hatchet.[37] The Moravians interpreted this cultural clash through the lens of good and evil; they treated resistance to their efforts as the work of the devil. Rauch reported, "it appears as if the devil had strongly fortified his kingdom amongst them, and shut out every good impression."[38]

The missionary persisted and by the end of 1742 had baptized twenty-nine Indians in the area.[39] The Moravians had similar success among the Wampanoag tribe in Connecticut. White opposition only intensified. According to John Heckewelder:

> their white neighbours began to trouble, and even to persecute them. . . . Now that it was manifest that a number of them [the Indians] had embraced Christianity, and lead a Christian life, they [the whites] would not permit them to enjoy Christian privileges; every device was resorted to, to have these missionaries banished out of the country.—The loss the whites sustained in not having these Indians in their interest and under controul as formerly, when they were accustomed to take unlawful liberties and advantages of them, by defrauding them of their just due for labour, by imposing liquour upon them, thereby encouraging intoxication for the sake of gain, was considered by them as a serious loss; added to this, the Indian converts would frequently detect and reprimand offenders, which these white men could not relish; and ascribing the cause of the change in the life and morals of those Indians, to the missionaries, they sought by every stratagem to get rid of them, and some even offered liquour to any Indian that would kill them."[40]

Local whites charged the missionaries with disaffection from the governments of New York and Connecticut. Consequently, civil and religious authorities harassed the missionaries and moved them from place to place for examination. In the winter of 1744–1745 authorities prohibited missionaries from holding meetings at Shekomeko and ordered them to appear at Poughkeepsie. Charges ranged from being closet Catholics to spying for France. Henry Rimius would have been proud of his colonial cousins.

Zeisberger experienced this personally en route to the Iroquois League/Six Nations as a member of a two-man team with Christian Frederick Post. They lacked passes from the New York colony to travel among Indians. On the way to the Mohawk in 1745, local authorities in Albany arrested and jailed them, accusing the missionaries of having "treacherous views."[41] The mayor even threatened to have them whipped should they reappear without a pass.[42] They were eventually sent to New York, charged with refusing to swear an oath of allegiance to King George. There, Governor George Clinton and his council examined both. The interrogation reveals qualities in Zeisberger that he would demonstrate throughout his life and is worth reviewing at length.

In New York, the missionaries were separated for questioning and Zeisberger went first. The council established his place of birth and the circumstances of his arrival in the colonies. Then it proceeded more directly to the church's intentions and motivations.

Council: "How far up did you go into the country?"
Zeisberger: "As far as Canajoharie."
Council: "Who sent you thither?"
Zeisberger: "Our Church."
Council: "What church is that?"
Zeisberger: "The Protestant Church of the United Brethren."
Council: "Do you all do what she commands you?"
Zeisberger: "With our whole heart!"
Council: "But if she should command you to hang yourselves, or to go among the Indians and stir them up against white people, would you obey in this?"
Zeisberger: "No, I can assure your Excellency and the whole Council that our Church never had any such designs."
Council: "What did she command you do to among the Indians?"
Zeisberger: "To learn their language."
Council: "Can you learn the language so soon?"
Zeisberger: "I have already learned somewhat of it in Pennsylvania, and I went up to improve myself."
Council: "What use will you make of this language? What is your

design when you have perfected yourself in it? You must certainly have a reason for learning it."

Zeisberger: "We hope to get liberty to preach among the Indians the Gospel of our crucified Saviour, and to declare to them what we have personally experienced of His grace in our hearts."

Council: "Did you preach while you were among them now?"

Zeisberger: "No, I had no design to preach, but only to learn their language."

Council: "Were you not at William's Fort? Why did you not stay there?"

Zeisberger: "We were there, but finding no Indians, as they had all gone hunting, we went further."

Council: "But their wives and children were at home; you could have learned of them."

Zeisberger: "That was not proper for me, being a single man."

Council: "You will give an account to your Church, when you come of home, of the condition of the country and land?"

Zeisberger: "I will. Why should I not? But we do not concern ourselves about the land; we have land enough of our own—we do not need that."

Council: "You observed how many cannon are in the fort, how many soldiers and Indians in the castle, and how many at Canajoharie?"

Zeisberger: "I was not so much as within the fort, and I did not think it worth while to count the soldiers or the Indians."

Council: "Whom do you acknowledge for your king?"

Zeisberger: "King George of England."

Council: "But when you go up among the French Indians, who is your king there?"

Zeisberger: "I never yet had any mind to go thither."

Council: "Will you and your companion swear to be faithful subjects of King George, acknowledge him as your sovereign, and abjure the Pope and his adherents?"

Zeisberger: "We own ourselves to be King George's faithful subjects; we acknowledge him as our sovereign; we can truly certify that we have no connection at all with the Pope and his adherents, and no one who knows anything of us can lay this to our charge. With regard to the oath, however, I beg leave to say that we are not inhabitants of this government, but travelers, and hope to enjoy the same privilege, which is granted in other English Colonies, of traveling unmolested without taking the oath."

Council: "You design to teach the Indians, and we must have the assurance that you will not teach them disaffection to the King."

Zeisberger: "But we have come at this time with no design to teach."

Council: "Our laws require that all travelers in this government shall swear allegiance to the King, and have a license from the Governor."

Zeisberger: "I never before this heard of such a law in any country or kingdom of the world."

Council: "Will you or will you not take the oath?"

Zeisberger: "I will not."[43]

Zeisberger's answers are short, factual, and still evasive. He did not say that he would not stir up the Indians against the whites at the direction of his church, only that he could not imagine the church issuing such an order. He dodged a question about swearing allegiance to the French king in French territory by simply stating he had no intention of going there. Yet, a few questions later, he artfully declined to adhere to a New York law requiring a gubernatorial travel pass because he was not familiar with a such a requirement in other colonies. When asked whether he would teach the Indians "disaffection" from the English king, Zeisberger replied as he had earlier: he had no intention of teaching at the moment. He left out the possibility that his intentions, or that of his church, might change. It was that kind of evasion that had driven Rimius and others to distraction in Europe. The governor's council eventually released Zeisberger and Post after fifty-one days.[44] Like so many other things about the United Brethren, their resistance to local political authority set them apart from their neighbors.

Colonial laws notwithstanding, all roads to preaching among America's Northeast Indian nations led through the Iroquois, who claimed suzerainty over many of them. The Moravians recognized and reconciled themselves to that reality, determined to build relations with the Six Nations, both to convert them and to ease the path toward converting others. Two embassies to the Iroquois, first by Zinzendorf himself and then by Bishop Spangenberg, advanced the cause, earning a wampum belt that functioned as both a symbol of good relations and a kind of pass to move about in Iroquois territory. Spangenberg in particular wanted to relocate the early mission at Shekomeko to Iroquois territory in the Wyoming Valley, where it might find relief from harassment by white neighbors.[45] However, he did not consult the Mahicans at Shekomeko about their relocation. They refused to go and instead founded small villages closer to Bethlehem. Those became Friedenshutten and Gnadenhutten. Follow-up meetings with the Iroquois in 1749 and 1750 resulted in permission for several missionaries to travel among the Six Nations to learn their languages but explicitly not to proselytize.[46] Of course, that was the Moravians' ultimate goal. In 1752, Spangenberg told Zeisberger, who had spent the prior years living and traveling amongst the Six Nations, that he was not to reveal these intentions to the Iroquois.[47] In other words, the United Brethren were not above duplicity.

In the meantime, Bethlehem and the nearby mission villages at Friedenshutten and Gnadenhutten flourished. Things were not well farther north. Zeisberger noted starvation stalking the land, particularly in the Wyoming Valley. As it does elsewhere, hunger produced refugees and the church took up their cause by providing relief.[48] This migration had several affects. It weakened the Wyoming Valley as a buffer between the Six Nations and whites; demonstrated that the Moravians had something practical to offer, namely food security; gave missionaries greater opportunity to proselytize among Indian nations subordinate to the Iroquois; and increased the flow of Indians toward the edge of white society.

Taken together, these things slowly changed the balance of power on the Pennsylvania frontier. The Moravians, by drawing the Nanticoke, Delaware, and Shawnee away from the Six Nations became a de facto, albeit unintentional, threat to Iroquois power in Pennsylvania. The Six Nations had to address the problem. In 1753, a delegation of Nanticoke, Delaware, and Mahican Indians arrived at Bethlehem asking to relocate the swelling population at Gnadenhutten, many of whom were Delaware or Nanticoke, to the Wyoming Valley, so recently emptied by hunger.[49] The Moravians put them off, but the question would not die.

Early in their missionary work, the Moravians converted two men critical to events in the 1750s: Teedyuscung, a Delaware, and Shabosh, a Mahican. Both men played important roles in bringing individuals from their nations into the Moravian fold. However, as the populations at Gnadenhutten expanded, they took up the cause of relocating to the Wyoming Valley, even attracting some followers who left with them. Both men had risen in the esteem of their Indian nations and could expect to exert greater authority the farther away from Moravian influence they moved.[50] Over time, the demands for the Delaware and Mahicans at Gnadenhutten to move to the Wyoming Valley would grow into ominous threats, reportedly from the Iroquois Council itself.[51]

Everything changed on the American frontier when competing claims between the French and English over the Ohio River Valley far to the west exploded into the French and Indian War, followed closely by Pontiac's War. Tensions had been building for years, but they had not significantly affected the Moravian communities. Braddock's 1755 defeat changed the strategic environment in which the Moravians had enjoyed their earlier successes.

While the English and French made their opening moves, Zeisberger returned to the Iroquois council fires at Onondaga, where he was welcomed. This time, he openly confessed his desire and intention to preach the gospel.[52] He stayed the better part of a year and returned to Bethlehem in June 1755, just as the frontier collapsed into spasms of widespread violence. The following month, an army largely consisting of Native American warriors and French officers defeated Major General Braddock on the banks of the Monongahela River. France had mobilized its strongest Native American allies to defend Fort Duquesne. While these included a smattering of Mingo, Delaware, and Shawnee Indians from the Ohio River Valley and Pennsylvania, more came from farther north and west: Ottawas, Wyandots, Hurons, Potawatomis, Mississaugas, and others.[53]

Braddock's defeat resulted in several Native American nations who had taken a wait-and-see approach to the conflict to side with the French. Delaware Indians, particularly those who had migrated west to the Allegheny and Muskingum Rivers, took up the proverbial hatchet and began attacking English farms and settlements on the frontier. Indians quickly struck Penn's Creek, Paxton Township, Great Cove, and Bethel Township.[54] The interest in raiding spread to those Indians who had converted to Christianity under the Moravian tutelage. Indeed, some who had followed Teedyuscung to the Wyoming Valley engaged in raids.[55] The missionaries' concern about those remaining behind led them to pay constant attention to the converts at Gnadenhutten, discouraging them from interacting with whites, purchasing shot, visiting trading posts, or going hunting, both for their own safety and to reduce temptation.[56]

In the war's early months, Moravian missionaries remained mobile, determined to move among frontier Indians, seeking to maintain the spiritual health of those who had already converted to Christianity and convert still more. Their mobility in a war zone only increased suspicions among whites who were retreating from the frontier under pressure from Indian war parties. Newspapers printed a letter allegedly written by a French officer and intercepted by colonial authorities. The letter writer asserted that the French were bound to conquer North America due to the assistance of Native Americans and Moravians.[57] The United Brethren insisted the letter was a forgery, but it still built animosity toward Bethlehem. Soon, more whites began proclaiming that the Moravians themselves were the enemy, even insisting that Bethlehem be burned to the ground.[58] (Bethlehem's leadership was forwarding news and reports of Indian affairs across the frontier to colonial authorities at Philadelphia, but this was unknown outside of Philadelphia's political elites.)[59]

The intentions of those Indians living in mission villages remained a problem throughout the war, further exacerbating tensions with whites. Indian recruiters moved among the converts, seeking more warriors to join them on raids.[60] Their successes and failures are not well known, but the recruiters and suspicious whites both remained a threat to the Christian communities, causing some internal turmoil. Despite their pacific intention and practices, the missionaries surrounded the town with a palisade as defense against both Indian raids and angry colonists. Yet, they had to live in a state of constant fear from within and without. Inside the palisade at Bethlehem, some converted Indians still argued for joining the war against the English, going so far as to threaten the chief obstacle to a warrior's path: the missionaries themselves.[61]

Understandably, first-person Moravian accounts from this period are circumspect on the topic. It is clear that some Indians left and engaged in behavior that the missionaries deplored. That comes through in how the missionaries responded to converts who had left the mission towns during the war and then sought to return at its conclusion. They were unclear, however, about the behavior of Indians who had adopted the Moravian faith, left the Christian community during the war, and then sought to return after the British victory. Most likely, they had joined the war against the English. Loskiel reported in his history of the missions that post-war returnees "were all lodged beyond the river Lecha, until they had given full proof of their true repentance and change of heart. When this was perceived, they were gladly readmitted to fellowship."[62] Loskiel further mentions that many of the returning Indians had "strayed during the troubles."[63] In 1762, word arrived that Abraham [Shabosh], who had left for the Wyoming Valley with Teedyuscung, was ill. Zeisberger visited him and preached a service. Loskiel reported, "They all listened with great attention to the Gospel; many lamented the woeful condition into which they had plunged themselves, by acting contrary to their convictions and the repeated advice of the Brethren."[64] As illness spread throughout the valley, so did the number of Native Americans repenting. Given that Teedyuscung and his followers had raided English settlements, it is likely that at least some of the deathbed confessions had to do with participation in the war.

After the 1755 massacre at Gnadenhutten, the United Brethren brought as many of their missionaries and congregants as could be found together at Bethlehem, while other frontier settlers fled to the town out of fear. The town's population grew by a third in just eight days.[65] So, the Moravians had to change their approach to life on the frontier. Missionaries could not move about the countryside as before and instead ministered to those already converted throughout New England and the refugees arriving in the areas around Bethlehem.[66] Thus, even as Indian recruiters visited the mission villages, the missionaries worked on dictionaries and grammar books of the various Indian languages and translated sermons that could be delivered, and songs that could be sung, in Native American languages. The first public service in Mahican was offered in January 1757 while portions of the Bible and several hymns were translated into Delaware dialects for various congregations.

Weak militarily and struggling to secure its frontier, Pennsylvania focused on diplomacy to secure peace with the Native American nations in eastern Pennsylvania, particularly those Delaware led by Teedyuscung, and then the western Delaware located in the Ohio River Valley. The Moravians played a role in advancing these efforts. Bishop Spangenberg participated in the development of Pennsylvania peace proposals; Zeisberger escorted a peace delegation part of the way to Iroquois territory, and a baptized Indian assistant joined the full delegation.[67] Zeisberger attended periodic peace conferences in Pennsylvania in an unofficial capacity.

Zeisberger's former New York cellmate, Christian Frederick Post, contributed to Pennsylvania's diplomatic overture to the western Delaware. Post was a misfit in the Moravian system. Born in Polish Prussia, he arrived in Pennsylvania with a group of Moravians in 1742. He spoke Mohawk, lived for over a decade with the Mahican nation, and had two Indian wives before marrying a white woman.[68] Although he associated with the Moravian Church's missionary work, he often worked freelance without a formal church appointment, going where he wanted, when he wanted.[69] During the first years of the French and Indian War, Post made his way back and forth to the Wyoming Valley, delivering messages to Teedyuscung and the Indians camped there in hopes of bringing the eastern Delaware to the negotiating table.[70]

In the summer of 1758, Pennsylvania's governor asked Post to carry messages to the western Delaware and Shawnee. He would operate under the direction of civil authority. At the time, a fraternal triumvirate of Pisquetomen, Shingas, and Tamaqua led the western Delaware, although the Iroquois declined to recognize their authority.[71] Post had the good fortune to travel with Pisquetomen, who was related to Teedyuscung. A Delaware accepted into the Moravian fold at Shamokin, baptized as Daniel, joined him.[72] (Shamokin Daniel later led raids against English farms during Pontiac's War.) Post stopped in the Wyoming Valley, where Teedyuscung tried to assert leadership of the entire Delaware nation, including those in the Ohio Valley. Traveling west, Post could not help but notice the emptiness of the lands around the Susquehanna River, where settlers had abandoned their homes and farms in the face of Indian raids. "It gave me great pain to observe many plantations deserted and laid waste; and I could not but reflect on the distress, the poor owners must be drove to, who once lived in plenty; and I prayed the Lord to restore peace and prosperity to the distressed."[73] Along the way, Post and his shrinking party detected other signs that war parties with captives had passed through.[74]

Post traveled up and down the Allegheny Valley north of Fort Duquesne to a mixed reception. In one instance, "The people of the town were much disturbed at my coming, and received me in a very rough manner. They surrounded me, with their breasts open, as if they wanted some pretence to kill me. I saw by their countenances they sought my death. Their faces were quite distorted with rage, and they went so far as to say, I should not live long."[75] Eventually, the Indians insisted that Post travel to a gathering of tribes at Fort Duquesne. Tamaqua was friendly and protective, but the reception there was decidedly chilly.[76] After several days, the French began demanding custody of Post. So, he took an opportunity to steal away from camp outside the fort's walls.[77] After following a roundabout route, staying off well-traveled paths, sleeping without fires, and hiding in bushes, Post eventually returned to Fort Augusta at Shamokin.

In October, the Six Nations and the eastern branches of the Delaware and Shawnee agreed to peace terms with Pennsylvania and New Jersey in the Treaty of Easton. Post set out to deliver the news in company with Pisquetomen and some Cayuga Indians representing the Six Nations. On the way he encouraged various Indians to visit Brigadier General John Forbes, whose campaign against Fort Duquesne involved building a new road through central Pennsylvania. The road upset many of the Indian nations on the frontier, who feared it presaged a mass movement of English settlers and land speculators into their territory.[78]

Post's second trip was as challenging as his first. He had to convince the western Delaware and their allies to accept the terms of the Treaty of Easton. While some Indians welcomed his messages of peace, others disregarded them and proposed acts of violence against him and his party. French officers also worked against him, highlighting Brigadier Forbes's approaching army as a threat. The Cayuga leaders who accompanied Post assured the western tribes that the English would drive the French off, beseeched the western nations to abandon the French, and promised that they would prevent the English from venturing beyond Fort Duquesne. By then, the French were already making preparations to abandon the fort.[79] The western Delaware faced the prospect of continuing the war without much support from their French allies. It was time for peace. Tamaqua and Shingas both attended a council meeting with Post, the former proclaiming, "Hearken, all you captains and warriors, here are our brethren, the English; I wish that you may give attention, and take notice of what they say. As it is for our good, that there may an everlasting peace be established, although there is a great deal of mischief done, if it pleaseth God to help us, we may live in peace again."[80] Post duly presented messages from the civil authorities at far-off Philadelphia and General Forbes.

The western nations debated amongst themselves, approaching Post for his thoughts. Their clear concern was that the English would settle the Ohio Valley—where the Mingoes, western Delaware, and

Shawnee lived—if the French were driven away. Pisquetomen, Shingas, and Tamaqua were increasingly willing to lead their branch of the Delaware down its own path and were careful and complete in their questions. After several days, Tamaqua finally addressed the council and indicated the Delaware would accept the terms of the Treaty of Easton. For their part, the English promised not to encroach on the Ohio Valley.[81] Separately, one of Tamaqua's chief advisors told Post that the Indians had resolved to jointly defend their hunting grounds on the Allegheny River and permit no one to settle there. He wished Post to deliver that message as well.[82] In short, an English failure to hold fast to the terms of the Treaty of Easton would promptly lead to a renewal of the war between the English and the Indians. Although the French and Indian War would continue for several years, it was largely over on the frontier. When Montreal fell in 1760, it became impossible for the French to provide trade goods to their erstwhile Indian allies and their position in the interior of North America started to collapse.

On his journey home, several Indians approached Post to inquire about preaching and indicated their desire to "hear the word of God," which they had avoided before lest it give the English an opportunity to turn them into de facto slaves. They extended an invitation for Post to return after the war and live among them. He made no promises but held out the possibility of returning for missionary work.[83]

Post eventually made good on his desire to proselytize. With the church's approval, he took a young assistant with him. John Gottlieb Ernestus Heckewelder was born in Bedford, England, in 1743. His father, David, emigrated from Moravia to Herrnhut before moving on to England. At a very young age, John attended a Moravian all-boys school. In 1754, Heckewelder's family left for the colonies but not before Zinzendorf encountered the young man and encouraged him to consider missionary work.[84]

Heckewelder attended another boy's school in Bethlehem and made slow progress, owing in large part to his lesser faculty with German.[85] He was not a native speaker, but German was the common language in Bethlehem. His parents served missions in several other towns before being sent to the Danish West Indies, where they died. Thus, at fourteen, Heckewelder was orphaned and on an academic track that would employ him in the fields before being apprenticed to a barrel maker. It was the Herrnhut system at work and Heckewelder was miserable. He recalled, "almost the only enjoyment I experienced during this period, and which tended in some degree to comfort my troubled mind, was the sight of so many Indians, who were frequently encamped near Bethlehem, and who at such times came into town for the purpose of trading."[86] The sight, and Zinzendorf's earlier words, sparked an interest in missionary work, despite the sorrow and tragedy so frequently passing through Bethlehem. Relief came in the person of Christian Frederick Post.

In 1761 Post returned to the western Delaware, who had moved to the Muskingum River Valley, farther away from the new British fort at the Forks of the Ohio, now known as Fort Pitt. He built a small cabin on the eastern tributary of the Muskingum River at a spot designated by the Delaware. (Today, this branch of the river is known as the Tuscarawas.) With the ground prepared, Post set out for Bethlehem to secure an assistant, principally to teach the children to read and write. Heckewelder, only nineteen and not prepared to be a proper missionary, fit the bill. The United Brethren agreed, and in the spring of 1762, Post and Heckewelder returned. On his westbound journey, Heckewelder noted that the countryside still had not recovered from the depredations of Indian raids: "scarcely had they passed Shippensburg, when the scene changed—the ravages committed by the Indians in that war, were now visible in almost every direction as they passed on. Farms laying waste, with stacks of chimneys standing in the midst of a heap of ashes, where the houses had been burnt down, presented a very gloomy appearance, and caused serious reflections on the fate of many of those unfortunate inhabitants, whose lot it had been to fall under the war hatchet and scalping knife."[87] They stopped at Fort Pitt, where the British officers supported their mission and provided them with some supplies, and then at the mouth of the Big Beaver River, where a Delaware leader named Koquethaqechton lived. Known as White Eyes among the English, Koquethaqechton provided them with additional supplies.

Post planned to live on the food he could raise at his cabin and hired a man in Pittsburgh to help clear three acres. This immediately caused a problem with the Delaware, who saw it as a sign of pending white encroachment. Post explained in council that he had to eat and did not wish to become a burden to the Delaware; this meant raising corn, which required large lots. Still, the Delaware were unconvinced, welcoming him as a teacher and messenger from God, but suspicious that other religious teachers who had visited them, namely French priests from Detroit, only required a small garden.[88] They noted that the French priests "without laboring hard, yet look well," and must have some other source of sustenance. Post should look to God to provide for him as those priests had, for surely God would do so. Post had little recourse but to agree to the larger garden plot that an Indian named Hopocan, Captain Pipe to the whites, personally stepped off for his use.[89] Heckewelder does not name Post's primary interrogator, but Hopocan would become the Moravians' chief tormenter among the Delaware in future years.

In the summer of 1762, Pennsylvania held another Indian conference in Lancaster and requested the presence of Post and the western Delaware. Tamaqua went, but Shingas feared he would be murdered and remained behind.[90] Originally, the elders at Bethlehem had secured a promise from Post that he would not leave Heckewelder behind. But the missionaries feared that, should they both leave, no United Brethren would be permitted to return. So, Heckewelder stayed.[91] The western Delaware clearly were still suspicious. Post left a few hymnals and books of sermons for his protégé to read but with strict instruction not to read them in front of Indians. According to Post, "The Indians are very suspicious of those white people whom they see engaged in reading and writing, especially the latter; believing that it concerns them or their territory. They say that they have been robbed of their lands by the writing of the whites."[92] Heckewelder quickly found himself destitute. His canoe, which had enabled him to fish and hunt on the river, went missing—he suspected stolen by Indian boys—and passing traders routinely robbed his garden. He visited an Indian trader's cabin on the east bank of the river but had to wade the waters and complained of often falling ill from the damp.[93] He also noticed "strangers among the real inhabitants" of a nearby Delaware village, whom he assumed were there to spy on him. He sent word back to Bethlehem via passing traders but remained in a state of abject misery for much of the summer.

Meanwhile, rumors of a new war spread along the frontier, reaching Heckewelder. One day, the local Indian trader who had helped feed the budding missionary called from across the river, telling Heckewelder to close up his cabin and join him at the trading post. The trader had been warned that an attack on Heckewelder was imminent. He kept the young man overnight then sent two men to investigate the next morning. Indeed, the cabin had been broken into and vandalized. That decided matters for the trader, who helped restore the missionary's health and prepared for his own departure. On his journey to Pittsburgh, which had grown up around Fort Pitt, he crossed paths with Post and the local Indian agent, Captain Alexander McKee, both bound for Shawnee towns. Heckewelder urged them to turn back, but the duo traveled on.[94] While Heckewelder made his way back to Pittsburgh and ultimately Bethlehem, Post and McKee saw clear signs that Indians were mobilizing for a renewal of war on the frontier. McKee, son of an Irish immigrant, had deep roots in the Shawnee nation and was safe for a time before he returned to Pittsburgh at the end of November 1762. Post, on the other hand, had to sneak away by rarely traveled trails.[95]

Pontiac's War began in earnest when the Ottawa attacked the British fort at Detroit in May 1763. It was prompted by several things. As the French and Indian War wound down in North America, the Crown economized. The British commander in the later stages of the war, General Jeffrey Amherst, saw most of his troops sent to other theaters and his resources reduced. He responded by severely curtailing the practice of giving gifts to senior Indian leaders and their Native American nations.[96] Amherst's policies caused real shortages of essential goods—notably guns, ammunition, and gunpowder.

Meanwhile, there was every sign that English settlers would continue to encroach on territories the Indians considered theirs. For example, the Delaware had already expressed concern about Forbes's army, yet the British settled in at Fort Pitt. A town grew up around it. By 1761, there were 219 men, 75 women, 38 children, and 160 buildings in Pittsburgh.[97] Farther east, Connecticut speculators pressed suspect land claims in the Wyoming Valley, even moving settlers there. Teedyuscung, who nominally had secured his followers' ability to live in the valley under the authority of the Iroquois at the last Easton conference in 1762, returned home to find the Yankees moving in.[98] The Iroquois drove them off, but the Connecticut-based Susquehanna Company was persistent and kept returning, creating a dispute not only with the Iroquois, but also with Pennsylvania. In April 1763, the entire town of Wyoming burned to the ground. Teedyuscung, by now in the final stages of alcoholism, burned to death with it while sleeping in his cabin. Suspicion fell on the land speculators, who moved in shortly thereafter.[99]

The pro-French Seneca sought to mobilize the western nations to change the situation, perhaps by recovering what the French had lost. In doing so, they came across Pontiac, likely a veteran of combat in the Ohio Valley during the French and Indian War's early years.[100] A native of the Detroit region, by 1763 he was knee-deep in mobilizing the western Indian nations to reignite the frontier war. Forts fell like clockwork west of the Appalachians, opening it up to additional attacks. The Delaware and Shawnee took the lead in attacking towns and settlers east of the mountains. Raids reached deep into Berks County, just sixty miles from Philadelphia.[101]

Pontiac's War exacerbated old threats to the Moravian community. It revived white suspicion and animosity toward the Moravian missionaries and their Indian congregations. The ground shifted suddenly as frontier ministers began equating all Indians with the Canaanites, whom God had commanded his people to destroy. The war was punishment for failing to do so.[102] Aggregating all Indians as enemies put the Moravian congregations at considerable risk. They were close to white settlements and easily reached. They had nominally foresworn violence, making them easy targets. They intermingled regularly with white people, creating new opportunities to attack them in isolation. Finally, they were economically successful and likely to hold onto land the church had acquired and which others might covet.

The Moravians sent an address to the governor affirming their abhorrence of the war and begging the governor's protection, which he granted.[103] (At the same time, belligerent Native Americans viewed missionaries as undermining the Indian way of life and saw potential recruits in their congregations.) By itself, the governor's protection would not be enough for the distant missions at Nain and Wechquetank on the Susquehanna. An early Moravian historian reported that "strange" Indians began circulating among the congregations, both to gather intelligence and to warn relatives of pending Indian attacks on the frontier. In August, a former parishioner appeared to sew discord among the congregations, warning them that whites intended to attack.[104] Soldiers later discovered him outside of town and killed him, along with his family, then threatened do the same to relations inside the mission. The missionaries and their congregations agreed to wear some signifier of their status as peaceful Indians in order to enable soldiers to distinguish them from raiding parties.[105] Meanwhile, the missions at Nain, Wechquetank, and Bethlehem continued to trade. All the traffic around the Moravian towns only raised suspicions among whites, increasing the danger to the Moravian communities. Indians had attacked a settlement eight miles from Bethlehem and killed a captain, lieutenant, several soldiers, and one civilian. The civilian's wife narrowly escaped. In the following nights, groups of white men assembled outside Nain but were apparently dissuaded from attacking the settlement. A different group of Irishmen assembled outside the mission of Wechquetank but also did not act on their intentions. Brother Grube, the local missionary, dissuaded them from attacking with both logical arguments and gifts.[106] The palisade went up again around Bethlehem and the missionaries themselves established a roll-call procedure to make sure their congregants were accounted for at all times and posted guards during services.[107] The Pennsylvania Assembly delegated several commissioners to look into the matter. In October they reported that the mission towns were indeed at risk from hostile settlers because people in the mission towns were secretly trading with hostile Indians and supplying them with arms and ammunition. They went one step further, implicating Moravian Indians directly in recent murders near Bethlehem in Northampton County. Yet, the commissioners did not embrace retaliatory or punitive raids against the mission towns.[108]

The Paxton Boys took their name from the Paxtang Presbyterian Church. They had asserted for months that the friendly Indians living on the frontier were in league with enemy Indians. They focused on the Conestogas but kept another eye on the Moravian missions, arguing that Indians residing there had also participated in frontier raids. As the Paxton Boys were conducting an unauthorized campaign against hostile Indians in October, they saw the results of an Indian massacre in the Wyoming Valley. They discovered the remains of nine men and a woman. The woman had been burned alive, after having two red-hot door hinges thrust into her hands. Men had awls pierce their eyes while their bodies were perforated by spears, arrows, and pitchforks.[109] The massacre led the militia to abandon its campaign and return home, no doubt frustrated and angry.

That fall, the Pennsylvania government summoned the Moravian Indians to Philadelphia for their own protection. They arrived in Philadelphia on November 11 to be housed at the city's barracks. Oddly, no one had informed the soldiers that the Indians were coming.[110] While the Indians waited in the street for the authorities to sort the matter out, "A dreadful mob gathered around them, deriding, reviling, and charging them with all the outrages committed by the savage, threatening to kill them on the spot, which they certainly would have done, had the Indians returned evil for evil."[111] Thus began a months-long trial of trying to find a place to hold the Christian Indians. The authorities eventually sent them to Province Island, the summer quarantine spot for smallpox outbreaks.[112] Living in quarantine huts was no guarantee of protection. Knowing this, they sought to move to New York, where British Indian Superintendent William Johnson might protect them, but New York rejected them and they were turned back in New Jersey and then sent once again to the city barracks and allowed to enter.[113]

Moravian fears were well-founded. The threat became all too clear on December 14, 1763, when the Paxton Boys rode into Conestoga Indiantown near Lancaster and brutally killed the six Conestoga Indians they found there and then burned the settlement to the ground. Local authorities quickly tracked down the remaining Conestoga Indians and took them to the Lancaster Work House, where they could theoretically be protected. The Paxton Boys followed and, on December 27, rode into town and killed the fourteen Conestoga Indians there—three married couples and their eight children.[114] The killings included scalping and dismemberment.

The Paxton Boys were not done, however, and marched on Philadelphia in early February 1764 to demand that the Moravian Indians be turned over.[115] At the barracks, near panic set in. On February 4, "Captain Schlosser came and reported to us that we should move to the second story with the soldiers, because there were no keys if the rooms should be broken into. Because the order regarding the moving of the soldiers came so late, a great confusion arose between them and our poor Indians, who were chased from one place to another, particularly when a couple shots happened outside the barracks, so that everyone got alarmed and made ready to fight. We then had our hands full with our Indians, getting them in their lodgings, and quieting them."[116] A city mobilized in its own defense and careful diplomacy from local ministers and the city fathers, including Benjamin Franklin, managed to turn the Paxton Boys back, but not before a delegation pressed into the city to "inspect" the Moravian Indians there and determine whether any had played a role in widespread frontier violence. Finding no individual suspects, the delegation eventually left the city as well.[117]

The Paxton Boys crisis was not the end of the Indians' tribulations. The city barracks, which had promised to be a refuge, became a virtual prison that locals visited to marvel at the spectacle of Indians from the frontier. At least the guards were kind.[118] The inevitable return of smallpox killed some 40 percent of the converts.[119] They were finally permitted to leave in 1765. Returning to Bethlehem was out of the question; it was not safe as white settlers had flooded the area during the war. Instead, the United Brethren moved their missions to the upper Susquehanna, deeper into Iroquois territory, and founded the new town of Friedenshutten with the condition that white traders not visit. Delaware and Mahican comprised the population. Nevertheless, the United Brethren largely abandoned their goals of converting the Iroquois.[120] Simply, it had proven too difficult a task. The French and Indian War and Pontiac's War had largely undone the Moravian missionary program in eastern Pennsylvania. The Iroquois, who had never been receptive to the idea of proselytization, were more thorough in their restrictions and the Indians among whom the Moravians had made converts were driven to the west by war, white animosity, and white land acquisition conducted in cooperation with the Iroquois. After the North American conflicts of the mid-eighteenth century, home for the United Brethren and their mission lay farther west, in the Ohio Country and, eventually, on the banks of the Muskingum River, where Post had built his first cabin and Heckewelder had undertaken his first mission.

Two

The Delaware at the Crossroads

In 1626 Peter Minuit purchased the island of Manhattan for the Dutch from local Indians for the tidy sum of $24. Minuit likely paid a band of the Lenni Lenape.[1] At the time, the Lenni Lenape occupied a vast stretch of territory centered around the Delaware and Hudson River Valleys.[2] Lenape can be translated in several ways, but most simply as "the people." In the early seventeenth century, an English sea captain entered a large bay and named it "de la Warr Bay" in honor of Virginia's governor, Sir Thomas West, Lord de la Warr. Europeans applied the name to the river at the head of the bay and then to the people living along its shores.[3] According to tradition, the Lenape accepted the name "Delaware" rather than listen to Europeans butcher the pronunciation of "Lenape."[4] No Native American nation would figure more prominently in the future of the Moravian missions during the Revolutionary War.

The Lenape lacked the kind of hierarchical political cohesion associated with Europeans. Despite the English practice of designating certain leaders "king," the Delaware did not have a centralized leadership. Indeed, the nation itself was extraordinarily diverse, fluid, and decentralized, a nation primarily in the sense of ethnicity and some common cultural elements. While their language fell into the Algonquian family, Lenape dialects were different and distinct enough that some groups could not readily understand one another.[5] Thus, the words "nation" and "tribe" imply too much organizational structure, but as we have nothing better, we often use them interchangeably.

Society was organized around villages or towns with family and kinship ties providing continuity.[6] Family relationships were matrilineal, meaning descent was traced through the female line. At marriage, a man went to live with his wife's family and became a member of her social group. Individual towns or villages generally had a leader, a sachem, who was more the head of a community than a formal political leader.[7] Particularly charismatic, wise, smart, or accomplished leaders could be elevated by attracting followers, who might defer to them or seek their counsel on matters of social importance. A distinguished family history might help would-be leaders as a mark of importance. Successful leaders were expected to work for the interests of their entire community by exercising good judgment and promoting such things as trade, wealth, health, and spiritual satisfaction. This often involved a good knowledge of tribal ritual and ceremony. Europeans tended to refer to such individuals as chiefs and think of them in the same way they viewed European political leaders. But the political authority of such Delaware leaders was less formal; these so-called chiefs often had difficulty making binding decisions on behalf of the entire tribe and were in constant contact with other "chiefs." Normally, the sachem was a political leader; during times of war or crisis, the social group would turn to a war leader.[8]

Familial ties could be aggregated, which often coincided with a particular territory. In his history of the Native Americans, John Heckewelder named three principal phratries, or divisions, in the eighteenth century: the Unamis/Turtle clan who lived along the Delaware; the Wunalachticos/Turkey clan of the coasts; and the Monseys/Munsee/Wolf clan of the highlands. More recent scholarship indicates there was a significantly larger number of groupings, but these three dominate Moravian accounts.[9]

The Iroquois rise to prominence led to their dominance over the Delaware, who lost the authority to conduct an independent policy vis-à-vis the whites, including the ability to buy and sell land.[10] The new relationship also facilitated the Penn proprietorship's purchase of land from the Indians. Rather than dealing with multiple tribes, the colony could simply deal with the Iroquois, who readily sold territory traditionally occupied by the Delaware.[11]

Many Shawnee and Delaware responded by migrating. When some Delaware communities and other eastern Indian nations moved westward in the early 1700s, their societies became part of the Ohio Country, more easily integrated with the western Indian nations and French society that dominated the Great Lakes and Mississippi basin than the English along the Atlantic coast. Relocation had the added benefit of putting more distance between those Delaware and the Iroquois, which would give them greater independence. The western nations could play the English against the French, and vice versa, beseeching each for protection from the other and demanding higher quality trade goods, lest the Indian nations be forced to side with the one European power or the other. When the French and English went to war over the Ohio Valley and the French demonstrated greater military prowess, the western Delaware sided with them, even though their nominal "superiors," the Iroquois, remained neutral or pro-British. Within months of Braddock's defeat, Shingas was one of the most feared war leaders on the frontier, raiding Virginia, Maryland, and Pennsylvania.

In 1758, Teedyuscung, the lapsed Moravian convert who still led some eastern Delaware, sought to use negotiations with the Pennsylvania government to elevate himself and secure the Wyoming Valley for his followers, regardless of the Iroquois position. His involvement in the war on the French side ran counter to Iroquois policy, but the Six Nations could not prevent it. As the French and Indian War wound down in Pennsylvania, the Iroquois decided to reassert their authority over the Delaware. At the 1758 Easton Conference, Teedyuscung tried to recover land along the Delaware River acquired by Pennsylvania in the controversial Walking Purchase of 1737, in which William Penn's sons defrauded the Delaware. Teedyuscung, who was often roaring drunk during the conference, first denied the legitimacy of the Penns' claim and then the authority of the Iroquois to agree to it. The Iroquois responded by walking out on him; they would deal with the Pennsylvanians without Teedyuscung's input. When the Delaware leader sobered up, he threw himself, and the future of his followers in eastern Pennsylvania, on the mercy of the Six Nations and the Pennsylvania government, announcing:

> Uncles, You may remember that you have placed us at Wyomink, and Shamokin, Places where Indians have lived before. Now I hear since, that you have sold that Land to our Brethren the English; let the Matter now be cleared up, in the Presence of our Brethren the English.
>
> I sit there as a Bird on a Bow; I look about, and do not know where to go; let me therefore come down upon the Ground, and make that my own by a good Deed, and I shall then have a Home for ever; for if you, my Uncles, or I die, our Brethren the English will say, they have bought it from you, and so wrong my Posterity out of it.[12]

The Easton Conference in 1762 confirmed the eastern Delaware would have no voice in determining their future in Pennsylvania.[13]

When Teedyuscung made peace in the east, he claimed to do so on behalf of all Delaware. But Shingas and Tamaqua denied his claims and explicitly told Pennsylvania's messenger, Christian Frederick Post, not to repeat them in front of the French.[14] Even as they spoke, six Delaware had joined an eastbound war party.[15] The western Delaware were integrating themselves into the Ohio Country, with different allies. Rather than isolating themselves, Tamaqua, Shingas, and another Indian leader known as "Delaware George" told Post, "we alone cannot make a peace; it would be of no significance; for, as all the Indians, from the sunrise to the sunset, are united in a body, it is necessary that the whole should join in the peace, or it can be no peace; and we can assure you, all the Indians, a great way from this, even beyond the lakes, are desirous of, and wish for a peace with the English, and have desired us, as we are the nearest of kin if we see the English incline a peace, to hold it fast."[16] The western Delaware position might well determine the strength of the western Franco-Indian alliance. Even the Ottawa, firmly allied with the French, recognized this and rejected a French plan to preemptively remove the Delaware chiefs and replace them with leaders more amenable to continuing the war.[17]

For the Moravians, Post's mission represented an opportunity to ingratiate themselves with the colonial government and open the door to proselytization. But for the western Delaware, the missionary-turned-messenger's mission was an opportunity to draw a line. The western Delaware were reconsidering their strategy and warning the English that they were taking more control over their own affairs. On Post's departure, he passed through a town of mixed Shawnee and Delaware Indians where he encountered Koquethaqechton and Bemino, known as Killbuck or John Killbuck, Sr. Both would play important roles on the Ohio frontier during the American Revolution and expressed their support for Post's continued peace efforts.[18]

Tamaqua, Shingas, Pisquetomen, and Delaware George traveled a way with Post on his return and laid out their concerns that whites, both French and English, were really fighting for possession of the Ohio Country, despite promises from both sides that they coveted no Indian land.[19] They had reasons to be suspicious. A conference with Braddock during the war's first weeks had not gone well after the general admitted that the English laid claim to the Ohio region and "No Savage Should Inherit the Land."[20] Post could only repeat the platitudes he had been sent to deliver and announce that he personally possessed no land and did not seek any. He encouraged the western Delaware to meet with the governor, who Post believed would stand by the agreement made with Teedyuscung.

Eventually, the western Delaware agreed to the Treaty of Easton. Hindsight demonstrated that the Delaware chiefs understood the Pennsylvania government's likely course of action better than Post. Brigadier General John Forbes eventually captured Fort Duquesne, renamed it Fort Pitt, and made preparations to stay. Shortly thereafter, Forbes left, leaving Colonel Henry Bouquet, George Croghan, Andrew Montour, and his army behind to reconcile with the Ohio Indian nations.

Tamaqua confirmed the Delaware intention of joining the peace and reaffirming that "he [General Forbes] should go back over the mountains; we have nothing to say to the contrary." Some English middlemen, however, muddied the water. Neither Croghan nor Montour passed this message on to Bouquet in Post's presence. Instead, they tried to enlist Post to change the Indian stance. Post approached Tamaqua and Shingas, asking if they wanted to alter their message. But they replied, "We have told them three times to leave the place and go back; but they insist upon staying here; if, therefore, they will be destroyed by the French and the Indians, we cannot help them."[21] Croghan asked Post to inform Bouquet that the Indians had changed their position, but the missionary refused until he heard it from the Indians themselves. Croghan later enlisted an assistant to approach the Indians and ask them to change their message. Again, they declined.[22] Separately, one of Tamaqua's chief advisors told Post that the Indians had resolved to jointly defend their hunting grounds on the Allegheny River and permit no one to settle there. He wished Post to deliver that message as well.[23] In short, an English failure to remain east of the Appalachians would promptly lead to a renewal of the war between the English and the Indians. So, the stage was set for another conflict. Whereas Post left the Appalachians having opened the door to missionary work, his departure coincided with a firm attempt by the Delaware to draw lines in the sand over English expansion.

European encroachment in the Hudson, Delaware, and then Susquehanna River Valleys caused considerable turmoil in Delaware society. The emigration to the Ohio, the war, the changing relationships with the English and the French, and English economic policy caused significant social dislocation. Meanwhile, the western Delaware had risen to greater prominence, largely as a result of Shingas's war-time leadership and the consolidation of the Lenape west of the Alleghenies. Such dramatic internal change made the Delaware ripe for a new direction.

Several spiritual leaders stepped into the mix, either as spurs to further cultural dislocation, symptoms of it, or both. They often mixed traditional Lenape beliefs with Christian concepts. They symbolized the Delaware's spiritual and cultural dilemma: whether to adopt or modify European value systems for the Delaware or to reject them outright and return to some purer form of what it meant to be an Indian. John Papunhank was one Munsee Delaware preaching on the Susquehanna who represented the former approach. He promoted a new concept of morality among the Delaware, which had to be followed in order for one's spirit to enter a place of "good spirits," i.e., heaven.[24] But Papunhank's followers indulged in "vices," which he confessed he was also unable to resist. Papunhank spoke of a supreme being, but reportedly upon hearing the Moravians at Nain preach about God's universal love for man and Jesus's sacrifice, he declared that was the faith he wanted to adopt. Thus, he traded in his homegrown faith and embraced Christianity.[25] Papunhank and his followers became frequent visitors to Bethlehem, but the Delaware leader would not submit to the authority of the Moravian church. Missionaries continued to suspect the sincerity of his faith, believing that he perhaps preferred the role of leader and teacher to that of penitent Christian.[26] Nevertheless, Papunhank and his congregation remained friendly toward the Pennsylvania government, joining the Moravians in Philadelphia during Pontiac's War and pledging their continued friendship, goodwill, and thanks to the governor at its conclusion.[27]

Farther west, on either the Muskingum or Cuyahoga River, another Delaware spiritual leader named Neolin emerged, preaching opposition to white society and a return to Indian traditions. It was a more confrontational approach. Neolin claimed to have had a vision of a world with no whites in it, in which Indians had direct access to heaven before the coming of Europeans. They had lost such a path when the Europeans arrived and spread vices among the Native Americans.[28] The solution was to separate from the whites, cease interaction, and return to pre-Columbian social practices. Only then could Indians find their way to the "Great Being" via his "Little Son." The parallels with Christianity were obvious and it seems Neolin mixed his spiritual nativism with Christianity in much the same way Papunhank did. As important, Neolin called on different Native American nations to stop making war on one another, a necessary step in building a common Indian identity. Neolin's message spread and other like-minded prophets cropped up. Violence was the logical outcome and Neolin knew it. Indeed, the Ottawa leader Pontiac reportedly adopted Neolin's teaching in motivating the Great Lakes tribes to launch the war named for him.[29]

Pontiac was not a commander-in-chief of Indian forces, but his charisma and leadership encouraged other tribes to follow the Ottawa in the war, each for their own reasons. In early May 1763, a large community of mixed Indian nations dominated by the Ottawa near Fort Detroit killed all the white traders and settlers outside the fort and laid siege. English forts fell like clockwork. Fort Sandusky fell to the Wyandot and Anishinabeg.[30] The Potawatomi captured Fort St. Joseph and massacred most of the garrison. Miami Indians seized Fort Miami, also killing most of the garrison. Weas, Kickapoos, and Mascoutens forced Fort Ouitanon to surrender, but they were on friendly terms with the garrison and treated it relatively kindly. Chippewa and Sauk Indians attacked Fort Michilimackinac at the junction of Lakes Huron and Michigan on June 2 and massacred the English garrison.[31] Fort Venango on the Allegheny fell in mid-June. Mingo Indians killed its garrison, burning the commander alive.[32] Most of the forts were small, isolated outposts with modest garrisons, meant more to show the flag and provide supplies to larger forces expected to move into the Illinois Country and Mississippi. But the speed with which they fell and the diversity of Indian nations involved in capturing them clearly indicated a widespread war was underway.

Word that the Ottawa and their allies had attacked across the Great Lakes territory arrived on the eastern branch of the Muskingum in late May 1763. The Delaware quickly joined the war.[33] Local leaders warned the traders who had assisted John Heckewelder during his stay on the Muskingum the year before that they must leave. Thomas

Calhoon and his men packed up their goods and set out for Pittsburgh but were attacked on the Beaver River. Only two survived.[34]

Delaware war parties quickly set their sights on isolated frontier farms and communities, resurrecting their strategy from the French and Indian War. They hoped to drive the English back across the Alleghenies by making the territories to the west of the range uninhabitable. They fell on a plantation on the Youghiogheny and killed all but three people, who escaped to Fort Pitt. Two more men were scalped at a nearby sawmill.[35] It was not initially clear to authorities at Fort Pitt who was responsible for these attacks. The garrison commander exchanged messages with Tamaqua and Shingas, who attributed them to rash young men. Intelligence also arrived that the tribes from farther west (Wyandot, Ojibwa, Miami, and Ottawa) were raiding the area.[36] Yet, warriors generally thought to be Delaware struck Fort Ligonier.[37] While the Delaware and English at Fort Pitt sized one another up, Great Lakes Indians captured Fort Le Boeuf on a tributary of the Allegheny River and Presque Isle, on the shores of Lake Erie. With that, Fort Pitt was largely isolated and Delaware Indians began raiding farther east, killing civilians in the areas of Fort Bedford on the Juniata River and Fort Cumberland on the Potomac.[38]

As the siege of Fort Pitt droned on, Delaware chiefs on good terms with its commander tried to talk the English into surrendering. Native Americans lacked the artillery needed to properly reduce a fort and could only attempt to starve a garrison out or capture it by ruse, which is how many of the British posts fell. Naturally, Fort Pitt's commander declined to surrender but sent the chiefs away with gifts of alcohol, food, handkerchiefs, and blankets. The latter were from the hospital and had been used by a man infected with smallpox. Lord Amherst, not knowing of the garrison's actions, would recommend it himself.[39] Whether from this source, or the increased interaction among Great Lakes and Ohio Valley tribes, the "gifts" correlated with a smallpox outbreak among the Ohio Valley Indians in the fall of 1763. Shingas and Pisquetoman disappear from contemporary records about this time, suggesting they may have fallen victim to the latest epidemic.

That summer of 1763, with the British position on the frontier largely reduced to Fort Detroit, Fort Pitt, and Fort Niagara, Colonel Henry Bouquet marched down the Forbes Road to relieve Fort Pitt. In early August, he was ambushed at a place called Bushy Run. Bouquet, his officers, and his army took heavy losses but managed to defeat the Indians and eventually relieved the fort. In the meantime, the war had continued to spread eastward and northward to the Susquehanna Valley, where the late Teedyuscung's son, Captain Bull, led raids throughout the region. The eastern Delaware had joined the war.[40]

When Lord Amherst was recalled, General Thomas Gage replaced him and promptly turned to Sir William Johnson, already a legendary Indian agent close to the Iroquois, for strategy. Whereas Amherst had looked down on the Iroquois, leading them to sit the war out, Johnson embraced them and enlisted them in the British cause. He turned Andrew Montour and a force of Iroquois loose in the Susquehanna Valley, where they promptly captured Captain Bull and drove most of the remaining Delaware westward.[41]

In the Ohio Valley local settlers organized volunteer militia groups while the Pennsylvania legislature dusted off militia laws from the French and Indian War and approved scalp bounties for Indian men and women. For its part, the British army aimed two columns at the Ohio Country. Colonel John Bradstreet would advance against the Shawnee on the Scioto River via Lake Erie and the Sandusky River while Colonel Bouquet would head west from Fort Pitt into the Muskingum River Valley, heart of the western Delaware.[42] With both columns advancing, Fort Detroit and Fort Pitt still in British hands, and the French declining to enter the war, the western Delaware decided to make peace. But it was not a unified or solitary decision. Reflecting the dispersed nature of political authority among the Delaware, it was a long, drawn-out process involving message exchanges and discussions with Bradstreet, Bouquet, or their representatives. After the death of a messenger, a rising Delaware war leader, Hopocan, was taken prisoner and threatened with execution if English messengers were killed while performing their duties.[43] This was the same man who had paced off Christian Frederick Post's garden on the Muskingum a few years earlier.

The Delaware managed to secure reasonable terms with Bouquet. The main sticking point was captives. James Smith accompanied Bouquet's expedition as a lieutenant in the Pennsylvania Line and reported that the Muskingum Indians delivered three hundred prisoners at the time, with more promised in the spring.[44] Bouquet reported closer to two hundred returned captives and admitted some of them were reluctant to return to white society.[45] In the meantime, the Delaware agreed that several of their chiefs would remain with the English as hostages against the return of additional white captives. By November, Bouquet was sufficiently satisfied with the Delaware and began his return to Pennsylvania, having met with Packanke of the Wolf clan, Tamaqua of the Turkey, and the brother of Netawatwees, representing the Turtle, as well as Bemino.[46] Netawatwees, also known as Newcomer, was a senior Delaware chief and had outsized influence among his fellow Delaware. Bouquet was predictably not satisfied with Netawatwees's absence and directed the chiefs present to select another leader for the Turtle people. They largely ignored him.[47] By May, the Delaware had concluded a final peace with the English under the auspices of Sir William Johnson, who even released Teedyuscung's son, Captain Bull.[48] Pontiac's war went on in the west, but peace had returned to the Ohio Valley.

Neolin's visions had not restored the Delaware way of life or ejected whites from North America. To be sure, Bouquet's expedition to the Muskingum had signified Delaware vulnerability, but the nation was far from defeated. At the same time, war had pushed more Delaware out of eastern Pennsylvania and geographically consolidated the Lenape west of the Allegheny. They might hope to build greater tribal unity in the face of future threats. For his part, Pontiac had shown the western tribes that it was possible to coordinate actions for mutual benefit against the English. The Six Nations' hold had been weakened as the Delaware moved farther away from them and found allies in the west. With that, Netawatwees led efforts to reposition the Delaware as mediators on the frontier. That role satisfied Iroquois claims of suzerainty. Netawatwees further insisted on direct dealings between Pennsylvania authorities and the Delaware; he would no longer accept Iroquois authority in such things, although he avoided an explicit break with the Six Nations. It would be a slow process, involving tactical, political shifts in the years between Pontiac's War and the outbreak of the American Revolution.[49]

Neolin eventually reconciled himself to English ways, even living in an English-style cabin. But the war nevertheless exacerbated the social and cultural turmoil among the Delaware. Neolin, for example, did not stop preaching or pressing Native Americans to stop behaving in ways he thought destructive. Reverend Charles Beatty, a Presbyterian minister exploring the region for preaching opportunities in 1766, noted:

> A serious thoughtfulness about the great affair of religion, and a diligent attention to the word preached among them, seems to prevail with a number of these poor savages . . . several came to our lodging, and sat and heard, while I told them about the bible and the great things it contains. They appeared very grave and attentive. Among these was Neolin, a young man, who used some time past to speak to his brethren, the Indians, about their wicked ways, who took great pains with them; and, so far as we can understand, was the means of reforming a number of them.[50]

New prophets arose and embraced the kind of nativism Neolin represented. Wangomen was one such leader.[51] He lived on the Upper Allegheny River, where the Moravian missionary David Zeisberger met him on an exploratory tour in 1767. On the way, Zeisberger stopped and visited with some Seneca chiefs, who already knew him by reputation. Informed he was visiting the Delaware, they warned him, "The Indians at Goschgoschunk bear a very bad character they use the worst kind of sorcery, and will not hesitate to murder you."[52] Undeterred, Zeisberger proceeded, convinced he was needed more than ever.

The settlements along the Allegheny were relatively new, founded after Pontiac's War. At first, Zeisberger was a welcome visitor and object of curiosity, but it did not last. Wangomen, whom Zeisberger identified as his chief spiritual adversary, held sway. According to the Moravian, "I have never found such heathenism in other parts of the Indian country. Here Satan has his stronghold! Here he sits upon his throne! He is worshiped by savages and carries on his work in the hearts of the children of darkness! Here God's holy name is blasphemed at their sacrificial abominations, at which they venture to take it into their unclean mouths, and to say that what they do is to His honor!"[53] Zeisberger's condemnation aside, Wangomen's argument that Indians had their own way to God found support among the younger generation.[54] Zeisberger sought to counter the notion of racial uniqueness that both Neolin and Wangomen preached, insisting in a crowded council hall that "All men, whether white or black or brown, must come to Him if they would be saved,—must feel that they are sinners, and seek forgiveness of Him."[55] The Moravian's theological refusal to distinguish among races found some purchase. Yet, when he returned in 1768, he detected even more resistance and was warned that the Iroquois did not approve of his presence.[56]

Rather than giving up his mission, Zeisberger investigated. He sought to determine for himself what the Six Nations thought of his presence on the Allegheny. Ironically, the Delaware opposed his efforts as they implied that the Six Nations exercised some authority over events on the Allegheny.[57] Nevertheless, he went into Iroquois territory and reminded the Six Nations of his strong relationships among the Iroquois leadership and the benefits of his mission work. The Iroquois assured him they had no opposition to his presence among the Delaware. Another important development occurred in the fall when Zeisberger received word from three Delaware chiefs farther west: Netawatwees of the Turtle, Amochk (whom Zeisberger called King Beaver) of the Turkey, and Packanke/Custaloga of the Wolf clan. They did not recognize Seneca claims of authority and would be glad to see Christian Indians occupy the lands around Goschgosching.[58] The message made Zeisberger's mission easier for the moment and the Indians inclined toward Christianity began to relocate their huts around his mission house.[59]

The missionaries had walked into a power struggle among the Seneca, the Six Nations, and factions of the western Delaware. Each party sought to make the other responsible for Moravian difficulties. Each had its own purposes. At least some of the Delaware opposed the Moravians because Christianity undermined their nativist message and influence within the tribe. For them, Iroquois animosity, real or simply perceived, helped. The Iroquois wanted their suzerainty over the Delaware acknowledged. Requiring their permission as a precondition for Moravian preaching among the Delaware served that purpose. For Delaware who already possessed authority, such as Netawatwees, Packanke, and Amochk, the key object was to establish their independence from the Iroquois. The critical task for them was to exercise, and be seen to exercise, ultimate authority over whether the Moravian missionaries preached among the Delaware.

Thus, the Moravians and their congregations became ping-pong balls bounced between Netawatwees, Wangomen, and the Iroquois. In trying to sort out the truth, Zeisberger put his mission in the middle of the situation and became a wild card in the political game being played on the frontier. Moravian histories, however, do not always grasp this. They tend to place the blame for their difficulties on deceitful Indians under the influence of Satan. Wangomen and his nativist breed of spirituality became a particular focus, leading the missionaries to misinterpret the situation and their impact on the Delaware. That political conflict went part and parcel with Netawatwees's rise to leadership, largely fueled by his efforts to continue Delaware consolidation.[60] Events in the east would make that easier and begin the process of relocating many of the Moravian Indian mission towns to the Ohio Valley.

Greater interaction among whites and Indians after Pontiac's War increased tensions throughout eastern Pennsylvania.[61] In 1768, the Iroquois and Sir William Johnson, Britain's Indian agent, signed the Treaty of Fort Stanwix, moving the border between whites and Indians into the Ohio Country and helping defuse the situation between the Six Nations and the English.[62] However, the cession included land occupied by Moravian converts. As was their practice, the Iroquois sold land to the English on which other, allegedly subordinate, Indian tribes lived in exchange for significant payment. Just three years after their departure from the Philadelphia city barracks, where they had lived under the threat represented by the Paxton Boys, a significant number of Moravian Indians were homeless again.[63]

In the spring of 1770, Zeisberger moved his mission to the Beaver River at Packanke's request, naming it Friedenstadt.[64] Ever since the Moravians had arrived on the Allegheny, Glickhican had kept an eye on the new community. He was a well-respected leader among the Delaware. He had been a successful war captain, served as Packanke's chief advisor, and was a widely regarded speaker at the larger Delaware council. Quick of mind, he outfoxed Jesuits at Venango through the sheer power of his rhetoric. Heckewelder reported, "This extraordinary man was, by all who knew him, both admired and dreaded, on account of his superior courage as a warrior—his talents in council—and his unequalled manner of delivering himself as a national orator, or speaker."[65] The Moravians believed he had been sent to trap them and force them out.[66]

Glickhican did what any good rhetorician does. Rather than confronting the missionaries directly and being outmaneuvered by them in the moment, he studied his adversaries. He attended services and spoke at length with different missionaries, looking for inconsistencies. But, in dealing with Zeisberger, he faced someone equally impressive. The missionary had lived and traveled throughout Europe and the colonies for decades, spending years among various Indian nations. He had faced down threats to his own life with nothing more than the power of his rhetoric, strength of his logic, understanding of Indians, and courage of his convictions. He was well-educated and well-versed in his own theology, which had been tested by everyone from German professors and colonial authorities to Indian children and Iroquois chiefs. In the end, Glickhican decided that Zeisberger's spiritual system was the fullest explanation of beliefs he was coming to on his own. Eventually, he moved into Friedenstadt and was baptized under the name Isaac.[67] Glickhican's adoption of Christianity undermined Delaware nativism, although opponents of the Moravian presence continued to rear their heads.[68]

In 1771, Zeisberger undertook his first journey to Netawatwees's capital, Gekelemukpechunk, to meet with the chief.[69] By frontier standards, it was large, consisting of a hundred houses, primarily built of logs in the European fashion. Netawatwees's house had a shingled roof, wood floor, staircase to the attic, and a stone chimney.[70] There, the missionary preached against popular nativist beliefs.[71] Netawatwees eventually invited the Moravian to settle among the Ohio Delaware. Heckewelder explained the invitation as a response to a disease outbreak among the Delaware, which Netawatwees and his counselors attributed to witchcraft. According to Heckewelder, the council on the Muskingum resolved "that by embracing Christianity, the contagion would cease. That therefore they were unanimous, that this remedy should be resorted to; and that they hereby declared, that the word of God should be received by them; and further, that whoever should oppose the measure ought to be considered an enemy to the nation."[72] But that patronizing interpretation does not capture Netawatwees's entire motivation. Surely, professions of faith would make the invitation more appealing to the Moravians. But with Friedenstadt growing and Delaware arriving from the east, the appeal of such a group coming into Netawatwees's territory was obvious. It enhanced his authority over a larger number of Delaware, continuing the process of consolidating the nation in the Ohio territory. Indeed, the invitation included the Moravian congregations in the east. Later, Netawatwees reported that the Wyandot tribe, living farther west on the Sandusky River, joined them in the invitation, promising never to sell the land out from under the Christian Delaware, as the Six Nations had done.[73] This was an offer designed to encourage immigration, not merely one to encourage the spread of the gospel and avoid epidemics.

Zeisberger finally set out for the Muskingum with the first set of families in 1772. Arriving at a pre-designated site with a spring on May 3, they quickly set about clearing land for farms and a town, which they named Schoenbrunn (Fine Spring). Their arrival coincided with food shortages throughout the Ohio Country, which Netawatwees took the opportunity to blame on an Indian shaman who had promised a plentiful bounty the year before. With that in mind, he encouraged the Delaware to listen to the Moravian preachers and visit them in their new towns.[74] He may have recalled stories of the Moravian missionaries feeding Delaware and others in the Wyoming Valley during past food shortages.[75] Over the course of the next year, a broader emigration from the Susquehanna Valley followed, often over the objections of the Six Nations.[76]

In Pennsylvania, the rules governing behavior and beliefs at mission towns had been necessarily flexible within a general framework. After all, the missionaries were often moving into established Indian towns to preach the gospel at the sufferance of the Six Nations. Conflict and animosity from whites and Indians had made it important to maintain a degree of adaptability to accommodate outsiders. On the Muskingum, however, the Moravian congregations were starting from scratch and the missionaries opted to establish a stricter code, more reminiscent of Herrnhut.

In general, the rules read like a copy of the ten commandments with a few additions: temperance, debt avoidance, deference to authority on community matters, the receipt of parental permission before marriage, monogamy, and the like. Some of the rules were designed to maintain the community's integrity and cohesiveness in the face of frontier life's temptations. The Muskingum towns would not permit anyone to live with them without the consent of their teachers. No one attending dances, sacrifices, and heathenish festivals or using witchcraft to assist hunting could reside in the community. They would not risk harboring war parties, as may have happened during the French and Indian War and Pontiac's War. Similarly, no one could go on long journeys or hunts without first informing the minister or stewards. Keeping tabs on members of the congregations had helped the ministers defend their communities against white charges that Moravian Indians were participating in raids. During the American Revolution, the missionaries would add two new rules: no man inclined to war would be permitted to live in the towns and no one would be permitted to knowingly trade with war parties, which would encourage "murder and theft."[77] The rules were publicly read every year and no one was permitted to join the community without first swearing to abide by them. Over time, the Moravian

Indians shed the outward manifestations of their tribal identities and adopted the plainer and more European appearances of their Moravian teachers.

The rules did not represent a form of isolationism. The Moravians interacted constantly with the Delaware in a mutually beneficial relationship. Zeisberger and the other missionaries frequently met with Netawatwees and his allies. Potential recruits came and went from the towns to trade, catch up with family relations, and listen to missionary preaching. As important, the Muskingum Delaware acted as a kind of shield and protector for the Moravians. For their part, the Moravians and their congregations enhanced the power of the Delaware by contributing to Netawatwees's project of consolidating the tribe and giving it greater access to resources. For example, on one occasion the Moravian towns supplemented the Delaware supply of wampum, which acted as a kind of currency and was the chief ingredient in weaving belts used to communicate important messages.[78]

The arrival of Native Americans who had accepted the Moravian brand of Christianity quickly overwhelmed Schoenbrunn. So a group set out to found a second town lower on the Muskingum, naming it Gnadenhutten.[79] In Pennsylvania, the Moravians had converted people from several different Indian nations, which had often remained segregated by tribe. The practice continued on the Muskingum. Delaware would live at Schoenbrunn, the Mahicans at Gnadenhutten.[80]

By the time the Moravians began arriving on the Muskingum, Delaware efforts at consolidation were well underway. Netawatwees and Bemino most clearly recognized that the nation would have to change its strategy to preserve the tribe's integrity and cohesiveness. They confessed as much to a minister visiting the Ohio frontier in 1772 and 1773. Reverend David Jones, pastor at a Baptist church in Freehold, New Jersey, had ruminated for years on the Bible's admonition that the word of God must be spread among all nations.[81] To that end, he undertook two journeys to the Ohio Country, first visiting the Shawnee and then the Delaware. During his travels he met Koquethaqechton and formed an opinion of the rising Delaware leader: "He was the only Indian I met with in all my travels, that seemed to have a design of accomplishing something [in the] future. He told me that he intended to be religious, and have his children educated. He saw that their way of living would not answer much longer—game grew scarce—they could not much longer pretend to live by hunting, but must farm, &c."[82]

Jones asked to meet with Netawatwees, but the chief put him off. The Baptist killed time by visiting the Moravians. Jones remarked that the town he visited was well laid out and built, with a sound chapel and organized services. Zeisberger allowed him to preach, but as the two differed theologically, Jones did not tarry, preferring his hoped-for audience with Netawatwees.[83]

Instead, Jones had lengthy conversations with Bemino over several days. Jones described him as "a sensible Indian, and uses us with part of the complaisance of a gentleman. He speaks good English, so that I conversed on the subject of preaching."[84] During their discussions, Jones learned two Presbyterian ministers had visited the Delaware some years previously. They were not welcome to stay, but their visit planted the idea that the Delaware might want to change their approach to the rest of the world.[85] With that in mind, Bemino indicated that the Turtle division, at least, wanted a minister and a schoolmaster. Jones suggested the Moravians could play both roles. Bemino's response indicated that education and Christianity were not the only things on the Delaware's mind. According to Bemino, the "Moravians did not belong to our kingdom, being from Germany, and could not save their people alive in time of war."[86] He specifically highlighted the dangers from the Paxton Boys. That experience highlighted that the United Brethren did not have political sway in Pennsylvania and their faith could offer no physical protection for Delaware communities threatened in wartime. Instead, the Delaware were raising funds to visit England and seek the king's protection.[87] They would adopt the king's faith as a means of enhancing their security. Delaware leaders even sought assistance from the Moravian towns to make this trip.[88] Jones was skeptical that the Church of England would conduct missionary work on the frontier or that the Delaware would find value in its catechism or elaborate worship services.

Jones's journal hinted at several things about the Delaware. First, they felt insecure and hoped that adopting the right kind of Christianity would improve their situation. They recognized that the Moravians could not meet this need. Second, they had given up on colonial government and sought to appeal to higher authorities. This was sound strategic judgment. The Penn government reinforced Delaware subordination to the Iroquois and drove formal land acquisitions that moved the Delaware ever farther west. Appealing to the king meant going over the proprietorship's head. There was reason to hope for success. In 1763, the king had tried to resolve border disputes, and martial conflict, between whites and Indians by proclaiming the crest of the Alleghenies as a formal dividing line. The 1763 Proclamation Line had not held but it confirmed the king's interests differed from the proprietorship's and that he was willing to rule against it. Third, the tribe remained divided over how to deal with white society. Some, like Bemino, were willing to work with whites and chart a new course for the Delaware. Others remained innately suspicious. The plan to approach the king suggests the former faction was ascendant. Fourth, Jones's visit suggested some distance between the Delaware and the Moravians. Zeisberger and his fellow missionaries might have dreams of converting the Delaware nation, but Netawatwees and his supporters, likely speaking through Bemino, were primarily interested in conversion as a means of creating security through influence. Since the Moravians could offer neither, their invitations to come to the Muskingum had more to do with attracting their congregations than any spiritual embrace.

Reverend Jones's departure coincided roughly with the outbreak of a conflict between the Shawnee and Virginia over hunting grounds south of the Ohio River. In a series of treaties between the Six Nations and colonial authorities, the border separating whites from Indians advanced westward from the Proclamation Line to the southern bank of the Ohio River, all the way to the Kentucky River. Delaware fears had all come true. A series of robberies, murders, and blood feuds between white settlers and local Indians sparked the tinder and set the frontier afire once more. By the summer of 1774, Virginia and the Shawnee were at war.[89]

Dunmore's War, named after Virginia's governor, John Murray, the Earl of Dunmore, represented a considerable danger to the Delaware and their Moravian guests, who lay roughly between the warring parties. As hostilities escalated, Netawatwees and Koquethaqechton led a peace mission to the Shawnee in an attempt to alleviate tensions. It failed.[90] They also reached out to the Cherokee in the south, whose borders with the English were similarly contested. Seeking to play the mediator, the Delaware hosted a council meeting at Gekelemukpechunk in June 1774.[91] Representatives from the Wyandot, Cherokee, Christianized Mohawk, and Shawnee nations attended. Additionally, missionaries from the Moravian towns were invited and went. Netawatwees argued for peace. When the Shawnee pressed the Delaware to join them, Koquethaqechton took the lead in rejecting the overture.[92] The Shawnee would remain generally isolated, although small groups from the other nations would join their war effort.

Unlike the Moravian Indians, the status of the Moravian missionaries was uncertain, more tolerated than enthusiastically welcomed. The Moravian Indians sought warm relations with the Delaware, but Zeisberger admitted to his diary:

> as long as we have been here we still do not know how things stand between them and us. No Chief wants to acknowledge that he has called us White Brothers here, and we have thus not yet been recognized or accepted in Indian country for the reason we are actually here. [i.e., proselytization] Presumably we have only been tolerated because they think if they drive us away our Indians will not remain either. Sooner or later they will find a suitable occasion to drive us away, which many people would like to see.[93]

At a council meeting called to decide the issue, Glickhican, known as Isaac among the Moravians, spoke for them and found a welcoming audience in Netawatwees and Koquethaqechton. When the council decided that the Moravian missionaries should stay and continue their work, Heckewelder concluded that the Delaware had collectively endorsed the Moravian presence.[94] But, the need for the council and Zeisberger's uncertainty suggest that opposition to the missionaries' presence remained and that the Delaware were far from united in their tribal leadership. Zeisberger's interpretation—that the Moravian missionaries were welcome because they brought other Delaware with them to Muskingum—was on target.

The outbreak of war between Great Britain and her colonies caught the Delaware unaware. While minutemen were squaring off against British regulars in Massachusetts, Koquethaqechton was discussing his plans to travel to England and petition the king for a permanent settlement of the Delaware's borders.[95] The trip had been in the works for years but would never come to pass. After Lexington and Concord, the Crown and the Americans scrambled for influence among Native Americans. Lord Dunmore engaged his agent, John Connolly, to call a general council of Indian nations at Pittsburgh in June 1775. The Delaware left thinking Connolly and Dunmore would assist their meeting with the king, but they wanted more than promises.[96]

Unlike the British, who pressed the Ohio Indians to side openly with the Crown, the Americans hoped only to secure Indian neutrality. The Continental Congress wanted to sponsor a second council at Fort Pitt.[97] Captain James Wood traveled throughout the Ohio Valley in the summer of 1775 arranging it. He visited the Shawnee, with whom Virginia had just concluded Dunmore's War, then the Wyandot on the Sandusky River, and returned to Fort Pitt via the Delaware and Mingo tribes.[98] In each case, he delivered the same speech on behalf of Virginia, which had also named him as a commissioner to deal with the western Indians. In particular, he focused his attention on Hokoleskwa of the Shawnee (known as Cornstalk by whites), and Koquethaqechton and Gelelemend of the Delaware. (Netawatwees had "retired" at the close of 1774. Koquethaqechton ascended to prominent tribal leadership as a past war captain. Gelelemend of the Turtle Clan, who was Bemino's son, was also called Killbuck or John Killbuck, Jr. by whites.)[99]

Wood approached the Ohio Indians as "brothers" and proposed meeting to help resolve any differences left over from Dunmore's War. Koquethaqechton responded similarly, acknowledging a friendly attitude toward the Virginians and promising to spread the Virginia address. Later, he privately approached Wood seeking a land grant from the king to protect Delaware territory and sought Wood's advice about traveling to Williamsburg. Wood acquainted the chief with the growing conflict between England and its colonies and assured Koquethaqechton that he would accompany the leader and plead his case to the Virginia assembly. According to Wood, Koquethaqechton claimed "they were all desirous of living as the White People do and under their Laws and Protection."[100]

Koquethaqechton's approach to Wood marked the evolution of Delaware strategy. While it was consistent with a desire to seek protection from higher authorities, his willingness to live as the English under their laws and protection would require a complete overhaul of the tribe's way of life. Later in 1775, he declared to the Wyandot, "I for my part will be Strong and Prevent my young men from hunting thereon [in Kentucky] for I had rather they wou'd employ themselves in planting Corn in their Own fields than that any Mischeif shou'd happen by their hunting."[101] Where Neolin had encouraged the Delaware to "be more Indian," Koquethaqechton seemed to think they needed to "be more white." It was not far from Bemino's comments to Reverend Jones. The economic success of the Moravian towns on the Muskingum may have influenced Koquethaqechton's thinking. Delaware who had adopted white ways under Moravian tutelage were not experiencing hunger or poverty.

The American-led council at Pittsburgh finally opened in October with chiefs from the Delaware, Mingo, Wyandot, and Shawnee present. The Congressional commissioners attempted to explain the political situation, noting that all thirteen colonies were now united in a "great council," the Continental Congress, and that the Indians need not deal with them individually. The commissioners wanted to bury the past and start anew with the Ohio tribes. Koquethaqechton then rose and addressed the Indians as well, telling them that messages of peace from the commissioners were welcome and that the tribes should listen to them, discuss them, and then respond in twenty-four hours.[102] The Indian reply was not forthcoming due to a dispute over who could speak for the Native Americans. The Six Nations still wanted to assert their suzerainty over the Ohio tribes, but Koquethaqechton used the debate to separate further from the Six Nations. When the council reassembled, he announced he would speak for the Wyandot, Shawnee, Tawaa, and Delaware people. He welcomed unity among the colonies and then sent a direct message to them and the Six Nations. The Wyandot, uncles to the Delaware, had laid out territorial boundaries for the Delaware and given them the land. It was now theirs and he enjoined any from moving into it.[103] For all intents and purposes, the Delaware had declared their independence. More importantly, perhaps, they had joined the Wyandot, Shawnee, and Tawaa in an alliance of Ohio tribes. He attributed much of the initiative to the Wyandot: "I now also Acquaint you that my Uncles the Wiandots have bound themselves the Shawanesee Tawaas and Delawares together and have made us as one People."[104]

Writing for posterity, John Heckewelder described the address as bold and daring, which he attributed to Delaware confidence in the promises made by the American commissioners and his commitment to peace.[105] He also suspected that the Delaware chose the moment because the member of the Iroquois Confederation most likely to oppose their independence was the Seneca, who were also most likely to wage war on the Americans. Thus, Koquethaqechton and his allies could expect American assistance to preserve the Delaware's newly declared independence from the Iroquois. In other words, the Delaware would use the Americans against the Six Nations.

But that was Heckewelder's interpretation. Koquethaqechton also sought to build unity among the Ohio Indians, whose interests increasingly coincided with those of the Delaware. By declaring Delaware independence from the Six Nations and drawing a line around Delaware land, the Six Nations could not sell it out from underneath. The chief's next task was to secure recognition of that fact from all the major powers in the area: British authorities at Detroit, the Americans at Philadelphia, and the Six Nations' council at Onondaga.

With the close of the Pittsburgh Council, Koquethaqechton shifted his focus from King George III in London and Lord Dunmore to a meeting with the Continental Congress in Philadelphia. Having already determined the Delaware needed to "live as white people," Koquethaqechton wanted help from the new American legislature to make the transition. He asked for a minister, a schoolteacher, and help shifting to an agrarian lifestyle.[106] Congress received his petition on March 16, 1776, and referred it to a committee.[107]

By April 10, the ad hoc committee considered Koquethaqechton's request and proposed acceding to it, along with making sufficient resources available from the United Colonies to provide leaders among the Ohio Valley Indians with sufficient gifts to demonstrate the Americans' goodwill. Congress promised to do its best to provide the minister, schoolteacher, and a "sober man to instruct you in agriculture. . . . These things we agree to do, brothers, at your request, and to convince you that we wish to advance your happiness, and that there may be a lasting union between us, and that, as you express it, we may become one people."[108] In short, Congress accepted Koquethaqechton's notion of treating one another as equals. Then it pulled the rug out from under him. It acknowledged Koquethaqechton's assertion at Pittsburgh that the Wyandot had granted the Delaware a large tract of land in the Ohio Country, but it did not recognize Koquethaqechton's declaration of independence from the Six Nations or his nation's title to the land it claimed. Instead, it told him, "As we are informed that your uncles, our brothers the Six Nations, claim most of those lands, we recommend it to you to obtain their approbation of this grant to you from the Wiandots in public council, and have it put on record."[109] In the competition for influence among the Native Americans, the Iroquois were simply too important for Congress to anger.

Undeterred, Koquethaqechton returned to Pittsburgh in company with George Morgan, the Continental Congress's new Indian agent. Although he owned a farm near Princeton, Morgan was an experienced frontiersman and junior partner in a trading company that connected the Ohio Valley with the Atlantic world. A member of the American Philosophical Society, he was well-educated, known amongst Congressional leaders, and committed to the American cause.[110] Morgan's instructions were four-fold: secure friendly relations between the Ohio Indians and Congress to prevent raiding, promote general peaceful relations among Indians and whites living on the frontier (which involved settling local disputes), secure intelligence of pending raids, and promote trade between Indians and the emerging American country.[111] The two arrived at the end of April to find the British were already circulating among Ohio Indians and the Iroquois to hold a peace conference at Fort Niagara; the British and Americans had resurrected the English-French competition for Indian loyalty. It was having an effect.

While Koquethaqechton was in Pittsburgh and Philadelphia, internal schisms among the Delaware grew. He had exceeded his authority at Fort Pitt and then left the tribe for six months in order to make his case to Congress. In Koquethaqechton's absence, events moved rapidly. Netawatwees received word that the Wyandot and other nations had attacked white settlements and expressed a desire to attack the Delaware, leading him to prod the Moravians to establish a third town near his capital in the hope that it would offset domestic voices for war.[112] Meanwhile, Morgan and Koquethaqechton learned from a Quaker trader that "I fear they may be led to join the other Party—they seem [agitated in] great confusion & have false reports every day."[113] The trader requested Koquethaqechton to return quickly.

Heckewelder, who remained behind with the Moravian missions while Koquethaqechton went east, named Hopocan and the Munsee/Wolf phratry as the agitators. According to the missionary, the Munsees "pretended apprehensions, that the Six Nations would resent the liberty White Eyes had taken; and made this a pretence of withdrawing themselves from the councils of the Turtle tribe. . . . Nor did the Monsey chief, Newalike, rest until he had succeeded in detaching a number of their tribe from the Christian Indians at Schoenbrun."[114] His distaste for Hopocan was even more palpable. "Captain Pipe, at the head of his tribe, was glad to see a breach made, of which White Eyes was to bear the blame. Pipe was an artful, cunning man. Ambitious and fond of power, he endeavoured to create a mistrust in the minds of individuals of the nation—persuading them to believe that their chief (White Eyes,) had entered into secret engagements with the American people, for the purpose of having their young people enslaved, while they (the chiefs) were to reap the benefit thereof, and be lords over them."[115]

It went beyond that. After the fall 1775 council at Fort Pitt, Hopocan had been charged with joining the Seneca chief Guyasuta in delivering peace messages to the western tribes. According to Guyasuta, the Delaware never showed.[116] Hopocan's political tactics were proving effective. When Koquethaqechton returned to Delaware territory, the Delaware held a council meeting in May 1776 to discuss the Congressional response to his speech the previous fall. The Moravians were of decidedly mixed thoughts about Koquethaqechton's return. The chief had gone east to secure a schoolmaster, an agricultural instructor, and a minister. The missionaries were anxious lest the preacher not be of their faith and compete with them for influence over how the gospel would be taught. They went so far as to resolve to oppose Christian preaching in Goschgosching from any other sect. They were not alone; Gelelemend, for example, had already declared he would listen to no other missionaries.[117]

Koquethaqechton did not return to the Muskingum with either a teacher or a minister. Their presence required the entire tribe's assent, indicating that the question had not been settled before the Fort Pitt conference of 1775 and that Hopocan's sewing of discord was succeeding. Moravians attended the council, which resolved nothing, but broke up for private discussions.

After the council meeting, leaders within the tribe assailed Koquethaqechton from all directions. Hopocan undermined his strategy altogether while the Moravians questioned his actions with regard to its implementation. They challenged him publicly on the matter of bringing a non-Moravian minister onto tribal territory, going so far as to make many of the same accusations as Hopocan. Zeisberger, in particular, had a rather low opinion of the leader, although Heckewelder admired him in retrospect.[118] Zeisberger recorded a visit the chief made to the new Moravian town, which they had dubbed Lichtenau.

> White Eye was very friendly and also obliging towards us, but he looked dejected and restless. He stayed here for several hours, went into the bush alone with Brothers Wilhelm and Isaac, and talked and discussed with them. From all his talking and questioning, however, you could see that he has gotten very distracted from the main concern; his thoughts were gloomy and focused on secondary issues and Projects of great undertakings he is still planning to accomplish with the Indians in order to turn them into a respected and rich people. He hopes in vain that the great people in the country will help him do this. In contrast, the Brothers and their work seem too lowly to him, to speak plainly, and he does not like poverty and baseness. . . . He complained that he had to suffer much since his return home; everyone was against him and he had to listen to almost more than he could bear.[119]

From Zeisberger's standpoint, Koquethaqechton could only realize his goals through an embrace of God's grace as interpreted by the Moravians; everything else would come afterward. Zeisberger missed the point of Koquethaqechton's strategy. Christianity was not the Indian's goal. He was trying to establish his tribe's independence from the Six Nations, earn recognition of its sovereignty from English and American authorities, and provide it with security in the face of an approaching wave of violence, the first ripples of which had already brushed up against the Ohio Country. Christianity was the means to his end and, as Bemino had told Reverend Jones in 1773, the Moravians were not the best tool. For Koquethaqechton, the Delaware needed preachers with more political sway and a relationship with those who held power in the east.

Despite the turmoil and disagreement at home, Koquethaqechton was not ready to quit. Rather than pressing the matter of independence from the Six Nations or allying with the Americans, he changed tactics, trying to build on the mediators' role. In the summer of 1776, he led a delegation west to spread an argument for peace among the western nations, in particular the Shawnee and Wyandot. The Continental Congress had requested his assistance in that task and it was in the Delaware self-interest to succeed.[120] Preserving the neutrality of the western tribes would take pressure off the Delaware to declare for either the Americans or the British, possibly ameliorating some internal divisions.

Unfortunately, Koquethaqechton's trip revealed that the western tribes were already moving into the British camp and the Delaware peace faction was more isolated than it realized. While George Morgan traveled to the Scioto to negotiate with the Shawnee and nearby Mingo, Koquethaqechton traveled west with an American delegate, William Wilson, to meet with the Wyandot and such Indians as would receive him.[121] They were forced to meet with the Wyandot at Detroit in front of Lieutenant Governor Henry Hamilton. Just as Post had delivered English messages to the Indians in front of the French, putting the Americans and the British in a room together underscored that the Indians were capable of joining either side. But Hamilton's actions were hardly diplomatic. Koquethaqechton made the customary opening speech and presented his wampum belts, stressing the importance of his peaceful message. Before the Wyandot could retreat to discuss the message, Hamilton took the wampum belts and cut them into pieces, threw them on the ground, and commanded the Delaware representatives to leave immediately. He berated the delegation as de facto Virginians—essentially, enemies of the Ohio nations—and insulted Koquethaqechton personally, threatening bodily harm if he did not depart immediately.[122] Technically, the Delaware were still mediators among the western tribes, as designated by the Six Nations. Hamilton's actions were thus rude and dismissive, which even the Wyandot should have found disconcerting.

Hamilton had reason for such behavior. The American invasion of Canada in 1775 had temporarily closed the St. Lawrence River to major shipping, reducing the amount of trade goods, including gunpowder, that the British could supply to the western tribes. When the Americans abandoned Montreal in the spring of 1776, the British were able to move supplies to the western tribes again. Hamilton enjoyed more bargaining power than the British had possessed early in the war. The western tribes needed his gunpowder, which the Americans could not offer.

The Moravian villages learned of Koquethaqechton's failed peace mission when he returned in September. Rumors quickly spread among the Delaware and Americans that a general Indian war was beginning. Reports circulated all autumn that Wyandot and Mingo war parties were crossing the Ohio to raid American settlements. Indeed, that summer, a war party had famously captured Daniel Boone's daughter, Jemima, and two other girls outside Boonesborough, Kentucky.[123] (Boone eventually rescued them.) In response, small American militia units began to cross the river as well, looking for Indian war parties, which strengthened the British argument that the Americans intended to invade.

Morgan stepped into the middle, trying to restrain militia crossing the Ohio and assuring Shawnee and Delaware leaders that the Continental Congress, at least, still desired peace. He also sought another conference. For their part, pro-peace Indian leaders sought to separate the actions of their warriors from the tribe as a whole and passed intelligence about Indian affairs in the west to American authorities.[124] Rumors flourished and spread quickly as tensions rose. By September, the mission towns on the Muskingum felt compelled to provide Indian escorts to the white missionaries moving back and forth between Indian and white territory.[125] Word eventually reached the missions that the Wyandot, for all intents and purposes, had gone to war. Zeisberger recorded, "Many Wyandot and Minque are crossing the Ohio where they are doing much harm. We heard that on one field thy killed 11 people at one time."[126] Inevitably, war parties started moving in and around Delaware villages and the Moravian towns. Indian converts might feel some degree of safety, but the white missionaries and their families feared for their lives. Zeisberger noted on October 31 that "A Company of warriors passed close by Goschgosching and went to the Settlements. Isaac, who had been down the river a way, returned and brought news that a party of Wyandot had returned with 3 Scalps." The next day, he wrote, "Last night hostile Indians were seen in Goschgosching and people also observed things like this here. They sneak around in the Towns during the night to see if they can perhaps see and track down White people . . . they hope to get some here. Therefore we commended ourselves every day and night to the protection of the dear heavenly Father and to the dear angels."[127]

As time passed, Indian war parties grew still bolder in Delaware territory. On November 12:

> When Brother Heckewelder got up at daybreak and opened the doors, 6 Minque warriors were standing directly across from our house. It was a while before one of the Indian Brothers went to them, because everyone was still sleeping. When asked what they wanted here, they replied, We are looking for White people so we can beat in their heads. At first the Indian Brothers told them there were no White people here. Why were they looking for White people in the Delaware Towns? They replied, We know some are here and we want to see them. The Brothers told them there were none here except for their teachers, and they were their friends. They would not allow anyone to harm them. The warriors answered, We know they are there (and pointed to our house) and if we had wanted to kill them, we would have done so before you knew anything about it.[128]

The Mingo were nominally looking for a white trader who had vacated the premises only a day earlier, but the implied threat to the Moravian missionaries was clear, as was the explicit blanket of protection thrown over them by the Delaware. Unfortunately, in coming years, this kind of confrontation would only become more frequent and more threatening while the Delaware protection weakened.

Morgan held another council in October 1776. To his regret, rumors among the western nations that the meeting was called to ambush Indian leaders spread widely. Rough treatment of Indians visiting Fort Pitt by local soldiers and citizens lent them credence. Still, Delaware, Shawnee, Mahican, and some Iroquois representatives attended.

Koquethaqechton and Gelelemend met first with Morgan and expressed their concerns that Hopocan was in separate correspondence with the Wyandot, then passed on a rumor that the Wyandot intended to attack. Hopocan met separately, assuring Morgan that the Wyandot had no such intentions and denying knowledge of Wyandot war parties in the field. More importantly, perhaps, he warned Morgan, "The reports you hear about us Indians are much like those told to us about you—but I hope the wise people of neither side believe them there are many people on both sides who to answer their own purposes endeavour to raise evil reports and to sow discord between you and us, let us not listen to such people."[129]

The divisions among the Delaware were there for all to see. Koquethaqechton thought his nation needed to adopt white ways, secure independence from the Six Nations, and seek recognition from American authorities. That meant finding patrons in Philadelphia. But his reception on returning from Philadelphia indicates the leader had gotten ahead of his tribe. Gelelemend sought neutrality in the war but objected to Koquethaqechton's tactics and the possibility of non-Moravian ministers and teachers coming amongst the Delaware. For his part, Hopocan was Koquethaqechton's rival for leadership. While Koquethaqechton was in Philadelphia, Hopocan focused on politics inside the Delaware and amongst the western nations. He had enlisted allies among the Turkey and Turtle phratries, effectively undermining Koquethaqechton's status.[130] He also built relations with the Wyandot, who, for the moment, remained formally at peace but were clearly closer to the British.

The conference concluded with public promises of peace all around, in part by papering over diverging interests. Everyone blamed renegade Mingo for causing problems, particularly those following a young, dispossessed Mohawk leader known as Plukkemehnotee, or Pluggy, who made his home on the Scioto River. Pluggy and his followers were not accorded the status of an Indian nation or tribe but were simply referred to as Pluggy's "gang." The inability of either the Six Nations or the Ohio tribes to restrain Pluggy's gang left white settlers distrusting all Indians and feeling they could take matters into their own hands. Second, the Shawnee leader Hokoleskwa expressed particular displeasure at white settlement of Kentucky. The Ohio nations all saw Kentucky as a test of American intentions. Morgan lacked the power to address it and could only forward the issue to John Hancock and the Continental Congress.[131] Third, the absence of the western Indians, such as the Wyandot and Potawatomi, was troubling, as some war parties were operating in the Ohio Country. So, even though they had not formally gone to war against the Americans, the western tribes were an active threat with the potential to grow quickly. Fourth, the Delaware were internally split. Finally, it was apparent that war in the Ohio Country might start and grow from the bottom up. Indian and American leaders could not restrain their hot-heads. Indian war parties and militia readily crossed the Ohio and threatened messengers from each side, all in disregard of the aims, desires, or guidance from their leaders.

The 1776 peace council resolved very little. Netawatwees, already an extraordinarily old man, died at its conclusion. Although he had not been baptized, the retired chief reportedly proclaimed the superiority of Christianity as preached by the Moravian missionaries and encouraged the Delaware to adopt it wholesale. At that point, Koquethaqechton allegedly picked up a bible and declared that they should pray for divine revelation and mercy for themselves and future generations.[132]

The next two years would be perilous for the Delaware. Netawatwees's death widened the floodgates of factionalism that had stalked the tribe since the Revolution's outbreak. The pro-peace faction spent more time visiting their fellow Delaware who had converted to the Moravian faith. Zeisberger suspected that Koquethaqechton and his allies viewed the missionaries and their congregations as helpful in maintaining Delaware neutrality, but there was still a rift between the missionaries and Koquethaqechton.[133] For him, religion remained a means to an end: independence and peace. In his mind, the converted Delaware were still part of the tribe and should join his agenda. He did not fully appreciate the spiritual influence the missionaries were having on the Delaware. For the missionaries, peace had value in and of itself, but it was also a means to a higher end, namely, protecting the mission towns they believed were critical in spreading the gospel. (Nothing was that black and white, of course. Koquethaqechton seems to have been affected spiritually by Christianity and the missionaries clearly cared for the people among whom they lived.) Zeisberger later summed it up: "They often talk about how we are supposed to become one people with them. However, if this is going to happen, then they must become one people with us. If we are to become one people, they must convert to our ways; we will never be converted to theirs."[134] Neither side wanted to force the issue lest clarity destroy the value of the middle ground.

Throughout the spring of 1777, Zeisberger and the missionaries heard rumors that Hopocan's Wolf phratry, the Munsee, wished them ill and blamed them for the peace faction's success in keeping the Delaware out of the war.[135] In March, Hopocan pressed Koquethaqechton and Gelelemend to move away from the Americans. He had already opened negotiations with the Wyandot. Koquethaqechton faced him down.[136]

The internal Delaware debates also coincided with the shift to a more aggressive British posture. On June 16, the British Lieutenant Governor and Superintendent for Indian Affairs, Henry Hamilton, received a message from Lord Germain via Governor Guy Carleton. It read, "It is the King's Command that you should direct Lieut. Governor Hamilton to assemble as many of the Indians of his District as he conveniently can, and placing proper persons at their head . . . employ them in making a Diversion and exciting an alarm upon the frontiers of Virginia and Pennsylvania."[137] Hamilton wasted no time calling the Indians together in a council. Several of the western Indian nations attended: Ottawa, Huron (Wyandot), Chippewa, Potawatomi, Miami, Shawnee, and some Delaware. He estimated he would have a thousand Indian warriors raiding the Virginia and Pennsylvania frontiers within a month.[138] Hamilton also sought to force those on the frontier to choose between the Americans and the British. He printed a proclamation promising amnesty and a reward to all who appeared at a British post and would take up arms against the American "Rebels and Traytors" and had it widely circulated.[139]

On the Muskingum, the missionaries noted still more war parties moving through. Zeisberger recorded, "A couple of Sisters from Gnadenhutten came here on business. They had almost been caught by a party of warriors yesterday evening. They ran quickly, because they had heard their death screams, and they reached Goschgosching. The warriors passed by there this morning; it was Wyandot and they had a Scalp. Some of the sisters had also seen another party like this close by yesterday, marching toward the Settlments. They are trying to keep the peace negotiations from taking place and therefore are starting to commit more murders than ever before."[140] Yet, Delaware leaders held out hope that wiser heads would prevail and they could avoid the provocations of small bands. Much depended on how the Wyandot reacted to Hamilton.

On July 22, a long-awaited Wyandot embassy met with Delaware leaders. The Wyandot confirmed many of the rumors. Western nations from both sides of the Great Lakes had accepted the war belt from Hamilton and were uniting against the Americans. Dunquat of the Wyandot, known widely as Half-King Pomoacan, handed a war belt to the Delaware, essentially inviting them to join the war, and then asked what the Delaware would do. He suggested the Delaware move west and offered to prepare a place for them.[141] Delaware leaders withdrew to consider their options and then declined to join the war, instead reminding the Wyandot of the peace agreements made at the end of Pontiac's War. Dunquat was not satisfied, threatened to force the Delaware to join the war, and then left. Zeisberger correctly anticipated that war parties in the area would increase yet again.[142]

The missionary promptly informed the new commander at Fort Pitt, Brigadier General Edward Hand, of the Wyandot visit and its results. He also told Hand that the Delaware were counting on military support for their defense: "The Delawares flatter themselves that an Army will soon come out which is their only Hope yet, but should that fail I am afraid they cannot stand."[143] The Delaware were still hanging on to Koquethaqechton's logic from 1775, when he expected the Americans to support the Delaware in the face of external threats.

Koquethaqechton's faith in the Americans was misplaced. Although the Delaware warned American officers all along the frontier of hostile war parties, the raids took their toll. American settlers did not discriminate between pro-war and anti-war voices among individual Indians or tribes. The settlers who suffered from the raids shared the views of the Paxton Boys: all Indians looked the same and had the same murderous intent. Colonel John Gibson, posted at Logstown, reported that his garrison had been fired upon with one sergeant killed and one boy captured. Shortly thereafter, two Delaware risked their own lives to warn the Americans that war parties were in the field to attack Logstown and Fort Pitt. Gibson reported, "if White Eyes [Koquethaqechton] passes this way he will Be in danger of Being killed, it was with the utmost Difficulty I prevented one of the men who Escaped from killing the Delawares."[144]

In the fall of 1777, Hand attempted to raise enough of an army to move against the western Indians, but troops were scarce. The militia were reluctant to travel far from their homes and the Continental Congress lacked sufficient troops to defend the extended frontier, much less conduct offensive operations. Indeed, when Hand arrived at Fort Pitt in June, he found only two companies of the 13th Virginia available for service.[145]

In the end, the brigadier could not assemble enough supplies or soldiers to invade. But some of the troops had assembled at Fort Randolph on the old Point Pleasant battlefield from Dunmore's War. When two Shawnee leaders presented themselves at the fort in October, the local commander arrested them. He similarly confined Hokoleskwa when that chief inquired about his fellow Indians. Like Koquethaqechton, Hokoleskwa was a voice for peace within his nation, but Americans living on the frontier were less inclined to credit any Indian with such intentions. In November, Indian warriors struck a small party of soldiers hunting outside the fort, killing one. Enraged, those soldiers then stormed back into the fort and murdered Hokoleskwa and his fellow prisoners.[146] When word reached General Hand, he feared it would provoke the Shawnee into formally joining the war. But, desperately short of soldiers, he took no immediate action against the militiamen who committed the murder. Virginia Governor Patrick Henry shared Hand's concern and sought to assuage the Shawnee by condemning the murderers and offering a reward for their apprehension.[147] It was not enough, and the Shawnee joined the western nations in a general Indian war. The Delaware were more isolated than ever.

It was an opportune moment for Hopocan if he wanted to go to war, but he chose not to exploit it. When a band of Frenchmen traveled to the Cuyahoga River, where Hopocan made his home, they convinced some of the Delaware there to raid Fort Ligonier. Hopocan was absent but quickly caught up with the band on the way. He berated the French as having no power to invite the Delaware to war, insisted no one could force him to take up the tomahawk, and led most of the Delaware in the war party back home. He and Gelelemend then traveled to Detroit, suggesting Delaware efforts to maintain some semblance of unity and peace on the frontier had not exhausted themselves.[148]

Unfortunately, the American peace efforts began to fall apart. Americans in Pittsburgh freely accused one another of having Loyalist sympathies. By December, Hand ordered the arrest of George Morgan, Colonel John Campbell, Captain Alexander McKee, and Simon Girty, who had been accused of conspiracy.[149] Morgan continued to try and do his job, hamstrung by house arrest. McKee and Girty, however, were more challenging cases. McKee had been a British Indian agent for the Ohio Country for years before the Revolution. He nominally disavowed his royal connections as the war got underway, largely to protect his substantial holdings in Pennsylvania.[150] But he had close ties to the British government, under which he had profited considerably, and the Shawnee nation, which he considered a second family. For those reasons, Lord Dunmore sought to enlist McKee in the crown's cause early in the war, which made him suspect among the Americans. To complicate matters further, Dunmore and other frontier Loyalists assumed McKee remained loyal. When it came to choosing sides, others were picking McKee's side for him.[151] With Hokoleskwa's death, he had ample reason to go along with them.

Simon Girty was born in 1741 to a Susquehanna-based fur trader. During the French and Indian War, the family was captured with the fall of Fort Granville on the Juniata River. After torturing Girty's stepfather to death, the Indians divided up the family among the Delaware, Shawnee, and Seneca.[152] Thereafter, the Girtys became permanent fixtures on the frontier as scouts, translators, and assistants to Indian traders like George Morgan and Alexander McKee. The Girtys were among those Indian prisoners returned to white society at the conclusion of Pontiac's War. Speaking several languages, they naturally attracted McKee's attention in his roles as both a trader and agent for the British government.

When the American Revolution started, Girty continued in his role as messenger and scout but now for the new American authorities on the frontier, including George Morgan.[153] (He was joined by another frontiersman with long experience in the Ohio Country working with British authorities, Matthew Elliott.) He accompanied Captain James Wood as interpreter during his 1775 tour of the western nations, served as interpreter during many of the Indian councils at Fort Pitt, helped raise troops for the American cause, and then received a commission as a second lieutenant.[154] (He did not travel to Charleston with his company and resigned his commission.)

Magistrates examined Girty and eventually exonerated him of the conspiracy charges, but they must have left a mark. Still, when Hand finally launched an offensive against a suspected British supply depot on the Cuyahoga River in mid-winter 1778, Girty accompanied his force as an interpreter and guide. Hand lacked much in the way of Continental resources, so he turned largely to the Pennsylvania militia. Roughly five hundred militia from Westmoreland County turned out.[155] Hand's army marched about forty miles up the Beaver River when he decided it lacked adequate supplies to reach the Cuyahoga. Before turning around, however, scouts reported a small village of Indians camped at the confluence of the nearby Neshaneck and Shenango Rivers, which he concluded was a raiding party. So, Hand set out to surround the Indians. Demonstrating poor fire discipline, the militia attacked before they were in position. The "war party" turned out to be one older male Indian and several women and children—all Delaware. The man, Hopocan's older brother, stopped to fire at the attacking militia while his family and several women fled through a gap in the militia lines. He hit one militia captain before being brought down himself and then tomahawked. Of the women in camp, two were related to Hopocan. One was his wife and one was his mother. They were both wounded. While trying to escape, a militiaman scalped one woman and another one shot her. The other woman was captured. Hand could only report, "to my great Mortification [we] found only one Man with some Women & Children. The men were so Impetuous that I could not prevent their Killing the Man & one of the Women. Another Woman was taken & with difficulty Saved. the rem[ainder] escaped."[156] To make matters worse, the female prisoner informed the militia that another group of Delaware was making salt roughly ten miles away. Hand dispatched more men to round up those Indians. Again, they found no warriors but captured one woman. Later, on the way back to the general, they encountered a boy shooting birds and killed him.[157] Thus, the first major American offensive from the Forks of the Ohio had taken two women prisoner while killing one man, one woman, and a boy, all from a neutral tribe. Forever after, Hand's campaign was known dismissively as the "Squaw Campaign." It had done more harm than good to the American cause.

Congress responded to the worsening situation in 1777 by dispatching commissioners to sort things out. They arrived in March 1778, just as Hand returned to Pittsburgh from his ill-advised attack on local Indians. Whether it was a consequence of Hand's expedition or arrival of the Congressional commission, McKee, Girty, Matthew Elliott, and four others chose March 25 to abscond from town, bound for Detroit and the Loyalist cause. First, however, they stopped in Delaware territory on the Muskingum. On their flight Girty, McKee, and Elliott spread stories that the Americans meant to exterminate the "whole Indian race, be they friends or foes, and possess themselves of their country; and that, at this time, while they were embodying themselves for the purpose they were preparing fine sounding speeches to deceive them, that they might with the more safety fall upon and murder them. That now was the time, and the only time, for all nations to rise, and turn out to a man against those intruders, and not even suffer them to cross the Ohio, but fall upon them where they should find them; which if not done without delay, their country would be lost to them forever!"[158] McKee and Girty, at least, knew that story was exaggerated and reported to the British that a major offensive from the Americans was not imminent.[159]

Zeisberger recorded that the Delaware found the reports credible. "[T]he Chiefs were very upset by the news from the Deserteurs. . . . They were more influenced by what the Deserteurs said, that the Delaware really had reason to be on their guard because the militia on the Frontiers had been commanded and was prepared to march from Pittsburgh on May 1st and come into Indian country."[160] Delaware leaders specifically cited Hokoleskwa's murder and the Squaw Campaign as evidence of malicious American intent: "the Chiefs concluded that the gentlemen in the Fort were offering us peace with one hand and were using the hatchets against us with the other."[161]

It was a moment fraught with peril. Zeisberger recorded, "[The chiefs] were all very muddled and confused and not even in agreement among themselves. The situation was pretty extreme since this would determine whether they decided for peace or war."[162] War parties from the western nations had passed through Delaware and Moravian towns, scalps on their belts and captives in tow, for the better part of a year. Often, they managed to peel a few Delaware warriors away from the tribe to join them. While they had not enjoyed the same kind of success they had during Pontiac's War, it was clear that the Americans were unable to resist them.[163] Should the Delaware join the war on the British side, they might well repeat the success of Pontiac's War and perhaps secure a final victory. Meanwhile, the Americans had demonstrated a propensity to harm those most inclined toward peace with them. It was the perfect moment for Hopocan to again make the case for war. Koquethaqechton recognized it and quickly outmaneuvered his rival in council.

Rather than simply restating his case for peace, the wily Turtle war captain called for a national council and put the matter of war to it of his own volition. He asked first that they give the Americans a deadline to respond to the stories from McKee, Elliott, and Girty before making a final decision. The council agreed. Thus, he preempted an immediate decision for war and bought himself some time. Hopocan went along with the council but proposed that the Wolf phratry also determine that any Delaware opposed to making war on the Americans was an enemy of the nation. Not to be isolated so easily, Koquethaqechton agreed and promised to lead the Delaware in war, though he still thought it was the wrong path, and offered to be the first to fall should it come to that. The stage was set for a showdown between Koquethaqechton and Hopocan: peace or war.[164]

Back in Pittsburgh, the Congressional commissioners quickly cleared Morgan of all charges and he was free to minimize the damage he knew McKee and his colleagues were doing. He had already dispatched messengers all across the Ohio Valley, but, strangely, had none available for the Delaware council. Heckewelder and a colleague, returning to the Muskingum, volunteered, despite the large number of war parties operating in the area. For Heckewelder, "it appeared clear, that the preservation of the Delaware nation, and the existence of our mission, depended on the nation being at peace, and that a contrary course would tend to the total ruin of the whole mission."[165] Heckewelder and his fellow missionary traveled day and night, stopping only to feed the horses. They dodged a Wyandot war party outside Gnadenhutten, rested a few hours, and then rode straight on to Goschgosching, "where all was bustle and confusion, and many preparing to go off to fight the American people, in consequence of the advice given them by those deserters."[166] Behind them, the Moravian Indians were preparing to abandon Gnadenhutten and join the congregation at Lichtenau, where they hoped to find greater safety from roving war parties.

Heckewelder did not receive a warm reception at Goschgosching. Even Koquethaqechton and his pro-peace allies refused to extend a hand in greeting. Heckewelder concluded it was a matter of policy and not one of personal enmity when he noted some of Hopocan's spies in the crowd. Koquethaqechton had to appear strong and prepared to wage war in order to maintain his credibility. Much was riding on how his interaction with Heckewelder went; the leader needed the missionary and his message from the Americans to convince the majority of the tribe that they need not go to war, but he himself had to appear prepared for it in order to preserve his moral authority in the face of Hopocan's challenge.

Heckewelder understood his part and played it well. When he asked why he had been treated so coldly, Koquethaqechton replied that, according to McKee and his friends, "they no longer had a single friend among the American people; if therefore this be so, they must consider every white man who came to them from that side, as an enemy, who only came to them to deceive them, and put them off their guard for the purpose of giving the enemy an opportunity of taking them by surprise."[167] Heckewelder answered for himself, arguing he was a friend of the Delaware or he would not have been sent.

Koquethaqechton then demanded that Heckewelder tell the truth and asked a series of straw-man questions likely based on the stories McKee, Elliott, and Girty had spread: had the Americans been cut to pieces by the British? Was Washington dead? Had Congress dissolved and some members been hanged? Did the British control everything beyond the Appalachians? Had those few who had escaped crossed the Appalachians simply to kill Indians, including women and children? Heckewelder denied it all. He had lived among the Delaware long enough to command some respect and the directness of his response carried weight. He offered up the messages from Fort Pitt, but Koquethaqechton still refused to take them personally. This was a matter for the entire tribe, not just a chief and a general or Indian agent. Heckewelder took the hint and asked everyone whether they would listen to the messages. A majority loudly assented so Koquethaqechton asserted his authority and asked the question formally, receiving the same answer. His play for time had worked.

With that, a large group retired to the council house and Heckewelder translated the friendliest messages. Koquethaqechton interrupted to remind those assembled that the Americans had not called on them to go to war, as the British had, and that the Americans had advised them to remain neutral. Heckewelder also produced a newspaper relating the surrender of Burgoyne's army the previous fall, which Koquethaqechton seized upon and compared favorably with McKee's "song of a bird." With that, Koquethaqechton formally welcomed Heckewelder among the tribe. Others followed and Hopocan's moment had passed. Heckewelder returned safely to Lichtenau to everyone's relief.[168] A few days later, Koquethaqechton and several pro-peace leaders visited the missionaries at Lichtenau to request their help composing a response to the Americans.

Back in Pittsburgh, American authorities had also issued their own deadline to a query about Delaware intentions. It was among the messages that Heckewelder delivered, so Koquethaqechton traveled to Fort Pitt. His visit put the rumors of another militia foray into the frontier to rest, much to the relief of the Delaware and missionaries, but that relief was tempered by fear. Zeisberger recorded in May, "We were happiest to learn that the militia that was supposed to march into Indian country, which would have been one of the most dangerous things for us, has now been completely called off because they had carried out evil deeds and had not spared friend or enemy. One Colonel from the militia announced in Pittsburgh that as soon as they crossed the Ohio, one party would march directly to Gnadenhutten without letting anyone in the Fort know about it." As if the threat were not bad enough, Indian converts who had gone to the fort reported that, during their return trip, they faced hostile Indians before them and a pursuing militia force that wished them harm. It eventually gave up the pursuit and the converts managed to avoid the hostile war parties.[169] The incident was emblematic of the growing isolation of the Delaware, caught between warring Indian nations to their west and militia who did not distinguish between friend and foe to their east, and an early warning sign that some frontier settlers viewed the mission towns themselves as a threat, four years before the massacre, and that they viewed authorities in Pittsburgh as a constraint.

Farther west, the war was not going well for the British in 1778. Virginia militia led by George Rogers Clark had launched a lightning campaign into the Illinois Territory, conquering a range of small British posts on the Wabash and Mississippi Rivers. Hamilton was preparing to march south and recover some of that territory by mobilizing as many western tribes as possible. With that in mind, he wrote the Delaware insisting that they join the war on the British side, hinting that they would regret failing to take up the hatchet.[170] In a bit of rhetorical legerdemain, the Delaware replied that they had promised the British Indian agent, Sir William Johnson, that they would never take up the hatchet again against the whites. Johnson, of course, was dead and circumstances had changed, but the Delaware could legitimately claim they were true to their earlier promise to the British. At the same time, the Delaware and Moravians attempted to open negotiations with the Cherokee, inviting them to join their peace movement.[171]

A new Fort Pitt council finally took place in September, but only the Delaware attended. George Morgan and Brigadier General Lachlan McIntosh, Hand's replacement, represented the Continental Congress. Virginia and Pennsylvania were both supposed to appoint commissioners, but only Virginia fulfilled its obligation by appointing Andrew and Thomas Lewis, both with long experience on the frontier. Officers from the Eighth Pennsylvania Regiment and Thirteenth Virginia Regiment, both providing the bulk of non-militia frontier defenses, were there as observers. Koquethaqechton, Gelelemend, and Hopocan attended for the Delaware, accompanied by two Moravian missionaries. Morgan and McIntosh made a show of welcoming the Delaware, perhaps to offset the harsh treatment they often received at the hands of locals when visiting the fort. At the same time, the Americans were only too happy for the Indians to witness the growing number of soldiers they were gathering around Pittsburgh. McIntosh was preparing for an invasion of Indian territory under Continental leadership. Where Hand had failed to assemble an army in 1777 and then abandoned even a limited raid to the Cuyahoga River in the Squaw campaign, McIntosh intended to march a nine-hundred-man army all the way to Detroit. Thus, when the Delaware chiefs arrived, they faced the prospect of making a formal peace or facing an invading army.[172]

The Americans informed the Delaware that they were now allies and an American army would march through their territory. It was a jolt from the neutrality Americans had previously sought. Under the circumstances, the Delaware leaders had a weak negotiating hand. Koquethaqechton, however, played it very well. The Treaty of Fort Pitt contained six articles, the first of which declared essentially that both sides would forgive and forget past injuries. Article II announced a state of perpetual peace and friendship and created a military alliance "if either of the parties are engaged in a just and necessary war with any other nation or nations, that then each shall assist the other in due proportion to their abilities, till their enemies are brought to reasonable terms of accommodation."[173] One might be tempted to read this as unfair to the Delaware in that the Americans were fighting a war they viewed as just and necessary and needed Indian allies on the frontier. But it should be remembered that, for years, Koquethaqechton had anticipated the need for American military assistance. The constant presence of western war parties in Delaware territory and frequency of threats from the British and western nations made such an alliance with the Americans all the more necessary.

In Article III, the Delaware pledged to allow an American army to march through their territory to attack American enemies. Moreover, the Delaware obligated themselves to guide the American army on its march, supply it, and augment it to the best of their ability. For their part, the Americans promised to build and garrison a fort in Delaware territory at American expense in order to protect the Delaware while their warriors were away.

In Article IV, both sides pledged to forego imposing unilateral justice against individuals who committed infractions against them without some form of fair and impartial trial, as determined by the Continental Congress with Delaware assistance. Such a provision nominally could help prevent blood feuds from escalating, but it also afforded more authority to the Americans in American-Delaware relations.

Article V made the Delaware economically dependent on the United States by requiring all trade to occur through an Indian agent.

In some ways, this recognized reality since the British would not trade with an enemy tribe, but, again, it confirmed an unequal relationship. The Delaware were not free to choose when, how, and with whom they would trade in the future.

Article VI was perhaps the most interesting. The United States guaranteed to recognize and respect Delaware territory as sovereign to the Delaware, so long as the Delaware abided by the chain of friendship. This would require the United States to essentially nullify some long-standing land claims in the Ohio Valley made by private American citizens, some of which predated the war by decades. More remarkably, however, "It is further agreed on between the contracting parties should it for the future be found conducive for the mutual interest of both parties to invite any other tribes who have been friends to the interest of the United Sates, to join the present confederation, and to form a state whereof the Delaware nation shall be the head, and have a representation in Congress." On paper, the Americans were prepared to recognize a new, Delaware-led, fourteenth state. Koquethaqechton had achieved one of his fondest dreams: recognition of the Delaware as independent from the Six Nations. Andrew and Thomas Lewis, originally appointed only to represent Virginia, signed on behalf of the United States. Koquethaqechton, Gelelemend, and Hopocan signed for the Delaware. General McIntosh, Colonel Daniel Brodhead of the Eighth Pennsylvania, John Gibson of the Thirteenth Virginia, and several other officers present signed as observers.

The Treaty of Fort Pitt is often thought of as a travesty of fairness. It was one-sided and with an army gathered around, the Delaware chiefs had little room to maneuver. The Americans reportedly plied the Delaware with alcohol and kept them in a state of constant inebriation. Morgan announced after the fact, "There never was a Conference with the Indians so improperly or villainously conducted."[174] Gelelemend would later proclaim that the treaty had been improperly explained to them: "I have now looked over the Articles of the Treaty again & find they are wrote down false."[175] On a visit east in May 1779, several Delaware chiefs repudiated the treaty as having been falsely presented to them.[176] But it also reflected many of Koquethaqechton's goals. Congress never ratified it.

Developments moved quickly after the treaty was signed in September. McIntosh put his army in motion, moving up the Beaver River and promptly building a fort, aptly named Fort McIntosh. Members of the Wolf phratry, who had been threatening the Delaware peace faction generally and the missionaries specifically for months, began to panic. As Colonel Gibson led the advance on the Beaver, Zeisberger recorded in his diary:

> Some Munsee came here to pick up their friends because they said we all be killed by the Nations. They realize they did not receive the favorable answer from the General they had been expecting for some time, so now they all want to run away. They had asked the Wyandot for advice about what they should do, and they replied that they should go to them and not worry about all their corn and food, because they would find this at their place, though it is well known that the Wyandot themselves have little since they planted almost none. Despite the fact that the Munsee are so horrified and scared, they are still malicious. They had often before threatened is that after they defeated the army, they would all overrun and destroy us. Now they are saying they would not wait until the army came, but would do this first. First we White Brothers would either be killed or captured and taken to Detroit.[177]

On October 25, a Munsee chief, likely Hopocan, visited the Moravian towns, announcing that the Munsee Delaware no longer believed they were safe in their towns and would move west at the Wyandot's invitation. He wanted those Munsee who had joined the Moravians to come with them, as he feared for their safety.[178] The converted Delaware declined. The threats did not end, though. Two days later, Zeisberger reported, "We have to listen to horrifying threats about beating us to death, and all of this comes from the Munsee. They are fleeing now so they want to do as much damage as they can first. It would bring them great joy if they could make us all run away. From midnight last night until noon today, one piece of horrifying news after another arrived. In order to make it quite believable, they said they were forbidden to tell people here what was going on. . . . The Munsee are our greatest enemies."[179]

The next day, the Moravians learned that Hopocan and one of his allies, Wingenund, had left the area and joined the Wyandot. Rumors flew that after the western tribes, now including the Munsee Delaware, met and defeated the advancing American army, they would fall on the Moravian towns. With the Delaware dividing, Gelelemend sent messages to General McIntosh, asking him to send troops to defend those Delaware who remained on the Muskingum.

Rather than turning southward from his base at Fort McIntosh and heading for Goschgosching, however, the general proceeded westward to the eastern branch of the Muskingum, along which the abandoned Moravian villages were located. When it reached the river, the American army established Fort Laurens. With winter approaching, the army turned back, leaving behind a modest garrison. The fort was too far away from Goschgosching or Lichtenau to offer the Delaware much protection.

Koquethaqechton makes a sudden and unanticipated exit from the story at this point. He had come achingly close to achieving many of his goals during the first years of the American Revolution. The Moravians were slowly helping the Delaware make the economic changes he thought necessary. Pastoral farming was replacing the migratory agricultural practices that had dictated the seasonal rhythms of Delaware life. By establishing more modern towns, the Moravians were also helping the Delaware acquire skills critical to building a healthier economy. Education was an important feature of the United Brethren's doctrine and more Delaware were picking up its rudiments. While the Moravian church may have lacked the political influence he and Bemino had sought from a Christian church, the chief himself had found allies at Fort Pitt and succeeded in putting the Delaware on the Congressional agenda. With the Treaty of Fort Pitt, he at last had a written promise from the whites to recognize the Delaware nation's independence from the Six Nations. So it was natural for Koquethaqechton to join McIntosh's army and use it to provide the Delaware with security from the western nations and British, who had spent much of the prior year attempting to intimidate them into an alliance. Unfortunately, during the march west, Koquethaqechton died. The Americans reported he contracted smallpox.

In truth, many had reasons to be rid of Koquethaqechton. Hopocan and his faction already disagreed with the chief's strategy and were clearly unhappy with the Treaty of Fort Pitt. While Koquethaqechton remained alive, his demonstrated ability to foil the Munsee desire to align with the British was always in play. His death removed an obstacle. For that matter, even those Delaware who wished to remain neutral may have felt betrayed by a treaty that committed them to the American side. He was clearly an obstacle to the desires of the British and western nations to enlist the Delaware in the war. They would also benefit from his death. It is not difficult to envision an encounter between the western war parties and McIntosh's new Indian scout deep in the woods ahead of the army.

It is also quite possible that Americans killed the chief. Morgan believed the chief had been assassinated but declined to make specific accusations, suggesting he suspected whites.[180] As we have already seen, the American militia rarely discriminated between friendly and hostile Indians and it was common practice to shoot first and ask questions later. Koquethaqechton also may have been murdered by an Indian-hating soldier. Others may have blamed him for Delaware participation in raids on frontier settlements. The threats made against him by a militia colonel in 1777 and repeated to Zeisberger were quite specific. Other whites who hoped to acquire land in the Ohio Country may also have sought to undermine the statehood provision in the Treaty of Fort Pitt by killing its chief advocate. It is even possible he was simply murdered for some possession, i.e., he was in the wrong place at the wrong time. Or Koquethaqechton may have in fact died from smallpox, which was common in the armies of the day.

It is easy to conclude in hindsight that Koquethaqechton would fail to secure peace with the Americans, if not an outright alignment with the Continental Congress. Despite the efforts of Congressional agents and Continental officers to treat the Delaware well, Americans in general had proven unreliable and dangerous. In theory, the British had more to offer. Yet, Koquethaqechton and his peace faction clearly saw greater forces at work than their nation's immediate circumstances. Immigration to the frontier was not going to stop. He could no more turn settlers back and preserve a traditional way of life than he could stop the rising and setting of the sun. Simply, the Americans and their settlers could not be escaped. The Delaware would have to deal with them, one way or the other.

The Delaware had first submitted to white expansion, dictated in large part by the Six Nations. But over the course of the French and Indian War and Pontiac's War, they changed strategy, embracing military means and seeking greater independence from the Six Nations. Violence failed to deliver. Over time and several leaders, that approach evolved into seeking recognition as a people independent of the Iroquois and sovereign over a defined geographic area. To achieve those goals, survive, and thrive as a cohesive people, Delaware leaders concluded their nation had to change. It meant adjusting the entire Delaware way of life, taking up pastoral farming, embracing education, and adopting Christianity and white norms of behavior. The Revolution preempted Koquethaqechton's attempt to find assistance for that agenda from England, so he turned to the Continental Congress. Congressional promises to provide help in 1776 and the 1778 Treaty of Fort Pitt brought him to the brink of success. But after Hamilton's 1777 council unleashed a general Indian war on the frontier, the neutrality Koquethaqechton had originally sought became impossible. He spent the next year maneuvering between different frontier factions: the British and western nations at war, Hopocan's anti-American camp (many of whom left to join raiding parties at will), the converted Indians who followed the Moravian missionaries, the missionaries who had a slightly different future in mind for the Delaware, Americans representing the Continental Congress who had little to offer but much to ask, and the American militia, who blamed all Indians for the suffering they and their families experienced at the hands of the British and their allies. Sadly, with his death, the one man with the political skills that might have held the tribe together was gone and the Delaware split openly into pro- and anti-American camps. Afterward, others would determine the Delaware future, and, by extension, that of the Indians who had taken up the Moravian faith under the Delaware wing.

David Zeisberger (1721-1808), left. Taciturn and judgmental, he was the senior missionary to the Moravian Indian communities. John Heckewelder (1743-1823), right. Heckewelder helped Christian Frederick Post establish the first Moravian mission to the Delaware Indians and chronicled the story of the Moravian Indians. (*Moravian Church Archives*)

Col. Daniel Brodhead (1736-1809), left. He commanded the 8th Pennsylvania Regiment, fought on Long Island, served at Valley Forge, and commanded at Fort Pitt during the critical years of 1779-1781. Right, "Habit of a Delaware Indian," published by T. Jefferys, London, c. 1757-1772. The mix of Native American and Western clothing elements highlights the interaction between European and Native American communities and cultures. (*New York Public Library*)

"The Power of the Gospel: Zeisberger Preaching to the Indians," by Christian Schussele, 1862. The painting's religious themes stress the importance of faith to the missionaries and their perceptions of Christianity's power of conversion. In practice, the missionaries won more converts through simple conversation and teaching in small groups. (*Library of Congress*)

"Massacre of the Christian Indians,"1857. Images of the Gnadenhutten Massacre were highly conjectural, emphasizing the differences between the white raiders and their Indian victims rather than the similarities. For example, the Moravian Indians did not partially shave their heads, wear top-knots in their hair, or limit their clothing to breechcloths, but cut their hair short and adopted the dark, austere dress of the missionaries. (*New York Public Library*)

Three

Frontier Settlers

TODAY, WE VIEW THE MEN WHO CARRIED OUT THE GNADENHUTTEN massacre in 1782 as a group of depraved and vicious killers, dehumanizing them in much the same way they dehumanized their victims. While conjuring up such frontier monsters may dismiss their behavior as out of the ordinary, it begs the question: How were such monsters created? A good place to start answering the question is to let frontier settlers explain themselves.

When the Paxton Boys departed Germantown, they left someone behind to craft a document laying out their complaints about government policy.[1] This became "A Declaration and Remonstrance of the Distressed and Bleeding Frontier Inhabitants of the Province of Pennsylvania, Presented by them to the Honourable Governor and Assembly of the Province, Shewing the Causes of their late Discontent and Uneasiness and the Grievances Under which they have labored, and which they humbly pray to have redress'd."[2]

The *Declaration and Remonstrance* presented a white settler view of things from the frontier. It began with a profession of the Paxton Boys' loyalty to the Crown and an assertion of their commitment to defend the king against enemies of his interests and dignity, "Whether openly avowed or more dangerously concealed under a Mask of falsly pretended Friendship."[3] By that, they meant the Indians living closest to them on the frontier, particularly those sheltered by whites through agreement with the government: namely, the Conestoga and the Moravian Indians then in Philadelphia. The Paxton Boys went further, asserting repeatedly that Indians guilty of aggressive depredations along the frontier were among those false friends.[4]

The Paxton Boys specifically tied their suffering on the frontier to the Indians whom the governor sheltered in Philadelphia:

> During the late and present Indian Wars, the Frontiers of this Province have been repeatedly attacked and ravaged by Skulking parties of the Indians, who have with the most savage Cruelty, murdered Men, Women, and Children, without distinction; and have reduced near a Thousand Families to the most extream Distress. It grieved us to the very Heart, to see such of our Frontier Inhabitants as they have escaped from savage Fury, with the loss of their Parents, their Children, their Husbands, Wives, or Relatives, left destitute by the Public, and esposed to the most cruel Poverty, and Wretchedness; while upwards of One Hundred and Twenty of the Savages, who are with great Reason suspected of being guilty of these horrid Barbaraties, under the Mask of Friendship, have procured themselves to be taken under the Protection of the Government, with a view to elude the Fury of the brave Relatives of the Murdered; and are now maintained at the public Expence; Some of these Indians now in the Barracks of Philadelphia, are confessedly a part of the Wyalusing Indians, which Tribe is now at War with us and the others are the Moravian Indians, who living amongst us under the Cloak of Friendship, carried on a Correspondence with our known Enemies on the Great Island.[5]

The *Declaration and Remonstrance* indicted the entirety of Pennsylvania's frontier policy, which to the Paxton Boys favored Indians over settlers. They resented the practice of frequent presentations of gifts and annual subsidies to Native Americans, which were often required as part of a land purchase agreement. Moreover, the settlers complained that Indians whose cornfields had been destroyed in war asked for, and received, public subsidies for their care. Yet, the settlers observed that the government frequently failed to provide sufficient funding to defend the frontier or relief for frontier families displaced by Indian attacks, even as the Indians did not fully meet their obligations to return captives:

> Should we here reflect to former Treaties, the exorbitant Presents, and great Servility therein paid to Indians, have long been oppressive Grievances we have groaned under. And when at the last Indians Treaty held at Lancaster, not only was the Blood of our many murdered Brethren tamely covered, but our poor unhappy captivated Friends abandoned to Slavery among the Savages, by concluding a Friendship with the Indians and allowing them a plenteous Trade of all kinds of Commodities without those being restored altho' a spirited Requistion was made of them. . . . [T]he Hands that were closely shut, nor would grant his Majesty's General one single Farthing against a Savage Foe, have been liberally opened, and the publick Money lavishly prostituted to hire, at an exorbitant Rate, a mercenary Guard, to protect his Majesty's worst of Enemies, those falsly pretended Indian Friends, while at the same Time hundreds of poor distressed Families of his Majesty's Subjects, obliged to abandon their Possessions, and flee for their Lives at least.[6]

They further objected to the government's policy of discriminating between tribal war parties and the tribal nation writ large.

> Nor is it less Distressing to hear other pleading, that altho' the Wyanalusing Tribe is at War with us, yet that part of it which is under the Protection of the Government may be friendly to the English, and Innocent. In what Nation under the Sun was it ever the Custom, that when a neighbouring Nation took up Arms, not an individual of the Nation should be touched, but only the Persons that offered Hostilities? Who ever proclaimed War with a part of a Nation, and not with the Whole? Had these Indians dis-

> approved of the Perfidy of their Tribe, and been willing to cultivate and preserve Friendship with us, why did they not give Notice of the War before it happened, as it is known to be the Result of long Deliberations, and a preconcerted Combination amongst them? Why did they not leave their Tribe immediately, and come amongst us before there was ground to suspect them, or War was actually waged with the Tribe? No, they stayed amongst them, were privy to their Murders and Ravages, until we had destroyed their Provisions, and when we they could no longer subsist at Home, they came, not as Deserters, but as Friends, to be maintained thro' the Winter, that they may be able to scalp and butcher us in the Spring.[7]

The murders of the Conestoga Indians and *Declaration and Remonstrance* received support across the frontier. One pamphleteer, Reverend Thomas Barton, claimed "nine Tenths of the Inhabitants of the Back-Counties either tacitly, or openly, approve and support them—Every cool and well thinking Man, as well as Men among themselves, are sensibly concern'd that they were reduced to the Necessity of having Recourse to such Methods as might be deem'd an Insult to the Government and Laws of their King and Country."[8] Unlike the *Declaration and Remonstrances*, Barton chose to name names and offer evidence in the form of testimony and depositions regarding Indian depredations entered into the records of various towns in the "back counties," as Pennsylvania's frontier was often known. He specifically called out a Conestoga Indian named Will or Bill Sock. Barton offered less evidence against the Moravian Indians, only citing a sworn statement by Thomas Moore, a former prisoner of the Indians, that his captors had frequently received intelligence about English movements from the Indians at Bethlehem, who also visited and kept a continual correspondence with them.[9]

Pennsylvania's elites had a different take on the matter. Benjamin Franklin, for example, was one of the first to enter the lists with a pamphlet titled, "A Narrative of the Late Massacres, in Lancaster County, of a Number of Indians, Friends of this Province, By Persons Unknown." He called the Paxton Boys murderers and capitalized on

European racial, cultural, and religious prejudices by comparing them unfavorably with heathens, Indians, Africans, Turks, Muslims, and Saracens. More, he dismissed their accusations against the Moravian Indians: "I will not dissemble that numberless Stories have been raised and spread abroad, against not only the poor Wretches that are murdered, but also against the Hundred and Forty Christianized Indians, still threatned to be murdered, all which Stories are well known, by those who know the Indians best, to be pure Inventions, contrived by bad People, either to excite each other to join in the Murder, or since it was committed, to justify it; and believed only by the Weak and Credulous."[10]

But the jousting over how to interpret the Conestoga murders quickly got lost in a debate over the future structure of the Pennsylvania government and the proprietorship's role in it. The Conestoga murders, march on Philadelphia, and threats against the Moravian Indians became ammunition in those debates. That left the matter of the frontier and settler complaints about government policy unaddressed.

Pennsylvania's frontier settlers and colonial authorities in Philadelphia had markedly different approaches to frontier management, which exacerbated conflict among settlers, Indians, and authorities in Philadelphia. In theory, the Penn proprietorship was the only entity permitted to purchase land from the Indians, after which all who sought land would have to purchase it from the proprietor. Land sales from the Indians were expected to be consensual; there would be no seizure in Pennsylvania. Meanwhile, the government's control over county offices, surveying, and law enforcement ensured that transfers could take place in an orderly manner sanctioned by the government.[11] In principle, this approach would ensure that settlers had clear title to the plots of land they purchased, for which they would pay a "quitrent," a form of property tax. Penn hoped to minimize conflict in this fashion. When the colony passed from William Penn to his sons, they and the government continued the practice. It served the Iroquois well enough since the Penns preferred to deal through them and they received payment when the Penns acquired land, often without regard to the people who lived on it, as we have seen with the Delaware. The practice did not sit well with the settlers flooding into Pennsylvania. Patrick Spero noted, "By 1740, recent non-English arrivals composed nearly half the population."[12] The flood did not stop then. In his landmark study of immigration, Bernard Bailyn found that the population of Pennsylvania rose 40 percent between 1760 and 1776. Many of the immigrants headed for the frontier in the years before the American Revolution. In 1771, some ten thousand families lived in Pennsylvania's trans-Appalachian frontier and farms dominated the areas around Fort Pitt to a radius of 150 miles.[13]

A great bulk of the immigrants came from Germany, Scotland, and Ireland and were practicing Lutherans or Presbyterians. The Penn government settled them on the frontier, putting them between the more settled parts of the colony, dominated by Quakers, and the Native Americans living to the north and west. The Scots-Irish had a reputation for independence and, for lack of a better phrase, trouble-making.[14] Their preference was simply to head into the wilderness, stake out a plot of unused land sufficient to farm, and build communities, then assert ownership through occupation and development. Thus, "squatting" became a real problem for the Penn government, creating conflict between Scots-Irish settlers and the Indians or between settlers and the government.[15] From time to time the Pennsylvania government was forced to work through county officials to evict such squatters, who made little distinction between land nominally owned by Indians or the Penns. Tensions could easily escalate. Their location at the edge of the colony ensured that Indian raids fell first on these Scots-Irish communities. This put settlers at odds with both the Indians and the Penn family proprietorship, isolating them from both and giving frontier settlers a common cause around which to unite. Worse from the settler's standpoint, the Penn government's history of relying on diplomacy, gifts, and the Iroquois Confederation left it unprepared to defend those very same communities when war broke out.

When Major General Braddock led his forces to the Forks of the Ohio in 1755, Pennsylvania did not have a proper law governing the raising, provisioning, and regulation of militia. Indeed, it had lacked one much of its existence and continued to debate the matter after Braddock's defeat left the frontier open to attack.[16] A historian of Pennsylvania's military preparedness points out that "for most of its early history, Pennsylvania had little or no need for a colonial militia. Enabled by a substantial Quaker majority, the Pennsylvania Assembly in Philadelphia pursued an expansionist foreign policy based on tribal diplomacy and a complex network of alliances known at the time as the Long Peace. Natural barriers deterred external enemies and facilitated trade. Robust relations, first with the Lenape and later with the Six Nations, facilitated rapid territorial growth without recourse to war."[17]

Nevertheless, communities had relied on private "associations" of armed men for protection against significant threats. Members of these associations became known as "associators," and they created armed, organized, alternative foci of authority to the government in Philadelphia, although they, of course, still recognized the superiority of colonial government and the Crown. The first associator units were established in Philadelphia, but the frontier counties quickly followed suit. Pennsylvania's militia law had lapsed again by the time of the Revolution, but as tensions increased counties controlled by committees of safety quickly established military units patterned after the associators.[18] Even as frontier communities might have a tradition of militarizing quickly, the state of Pennsylvania did not have a well-developed system for commanding, controlling, or coordinating such military forces state-wide.[19] So, on the frontier, local militia retained a kind of independence from outside authority.

Whites and Indians often viewed each other through the lens of race and culture. Calling the Indians "savages" was commonplace, and whites threw the word about casually as a synonym for Indians. The *Declaration and Remonstrances* is rife with it. Reverend Jones, who sought to minister to Native Americans, described one predominantly Shawnee town as "the most remarkable town for robbers and villains, yet it pretends to have its chief men, who are indeed the very scoundrels guilty of theft and robbery without any apology or redress."[20] In describing the Shawnee as a people, Jones credited them with being "cheerful and merry," but then "at the same time perhaps they are the most deceitful that exist in human shape."[21] One observer referred to the Indians as "monsters, left to the wild impulses of the wildest nature."[22] Zeisberger announced that "the North American Indians . . . as I have learned to know them, are by nature (I speak of savages) lazy as far as work is concerned."[23] He went on, "They are proud and haughty, even a miserable Indian, capable in no respect, imagines himself to be a great lord. They hold themselves in high regard as if they were capable of great and wonderful things, in which respect they are much encouraged by dreams, held among them to be very significant and, indeed, it would appear that through dreams Satan holds the heathen bound and fettered and in close connection with himself."[24] For Zeisberger, "They are courageous where no danger is to be found, but in the face of danger or resistance they are fearful and the worst cowards."[25] Zeisberger, who one might expect to have a more favorable impression of Indians given his life's work, was typical. Most notably, this particular passage lumps all Indians together, despite his wide experience with different tribes. (He excepted "civilized" Indians who had adopted Christianity and European modes of living.) Such conflation was typical among whites, particularly among whites who had not spent time among differing tribes, which would complicate Continental efforts to maintain peaceful relations with the Delaware.[26]

But arbitrary and insulting generalizations were not the sole providence of whites. Indians were equally prone to call whites foolish and cowardly.[27] During the French and Indian War, Christian Frederick Post reported that suspicion of all whites was widespread and that the Native Americans viewed themselves as morally superior. Shingas, Tamaqua, Pisquetoman, and Delaware George told him, "We love you more than you love us; for when we take any prisoners from you, we treat them as our own children. We are poor, and yet we clothe them as well as we can, though you see our children are as naked as at the first. By this you may see that our hearts are better than yours."[28] The whites tomahawked to death and scalped in their homes or later as prisoners and the future adoptees who survived their beatings in the gauntlet might have disagreed. Just before the Revolution, Reverend Jones reported Indians "are very suspicious of us having some design to enslave them," and noted "It is said of the Cretians [Christians] that they were 'always liars, evil beasts, slow bellies.'"[29] John Heckewelder, the Moravian missionary, spent much of his life among the Delaware of Pennsylvania and Ohio and described their attitude toward whites:

> They [the Lenape] say that the hair of their [white] heads, their features, the various colours of their eyes, evince that they are not like themselves Lenni Lenape, an ORIGINAL PEOPLE, a race of men that has existed unchanged from the beginning of time; but they are a mixed race and therefore a *troublesome* one; wherever they may be, the Great Spirit, knowing the wickedness of their disposition, found it necessary to give them a great Book, and taught them how to read it, that they might know and observe what he wished them to do and abstain from. But they, the Indians, have no need of any such book to let them know the will of their Maker; they find it engraved on their own hearts they have had sufficient discernment given to them to distinguish good from evil, and by following that guide, they are sure not to err.[30]

Neither whites nor Indians, of course, lived up to their idealized versions of themselves or down to the other group's worst stereotype. But racial differences were a constant companion to conflict on the frontier. Such dehumanization is common in wartime, but its peacetime pre-existence among people who knew each other well as individuals set the stage for wartime barbarities.

During periods of warfare and open Indian raiding, fear was a constant companion to frontier settlers, which contributed to their general resentment of the Indians who were its proximate cause and the eastern elites who failed to create a secure frontier. J. Hector Saint John Crevecoueur was a Frenchman who made his first appearance in the Western Hemisphere as a soldier in the French army. At some point, he resided in Pennsylvania and then became a naturalized citizen in New York. In 1779, he attempted to return to France, was arrested by the British as a suspected spy, briefly imprisoned, and eventually allowed to sail for England, where he published *Letters from an American Farmer* in 1782.[31] Educated in France and England, Crevecoueur brought an outsider's eye to events in America, yet, like Lafayette and de Tocqueville, viewed Americans through a sympathetic lens. In *Letters from an American Farmer*, Crevecoueur attempted to explain the emerging United States to a European audience.

Crevecoeur's letters are those of a composite character, one drawn from his own experiences and travels, and not a first-person account. Still, they eloquently summarize the image Americans saw or wanted to see when they held up a mirror. His twelfth letter is entitled "Distresses of a Frontier-man," and captures the emotional state and experiences of settlers living under the constant threat of Indian attack for much of the last half of the eighteenth century.

> [W]e are almost insulated, and the houses are at a considerable distance from each other. From the mountains we have but too much reason to expect our dreadful enemy; the wilderness is a harbour where it is impossible to find them. It is a door through which they can enter our country whenever they please; and, as they seem to be determined to destroy the whole chain of frontiers, our fate cannot be far distant . . . almost all has been conflagrated one after another. What renders these incursions still more terrible is, that they most commonly take place in the dead of the night; we never go to our fields but we are seised with an involuntary fear, which lessens our strength and weakens our labour. No other subject of conversation intervenes between the different accounts, which spread through the country, of successive acts of devastation; and these told in chimney-corners, swell themselves in our affrightened imaginations into the most terrific ideas! We never sit down either to dinner or supper, but the least noise immediately spreads a general alarm and prevents us from enjoying the comfort of our meals. The very appetite proceeding from labour and peace of mind is gone; we eat just enough to keep us alive: our sleep is

> disturbed by the most frightful dreams; sometimes I start awake, as if the great hour of danger was come; at other times the howling of our dogs seems to announce the arrival of the enemy: we leap out of bed and run to arms: my poor wife with panting bosom and silent tears, takes leave of me, as if we were to see each other no more; she snatches the youngest children from their beds, who, suddenly awakened, increase by their innocent questions the horror of the dreadful moment. She tries to hide them in the cellar, as if our cellar was inaccessible to the fire. I place all my servants at the windows, and myself at the door, where I am determined to perish. Fear industriously increases every sound; we all listen; each communicates to the other his ideas and conjectures. We remain thus sometimes for whole hours, our hearts and our minds racked by the most anxious suspense: what a dreadful situation, a thousand times worse than that of a soldier engaged in the midst of the most severe conflict! Sometimes feeling the spontaneous courage of a man, I seem to wish for the decisive minute; the next instant a message from my wife, sent by one of the children, puzzling beside with their little questions, unmans me: away goes my courage, and I descend again into the deepest despondency. At last finding that it was a false alarm, we return once more to our beds; but what good can the kind of sleep of nature do to us when interrupted by such scenes![32]

Horror stories of Indians' atrocities spread widely, exacerbating those fears. Shortly after the Delaware joined the French and Indian War, Shingas took 150 Delaware to the east, where he raided settlements in Virginia and Pennsylvania. The Delaware approach to the war was not to risk large battles but to focus on raiding between and beyond a line of frontier forts. By falling on isolated settlements or individual farms, the Indians created a fear of imminent attack that caused settlers to abandon their homes and return east, essentially rolling back the frontier.[33] That, of course, made it harder for local authorities to raise militia or other defensive forces. One of the most infamous raids was the Penn's Creek Massacre, on October 16, 1755. Penn's Creek was a small community on the west bank of the Susquehanna, not far from the town of Shamokin. Raiding Indians, likely Delaware, first struck the farm of Jean Jacques Le Roy, rushing his house, tomahawking him, subduing his son, and taking both his daughters captive before feeding Le Roy's body to the hearth. They then moved on to the Leininger farm, killing all the males there and taking more captives. Altogether, the raid killed fourteen people and carried another ten off into captivity.[34] Six men from Paxton township were killed the same month. Then, on November 1, Indians killed forty-seven people at Great Cove. Fifty more died in Bethel Township. Such attacks would become commonplace, coming within seventy miles of Philadelphia. At Fort Duquesne, the French commandant counted five hundred scalps and some two hundred prisoners, mostly from Pennsylvania.[35] By mid-1756, some estimated that Indians had killed upward of three thousand settlers, usually in brutal ways that involved tomahawk strikes to the head, scalping, and mutilation of the bodies.[36]

A Delaware-led war party captured Fort Granville on the Juniata River in Pennsylvania, slaughtering some prisoners and carrying others off into captivity. Shortly thereafter, militia raided the Delaware town of Kittanning on the Allegheny River. During the raid, several prisoners attempted to escape. Some were recaptured and executed. But they were not simply killed. One woman was

> put to death in an unheard of way. First, they scalped her; next, they laid burning splinters of wood, here and there, upon her body; and then they cut off her ears and fingers, forcing them into her mouth so that she had to swallow them. Amidst such torments, this woman lived from nine o'clock in the morning until toward sunset, when a French officer took compassion on her, and put her out of her misery. . . . When she was dead, the Indians chopped her in two, through the middle, and let her lie until the dogs came and devoured her.[37]

More specific are the many affidavits registered with county officials across the frontier. Reverend Barton cited many of them in his defense of the Paxton Boys. Massy Herbeson swore out one such statement in Allegheny County, Pennsylvania. She lived about twenty-five miles from Pittsburgh, within two hundred yards of one of the many blockhouses in which families forted up when raiding parties were reported to be nearby. Just after sunrise, a war party fell on her home and the blockhouse, killing those men they found and dragging away those women and children they could catch. According to Herbeson, "a boy, about three years old, being unwilling to leave the house, they took it by the heels, and dashed it against the house; then stabbed and scalped it." A few miles away, "a boy of about five years of age, began to mourn for his brother: one of the Indians then tomahawked and scalped him."[38] Running the gauntlet was also a common occurrence for new captives and could result in death if a captive failed to reach the end.

Pontiac's War was even more terrifying, in part due to the speed with which British garrisons across the frontier fell. The raiding parties continued to strike farms around the Juniata Valley under the leadership of a western Delaware known to whites as Shamokin Daniel, a former Moravian convert.[39] His war party attacked the homestead of William White, firing into the building, wounding a few men, and then setting fire to it. Only one man escaped. Then they struck Robert Campbell's home, bursting into the house and shooting as Campbell and five other men sat down to dinner. Only one escaped. Other raiding parties, likely Delaware but possibly including Shawnee and some Great Lakes Indians, attacked the Anderson family in the Tuscarora Valley, killing them. Militia pursuit parties were ambushed, taking relatively high losses themselves.[40] In 1764, the western Indians continued to raid those frontier targets they could reach. Thirteen settlers were killed near Fort Loudon in Pennsylvania and a Delaware raiding party massacred nine children and their schoolmaster in the Conococheague Valley, then killed a pregnant woman nearby, mutilating her body and that of her unborn child in the process.[41] Those stories were shared widely along the frontier and became a commonly shared cultural touchpoint that persisted after hostilities ended.

For people living on the frontier, the war was small but very intimate. Although a few campaigns involving over a thousand soldiers took place, fighting mostly involved sudden raids on poorly defended homes and outposts or skirmishes between bands of warriors and modest companies of militia. Indian war parties generally contained warriors from multiple tribes and might number between six and forty. Sometimes they included white officers, but raiding parties required no oversight to raid the frontier. Once a large war party reached the frontier, it might separate into smaller groups to attack specific farms or villages. During the Revolution, Zeisberger noted that they frequently passed through Delaware territory on their way to and from the American settlements. On October 31, 1776, he noted a company of warriors in Goschgosching headed for the settlements and Isaac (Glickhican) reported a westbound group of Wyandot warriors passing through with three scalps. Moravians encountered another group nearby on November 6. Just over two weeks later, they identified another group of six warriors passing through with two scalps on a pole. Fourteen more frontier-bound warriors passed nearby on December 19.[42] On January 3, 1777, a party of Shawnee passed through on their way to the Wyandot towns. They carried three scalps and one prisoner.[43] On April 14, another party passed through with five prisoners: one woman and four children.[44] In May, he reported a large party of fifty warriors had gone eastward and already stolen three hundred horses. Two other parties of Wyandot, Mingo, and Munsee warriors followed before the month was out.[45] On June 18, a Shawnee chief passing through on his way to Fort Pitt told the Moravians that a large party of Minqo, Shawnee, and Wyandot warriors had just returned to Shawnee territory from the frontier, bringing with them eight prisoners and twenty horses.[46]

This was all before Governor Hamilton's grand council at Detroit escalated the war. Afterward, the number of war parties and intimidation tactics used against the missionaries grew. Twenty-three Mingo and Wyandot warriors passed through in July, threatening the Moravian Indians and their missionaries on the way east, and then parading three scalps, three prisoners (all children), and eight horses through town on their westbound return.[47] White fear and hatred toward Indians were predictable responses.

In August 1777, Dunquat of the Wyandot arrived in Delaware territory with a very large war party and stayed, turning Goschgosching and the Moravian towns into a forward base. The Moravians provided them with food and noticed one band had four scalps and a prisoner with it. With Dunquat in town, the Delaware and Moravians played de facto host to one side of the war. In less than a month, the number of pro-British warriors staying at Goschgosching had swelled from the low 80s to some 250.[48] Amidst all the feasting and provisioning of the war parties by the Moravians, Zeisberger looked for a silver lining: "If they stay much longer, they will eat us out of house and home. They do not seem to be in much of a hurry to go to the Settlements, much less to have a battle with the White people. If they turned back it would be worth the trouble of entertaining them for so long."[49] Some even attended services.

Glickhican approached Dunquat and his fellow chiefs, making an argument for peace and attempting to throw a blanket of protection over the missionaries themselves. The converted Delaware's words had an impact, no doubt aided by the Moravians' commitment to feeding the assembled warriors. Dunquat kept order among his warriors and they did not plunder Moravian resources generally or threaten the missionaries individually. When it was time to leave, the war chief "thanked the Brothers warmly for all the kindness that they had shown them and all the goodness they had enjoyed from us, and said they would not forget this."[50] Moreover, he pledged to inform the other warring tribes and Governor Hamilton of the hospitality his war party had received from the Moravians, ostensibly with an eye toward protecting them from other pro-British war parties. For their part, the Moravian missionaries attempted to extract a promise from Dunquat not to pass through their towns lest they become the object of retaliation by the Pennsylvania militia. He and his warriors generally ignored the request. The visit, uninvited as it was, could only revive settler suspicion and animosity toward the Delaware and their Moravian guests.

Things looked different from the settler's perspective. As was the case in the French and Indian War and Pontiac's War, the settler experience survives largely anecdotally and was not always recorded accurately at the time of events. A sampling of a few from 1777 and 1778, however, can give one a feel for how frontier settlers perceived their experiences of the Revolution as the frontier war intensified.

In 1777, the Grigsby family lived on the west fork of the Monongahela River. While Mr. Grigsby was away, a small band carried off his wife and two children. He and his neighbors pursued. Six miles on, he found the bodies of his wife and one child. Both had been tomahawked. Some time later, two young men watched two Indians scalp a young woman, Miss Coons, while she was working in fields near "Coons Fort." The Indians escaped.[51] In July, Colonel John Gibson reported to General Hand that two men stopped at George Baker's house near Beaver Creek in Pennsylvania only to find it standing empty, the entire family (Baker, his wife, and five children) missing and Indians about.[52] From Fort Pitt, Colonel William Crawford, a business partner of George Washington's who made his home on the Youghiogheny River and had fought in the east, reported to Congress:

> the late depredations and murders which were committed by the Indians at different places in this neighbourhood, makes it appear to me as if a general irruption was threatened. On the 6th and 7th instant, they killed and scalped one man at Raccoon Creek, about twenty five miles from this place; at Muchmore's plantation, about forty five miles down the Ohio, they killed and scalped one man, and burnt a woman and her four children; at Wheeling they killed and scalped one man, the body of whom was much mangled with tomahawks and other instruments suitable for barbarity; at Dunkard's Creek, one of the east branches of the Monongahela river, they killed and scalped one man and a woman and took three children; and at each of the above places they burned houses, killed cattle, hogs, &c.[53]

Similar reports rolled in all summer, an almost mind-numbing litany of personal violence. Even in winter, which usually dampened campaigning activity among both whites and Indians, war parties ranged across the upper Ohio Valley. Some twenty Indians had reached the Tygart Valley, where they attacked the Connoly family, killing the father, his wife, and several children before escaping with three prisoners. On the way home, they killed John Stewart, his wife, and his child while taking Stewart's sister-in-law captive.[54] In July, Hand received a report that a militia party investigating a raid "found the House and Barn in flaims they found one man & a Cheild Killd and scalped, seven other Persons waise Either Killd taken Prisoners he Could not be Possative which at the time He Give me the Enformation." This was, of course, followed by a plea for assistance as the commanding officer was short on supplies and soldiers, which might lead him to quit the frontier altogether.[55] It was how the settlers and Indians fought on the upper Ohio. On more than one occasion, the western tribes were even able to cobble enough forces to together to lay a loose siege against poorly manned and supplied forts along the frontier.

Inevitably, American attention turned to Detroit. Hand had been unable to gather sufficient forces in 1777, but the object had not been set aside. The same Congressional commissioners who investigated Morgan and may have prompted McKee, Girty, and others to flee Pittsburgh for Detroit in 1778 had also been charged with cooperating with General Hand to carry the war into British territory, namely Detroit.[56] When General Lachlan McIntosh replaced him, he also set his eyes on Detroit. The 1778 Treaty of Pittsburgh facilitated his advance to the Muskingum, where he built Fort Laurens. McIntosh's intent was to advance to Detroit in the summer of 1779. However, Fort Laurens came under siege in the winter of 1778-1779.[57] Still, it and the cold drew enough of the war parties away from Goschgosching and Lichtenau for the Moravian missionaries and Indians to begin relocating to their old villages farther east to ease overcrowding and hopefully provide an added degree of safety.

For much of 1778, western war parties had purposely built their primary war path through all of the Delaware towns, terminating at Lichtenau, where, as we have seen, the warriors might be fed. From there, war bands would break up into smaller parties and set out for American settlements across the Ohio. After the raids were done, war parties would follow the path in reverse, assembling first at Lichtenau. The missionaries feared that this increased the danger to both the Delaware and the Moravian converts, particularly from pursuing militia parties. Heckewelder noted, "it might be expected that at one time or an other, the Americans, being in pursuit of warriors, who had committed murders on the south side of the Ohio, might, by following the traces of them along the path, be led straightaway into Lichtenau, and fall upon the Christian Indians, believing them to have been the aggressors."[58] It was a reasonable, and entirely accurate, concern. After all, it was just that kind of suspicion that had contributed to the Paxton Boys march on Philadelphia. In all likelihood, the western tribes hoped to provoke just such an event, which might be expected to lead the Delaware remaining along the Muskingum, converted or not, to join Hopocan or side with the British.

Militia concerns went well beyond that. The old suspicion that individual Moravian Indians were participating in raids or spying on white settlements returned during the Revolution. The case was circumstantial, as it had been before. First, the war path to Lichtenau was a problem. Second, the Moravians fed war parties passing through. In many ways, it was involuntary and meant to prevent the Delaware and Moravians themselves from being raided, but there is no doubt it made life easier for war parties. Third, when McKee, Girty, and others defected to the British, they made straight for the Delaware towns, where they expected to find a receptive audience. It was only Koquethaqechton's political skills, Moravian influence, and Heckewelder's ability to play the proper role that kept the Delaware from going to war at that moment. Fourth, individual Delaware had been reportedly participating in raids virtually since the war's beginning, even though tribal leaders sought to discourage it. The Delaware split after the Treaty of Fort Pitt made things even more problematic when Hopocan and the Wolf phratry moved west, closer to the British. Fifth, the militia failed to distinguish among tribes, let alone factions among the Delaware: pro-war Wolf, pro-peace Turkey and Turtle, and pro-peace Moravians. Just as Koquethaqechton viewed the Moravian Indians as part of his nation, so did frontier settlers, no matter how hard Zeisberger and Heckewelder fought to make it otherwise. Finally, the western nations and British had consistently pressured the Delaware to join the war.

The militia were largely unaware of mitigating factors. Zeisberger and Koquethaqechton went to some lengths to provide intelligence to American officials at Fort Pitt. Often, however, such assistance was kept secret at the request of both men. The British already suspected Zeisberger and the missionaries, so he was careful to remind Continental authorities not to spread word of his assistance. He wrote Morgan in 1778, "Inclosed you have a Message from Capt White Eyes, you will be cautious enough that it may not be known among the people at the Fort but such as ought to know of it why these Messengers who know nothing of the matter themselves, come to the Fort—for White Eyes & I are blamed & accus'd before the Governor at Detroit for giving you Intelligence of the Affairs in Indian Country, but I believe all this is the fruit of Mr McKee's labour at Detroit. I hope you have been careful concerning my Person while he was yet at the Fort."[59] Koquethaqechton also warned Continental authorities to keep his correspondence with them secret. When he corresponded with Morgan, Koquethaqechton used messengers who were unaware of the contents of the messages they carried. "I am blamed by the Nations that I betray them, therefore keep all what I tell you secret. These two Messengers I send privately & *none of my people knoweth of it but I, because I cannot trust them*, but am glad that I can inform you of this by these messengers."[60]

By the winter of 1779, things did not bode well for the Americans along the Pennsylvania frontier. First, McIntosh was still short of manpower, despite the relatively large number of troops he had revealed to Delaware leaders the prior fall. The general hoped to call upon the Virginia militia, but state authorities countermanded his summons, largely fearing its men could not be sustained.[61] Things were worse with the Pennsylvanians. McIntosh held a low opinion of the Pennsylvania militia and wrote the vice president of Pennsylvania's Executive Council, "I must observe to you, that all the Militia I had were from the State of Virginia, & none from Pennsylvania, nor would they be of any Service if they were willing, & had Joined me, as your present Militia Law, I understand, allows them, or which comes to the same thing, does not oblige them to serve above two Months, one half of which will commonly be taken up in collecting them together."[62] The reverse was also true. Frontier whites held low opinions of the Continentals, who failed to protect them, and continued to demonstrate that independent streak that had always frustrated eastern authorities' efforts to maintain peace with the Delaware.

Second, Americans could not maintain Forts McIntosh or Laurens. McIntosh went so far as to seek supplies from the more friendly Delaware at Goschgosching. Worse, he demanded a peace conference with them and the Indian nations farther west shortly after news of Koquethaqechton's death reached their towns.[63] When McIntosh declared that those who did not "heartily" take up the hatchet with the Americans "should be looked upon as Enemys of the United State of America," he was met with a "General Laugh."[64] Nevertheless, the nearby Delaware agreed to provide him with some supplies. Still, in January 1779 the fort commander reported "unless a Supply of Cloathing soon Arrives, I shall not have fifty men fit for duty in a short time."[65]

Third, the relationship with friendly Delaware was tenuous at best. As McIntosh had marched west in November–December 1778, Hopocan's pro-war Delaware continued mixing with those who had inclined toward Koquethaqechton's view of things.[66] Naturally, they encouraged their fellow Delaware to abandon the Americans. After McIntosh's departure, Colonel John Gibson, commanding the 13th Virginia at Fort Laurens, would report that John Killbuck (Gelelemend) was now a captain in the American service and brought seven Delaware into the fort where they were "heartily Sorry for the part they have [taken and are] inclined for peace," meaning some local Delaware were still not reconciled to the Americans.[67]

Hopocan himself sent mixed signals. The Americans sent messages to him and Dunquat asking to meet. Gibson received their reply via Gelelemend. Both begged off a face-to-face meeting and Hopocan appeared to set aside any grievances he might have over the deaths of his family members during Hand's Squaw campaign. When the Americans apologized, Hopocan replied, "I now inform you that I never thought of it, until your mentioning of it, put me in mind of it. I now acquaint that my heart is good and that I never meant to quit the hold I have of the friendship subsisting Between us. If you are desirous of Speaking of the Loss of my friends, who were killed at the Salt Licks, there is a great many of my Relations at Cooshackung; your speaking to them will answer the same End as Speaking to me."[68] Whether Hopocan's expression was meant sarcastically, deceitfully, or sincerely was a matter for interpretation. Both his and Dunquat's unwillingness to meet with the Americans face-to-face could have been out of honest fear for their safety; it could just as easily reflect a politician's desire to keep options open by avoiding an in-person discussion. In January, Gibson hired Samuel Sample as his agent in Goschgosching to arrange trade with the Delaware there. Sample visited the town with a caravan, only to have one man killed and scalped, three horses shot, and two stolen with their packs by Delaware Indians.[69]

Fourth, western Indians resolved to lay a loose siege on Fort Laurens. Zeisberger heard a raiding party was in the field in late January 1779, which he promptly communicated to George Morgan in Pittsburgh.[70] Simon Girty had indeed set out with a small party earlier that month, and raiders fell on a supply party returning from Fort Laurens late in the month, killing two, wounding four, and capturing one.[71] Girty was soon back near Detroit, trying to raise a force to mount a sustained siege. The British responded by sending a regular officer, Captain Henry Bird, to bring order to such an effort. Bird watched the western Indians torture, kill, and behead their captive and then listened to their plans.[72] Eventually, a force of Indians from several tribes set out and arrived at Fort Laurens on February 22. The next day, they surprised a work party outside the fort's walls, killing and scalping seventeen men and capturing two within sight of the fort's walls.[73]

Gelelemend denied that Delaware were involved in these attacks and blamed them on Girty. Moreover, he had dispatched messengers far and wide encouraging other Indian nations to have peace with the Americans. But average Americans had reasons to be suspicious. After all, Delaware warriors had been involved in the attacks on Gibson's traders at Goschgosching. Zeisberger also reported internally that Indian warriors involved in the siege of Fort Laurens circulated among the nearby Moravian towns. In March, a relief flotilla traveling by water had been ambushed at the mouth of the Muskingum.[74]

All spring, raids continued. McIntosh himself believed that Delaware warriors were involved in the siege of Fort Laurens and reported to Washington that a scalping party had penetrated to Turtle Creek east of Pittsburgh and killed or carried off eighteen people of all ages.[75] Heckewelder recorded that war parties were easily moving through the Moravian towns, writing in April, "The following parties have come from war through our towns within a fortnight: First a party of Mingoes with 3 children prisoners; a party of 10 Delawares and Shawanoes, with 2 scalps and 2 children prisoners, they also brought off a sucking child, which always crying they killed by Little Beaver Creek." When a party of Shawnee moved through the town with three prisoners, including an eighty-four-year-old man, the Moravians attempted to purchase his freedom but were rebuffed. He also reported that a party of Wyandot had moved through after killing two men on the frontier.[76] In April, reports circulated at Fort Pitt that a scalping party attempted to raid a farm on the Cheat River; a Mrs. Sampson's son was taken at his farm while another man and woman in the area were captured. Four men sent from Fort Pitt for Hannastown were found killed and scalped. Mid-month, David Maxwell and his wife were killed and scalped; their daughter had already been captured. The *Maryland Journal* reported that Indians attacked a settlement at "York Glades," killing four men.[77] Fort Hand was attacked, with one killed and two wounded while everything outside the fort was destroyed. Near Fort Ligonier, one man was killed, two were missing, and several houses had been burned and cattle killed or run off. Three men were killed south of Braddock's old road with six or seven more missing.[78]

Gelelemend's diplomatic efforts and his provision of information to the Continental officers and George Morgan were largely unknown to most Americans. The spring of 1779 felt as eerily similar to the violence of 1778 as it did to Pontiac's War. For them, the Treaty of Fort Pitt, McIntosh's advance beyond Fort Pitt, and the establishment of Fort Laurens and its garrisoning with Continental soldiers had changed nothing. Instead, frontier settlers knew only of raids, killings, and scalpings close to Delaware country, often involving Delaware warriors.

Colonel Daniel Brodhead replaced General McIntosh in March. He faced the problem of preventing precipitate action by whites on the frontier. One of his own Continental soldiers had killed a pro-peace Delaware while other frontier parties had assembled to murder Delaware chiefs bound for a meeting with the Continental Congress in Philadelphia.[79] Joseph Reed, president of Pennsylvania, expressed his regret that the state could not provide support to his forces, in part because no such support was available but also because he had doubt "whether the People in the Back Counties would suffer them to proceed, so violent are the Prejudices against the Indians. It has been with great Difficulty that we got the Indians back that came down lately; there were several Parties made up to destroy them on their Return, which were disappointed by the Indians taking an unexpected and circuitous Route."[80]

In the late spring of 1779, American attention turned away from Detroit and toward the Six Nations and Fort Niagara, which Americans blamed for raids in eastern Pennsylvania and New York. General Washington planned a multi-pronged campaign against the Iroquois under the command of Major General John Sullivan. The offensive would drive the Six Nations out of their traditional territories but precluded an offensive against Detroit. Indeed, Washington looked to those limited forces to march north from Fort Pitt up the Allegheny Valley and into Seneca territory, from where they might join Sullivan.[81]

Brodhead set out from Fort Pitt on August 11. He marched north to Seneca towns along the upper Allegheny, crossing the river several times. His column loitered three days destroying houses and despoiling some five hundred acres of corn crops. His force returned to Fort

Pitt in September with Brodhead convinced that "the counties of Westmoreland, Bedford, & Northumberland . . . will experience the good effect."[82]

Brodhead's expedition exacerbated the security dilemma for the remaining Delaware and Moravian communities along the Muskingum. The Treaty of Fort Pitt was predicated on an overland campaign to capture Detroit and building forts to protect the Delaware. Gelelemend had used the threat of an impending American invasion to good diplomatic effect. American inaction weakened Gelelemend's hold on the loyalty of his own nation. He wrote General McIntosh, "I am sorry to tell you, that as this has been made known to the Nations, and they finding nothing that has been done by you all this time, mock and make all the Game of me they Can, they try all they Can to disturb, and Convince my People that you are telling them, that which is not true, pointing to your not having fulfille'd your promise, and saying you were not able to do it, there being but a very few of you. . . . This makes me indeed much troubled, and disturbs my People greatly, thinking they might perhaps be really disappointed at last. Many have left me since last Fall for this Reason."[83] Brodhead recognized this in the spring of 1779 and raised it with Washington, but the commander-in-chief's changing focus rendered his arguments moot.[84] With that, Brodhead's campaign up the Allegheny required more men and he abandoned Fort Laurens, further undermining the Delaware peace faction.[85]

Not long after returning to Fort Pitt, Brodhead learned he had a problem with settlers crossing the Ohio River near Wheeling, building cabins and planting fields in territory that was Delaware land. As they had under the British crown, these squatters threatened attempts to promote peace between whites and Indians and they ranged from the mouth of the Muskingum all the way to Fort McIntosh and well up the Ohio River's major tributaries.[86] The problem was acute for Brodhead, who replied to a letter from Colonel David Shepherd, "I fear the imprudence or design of the Trespassers will involve the innocent in new Calamaties." More importantly, he pledged to take action against the frontier settlers: "I shall take the most prudent steps to prevent any ill consequence arising from such folly or villainy and in the mean time will endeavour to make an example of some to terrify the rest."[87] He implored Shepherd to enlist the aid of civil authorities in executing evictions but also ordered Continentals to assist with arrests as necessary. Next, he wrote to the Delaware council at Goschgosching, informing them of the trespassers and actions he had taken.[88]

Brodhead spent 1780 largely attempting to keep the Delaware gathered at Goschgosching and frontier settlers apart and his own Continental forces intact. The former required additional diplomacy and unkept promises to send traders among the Delaware. His difficulties on that score led Brodhead to propose that the friendly Delaware and Moravians move closer to Pittsburgh, where they might be more easily supplied and protected from the warring tribes to the west. Zeisberger, however, opposed the plan. His congregation had reason to avoid whites given their treatment during Pontiac's War: the Paxton Boys had, after all, explicitly blamed and threatened the Moravian Indians under protection at Philadelphia. He also feared that co-locating with a fort would more directly involve the Moravian community and Delaware Indians in the war.[89] Last but not least, he told Brodhead that the Moravians were reluctant to move their communities lest it require them to give up the work they had already done establishing themselves on the Muskingum.[90] It was a disingenuous argument given the number of times the Moravians had relocated already.

Brodhead's efforts to keep his own troops together as a fighting force resulted in constant pleading with authorities in the east—who had nothing to offer—and attempts to recruit locally, which conflicted with the work of county-based militia groups to maintain their own numbers. Meanwhile, he had to contend with ongoing raids in the face of growing evidence that some Delaware were participating.[91] Gelelemend denied it but conceded raiders were moving prisoners freely through his town, including one group of twenty children and three adults.[92] Heckewelder wrote separately that Dunquat of the Wyandot was leading raids and that Neeshawsh, a Mahican, was leading a group of Delaware warriors on raids.[93] For Americans on the frontier, it was easier to count the victims than track the tribal affiliations of the raiders. Brodhead reported to Washington that between March 1 and April 24, 1780, Indians had killed and taken forty-three men, women, and children in "the counties of Youghiogany, Monongalia, and Ohio."[94] The raids only intensified across the back country during the summer.

Militarily, Brodhead still wanted to take the offensive but shifted targets from Detroit to the warring Indian nations. He needed to demonstrate to frontier communities that he was addressing their security problem. Brodhead considered a march overland against the Wyandot while George Rogers Clark focused on the Shawnee.[95] Alas for Brodhead, and despite his frequent attempts to gather troops and resources during the summer of 1780, this offensive did not come to pass. Meanwhile, he was authorized by the state of Pennsylvania to offer scalp bounties, which he admitted concerned him, as they might lead local militia to collect scalps from friendly Delaware! All he could do was warn the Muskingum Delaware to be careful and avoid those places that put them at risk from whites, while encouraging them to attack eastbound war parties and collect their scalps for the bounty.[96]

Once again, the American failure to take up an offense against the western Indians undermined the American-aligned Delaware. The council wrote Brodhead in April, "I am so much mocked at by the Enemy Inds for speaking so long to them for You. Now they laugh at me, and ask me where that great Army of my Brothers, that was to come out against them so long ago, and so often, stays so long. They say to me, did We not tell that they had no Army and that we were nearly done killing them all, and yet You would believe them? They further desire me to tell You now to make haste and come soon, the sooner, and the greater Your Number the better."[97] Defections from the peace faction, which we can surmise based on the number of reports of hostile Delaware taking place in raids and the frequency with which the Goschgosching council either apologized for, or denied, involvement of their "foolish young men" in such raids, only weakened the peace faction further and undermined the only friendly Indian nation that the Americans might find in the Upper Ohio Valley. Thus, the Continentals' inability to take the offensive left both settlers and the Goschgosching Delaware dissatisfied and feeling vulnerable. It poured fuel into that independent streak that led frontier settlers and militia to take matters into their own hands.

Gelelemend had his problems, but the Continentals were in bad shape as well. As in the last two wars, armed frontiersmen saw all Indians as enemies or potential enemies not to be trusted. So, despite the assistance the Muskingum Delaware, including the Moravian communities, were providing to Colonel Brodhead, the indiscriminate hatred of Indians reared its ugly head in the Upper Ohio Valley again in the fall of 1780. Brodhead reported that a group of whites from Hannastown on the Allegheny had set out to destroy a group of friendly Delaware who had moved closer to Fort Pitt. To Brodhead's knowledge, it was led by former Continental officers who had joined the militia after their discharges. The colonel had posted guards to protect these Indians, who lived on McKee's Island below Pittsburgh and who caused the white raiding party to give up its plans.[98] Meanwhile, Brodhead's continued efforts to supply his forces and his need to resort to seizing provisions from local farms and merchants earned him no friends. He even heard rumors that some intended to resist by force of arms, worsening relations between his command and the local community.[99]

Brodhead's frustration with his situation was palpable, and he began looking askance at the local whites, suspecting a significant number of having Loyalist sympathies. At the same time, he felt adrift when it came to relations with the Goschgosching Delaware. He was unable to supply his own troops adequately, much less provide the Delaware with trade goods and supplies promised in the Treaty of Fort Pitt or make adequate use of those Delaware committed to the Americans. Squatting also remained a problem.[100] Moreover, he had concerns about growing animosity between the Delaware and the frontier settlers, about which he could do little.[101]

During the winter of 1780-1781, things went from bad to worse. Brodhead's foraging parties largely failed, sometimes going hungry themselves. So, he approached the Goschgosching Delaware, including those who had joined the Moravians, with an eye toward encouraging them to hunt on his behalf. They declined, much to his frustration. He could only tell Zeisberger, "I . . . am sorry to find that the proposal I made to obtain a quantity of wild meat was not accepted. It is probably that I said the Christian Indians declined assisting in the war, but I expected as a testimony of their attachment to American liberty they would not be averse to serving their country in affording supplies for the troops by every means in their power." Worse, he had heard that the Moravian Indians possessed a significant number of pigs that might help feed his troops, but they would only accept hard currency, which he lacked. Thus, he feared that the swine might end up feeding the British and their allies in Detroit![102] Brodhead's fears were warranted. Zeisberger reported that Indians hired by the English were in town at the end of the summer to trade for cattle and that Indians who had joined the church even herded their cattle to the western tribes on the Sandusky River.[103] In short, Brodhead's pleas for support from the Moravian towns were refused—he lacked the specie needed to pay for supplies—while the Moravian communities traded with the enemy. In all likelihood, his frustration was known to whites living on the frontier, giving them more reasons to distrust the Moravian communities. About the same time, the Moravian Indians, who had moved back to the eastern branch of the Muskingum, began leaving Lichtenau en masse and established a new town, which they named Salem.

The falling out between Brodhead and the Goschgosching Delaware only grew. Gelelemend had accepted a commission and was serving as a captain, leading him to relinquish some of his influence with the tribe. A leader who went by the name William Penn the Indian stepped up on behalf of the Delaware council. He informed Brodhead that it now desired a fort in Delaware territory, just when the colonel had no resources to build or man one, leading him to disappoint the tribe again.[104] Worse, Gelelemend had gone absent without leave.[105] It sparked distrust from the colonel, who wrote John Heckewelder, "Killbuck appears to have acted with duplicity . . . I conceive that much confidence ought never to be placed in any of the colour, for I believe it is much easier for the most civilized Indian to turn Savage than for any Indian to be civilized."[106] Thus, one of Brodhead's strongest allies among the Goschgosching Delaware was weakened within the tribe and unreliable as a captain in the Continental army, which provoked Brodhead's latent racism. And he was a man who had trusted Indians well enough to look to them for military cooperation and fill out any army he raised, although he was careful to hide this from the Delaware themselves. For his part, Gelelemend found himself walking in Koquethaqechton's shoes, trying to navigate the space between the white and Indian worlds during a time of war. He wanted to settle with the Moravians but was reluctant to give up his earthly roles in order to accept the spiritual demands that life as a United Brethren would make on him. The missionaries only advised him that he would have to choose between one or the other; he could not be both a Delaware chief and a Moravian communicant.[107] Thus, the bridge between the Americans and Delaware that Gelelemend and Brodhead had tried to maintain for nearly two years was weakening at both ends.

By February, events would prove Brodhead's skepticism, if not his racism, about the Muskingum Delaware correct. On February 26, 1781, the colonel received a letter from Gelelemend. First, it attempted to repair their personal rift. But, more importantly, it revealed that the Goschgosching Delaware council had been lying to the colonel for months. It had already dispatched emissaries to the Wyandot to declare for them and the British in the war. Gelelemend must have sensed the break coming, for when he returned to the Muskingum, he stayed in the Moravian towns: "I have been here all this time, The Council of Coochochking, have entirely stop'd my ears so that I know nothing." But he heard through the grapevine about the diplomatic mission to the Wyandot. Worse, some Goschgosching Delaware warriors had already gone off to raid white settlements on the frontier and a large party was gathering to follow.[108] Heckewelder, who had helped Gelelemend compose his letter, wrote separately confirming the intelligence.

> I could never learn what they were properly about, for they kept theer matters very Secret—Now it is almost publickly known, that

> they are about no good business, & have been very busy in trying to decieve you this long time they have, as I am informed, also told lies of Us brethren, I must wonder at their stupidity . . . I apprehend they will find themselves in the trap at last. I indeed believe that the greatest part of them will be upon you in a few days, they have already been stop'd once or twice, but I daile hear they will go soon, they have ranged themselves into three partys, & if I am right one party is gone of already but I hope they will recieve what they deserve.

Heckewelder explained that the council sought to further undermine Gelelemend's influence and concluded with a plea for the safety of those Indians who had converted to Christianity under Moravian tutelage. "Should it be concluded, on that a body of Men Shal march to Coochockung to punish these wicked People I trust that your honor will do all that lies in your power to prevent mislesting any body belonging to our Towns, and you may depend Sir, that in case any of your Men should have occasion to come by any of our Towns, that they would meet with much kindness from our People."[109]

Brodhead did not take Gelelemend's or Heckewelder's word for it but waited for additional intelligence to confirm that the Muskingum Delaware had joined the war against the Americans. With that, he forwarded the information to Continental officials and militia officers and announced his desire to conduct a campaign against Goschgosching, which his ongoing lack of supplies precluded.[110] Because he could not take an offensive unilaterally, Brodhead turned to the militia. While he waited, those Delaware who remained friendly to the Americans began filtering into the area around the Moravian towns (over the objections of the missionaries) and Pittsburgh, where they might receive some protection. Pennsylvania state authorities were receptive. Joseph Reed authorized Colonel Archibald Lochry of Westmoreland County to raise a force and place it under Brodhead's command during offensive operations.[111]

Finally, in April, Brodhead departed Fort Pitt with 150 Continental soldiers, moving down the Ohio to Wheeling, where he would rendezvous with a comparable number of militia under the command of Colonel David Shepherd and arranged into four companies under the command of reliable militia officials. From there, they crossed the Ohio, bound for Goschgosching. As an indication of the depth of the latest split among the Delaware, his force included at least two Delaware, likely acting as scouts. Oral tradition has it that one was related to Gelelemend and was murdered at Wheeling, but no documentary evidence has confirmed the story.[112] If true, it would further demonstrate the racial animus that the white militia held for all Indians without respect to an individual Indian's role in the war.

Brodhead made good time to the Muskingum, but high water prevented him from crossing immediately. Salem, the latest Moravian town to be built, was on his line of march, so Brodhead stopped at the river a few miles below town and sent a messenger by Indian runner requesting provisions and a meeting with someone there. The Moravians provided some supplies and Reverend Heckewelder rode out to meet him. When the missionary arrived, Brodhead asked whether any Moravian Indians were away from their villages hunting or in Goschgosching on business. Heckewelder indicated there were none, at which point Brodhead expressed his desire to make sure no Moravian Indians were molested.[113] According to Heckewelder, Brodhead assured him that the Moravian Indians had conducted themselves humanely during the war and neither the English nor the Americans could accuse them otherwise; the presence of Christian missionaries was an indicator of their peaceful intentions on the frontier. Given Brodhead's frustration with the Moravian communities earlier, his speech was probably meant for the militia, which had consistently demonstrated animosity toward the Moravian Indians. Indeed, at least one company of the militia with Brodhead threatened to march upriver and destroy the Moravian towns. Brodhead, aided by Colonel Shepherd, faced them down, but the occasion confirmed that frontier whites viewed the Moravian towns as a security problem.[114]

From the outskirts of Salem, Brodhead resumed his march to Goschgosching. A few miles from the town, the Americans took a prisoner, but two other Indians they encountered escaped. Fearing they would spread the alarm, Brodhead quickened his pace during a downpour. Upon arriving at the town's outskirts, the Americans destroyed those portions of the village east of the river, despoiled crops, and took many Delaware prisoners.[115] Pekillon, a friendly Delaware with the army, identified several as warriors who had attacked white settlements.[116] After dark that day, an American war council determined their fate. They were sentenced to death, bound, taken just outside the town, killed with tomahawks and spears, then scalped.[117] The remaining captives stayed with the army.

The next day, a Delaware leader reportedly came to the still-swollen river and declared he wanted peace with the Americans. Brodhead invited him and several other chiefs to cross the Muskingum to talk. After initially declining out of fear and receiving Brodhead's promise of safe passage, the Delaware chief crossed to speak with the colonel. While the two were conversing, a militiaman rushed up and killed the chief. After that, Brodhead's small army departed for Pittsburgh, but militiamen reportedly killed a large number of their prisoners on the return march.[118] On his way back to the Ohio, Brodhead invited those friendly Delaware in the area and the missionaries to join him at Pittsburgh where he might offer them some protection. Gelelemend and his remaining followers agreed, but the Moravians decided to remain on the Muskingum alone, without either the Delaware or the Americans to shield them.[119] Those Goschgosching Delaware who had declared war on the Americans and escaped Brodhead's force went west for the Sandusky.

The mind-set that would execute prisoners was well established among frontier settlers. For Brodhead and Shepherd, it was one thing to face down a company threatening mutiny to march on Christian Indians. It was another to protect enemy prisoners from revenge in the dark during a long march back to the Ohio River. Crevecouer described the cumulative experience of living under persistent fear on the frontier and the ultimate impact on rational thought: "I am seised with a fever of the mind, I am transported beyond that degree of calmness which is necessary to delineate our thoughts. I feel as if my reason wanted to leave me, as if it would burst its poor weak tenement."[120] Later, he admitted, "sentiment and feeling are the only guides I know. Alas, how should I unravel an argument, in which reason herself hath given way to brutality and bloodshed!"[121] In his view, one's perspective narrowed and was difficult for outsiders to appreciate. Instead of identifying with a wider society, the frontier settler living under persistent threat of random violence in the night begins to identify with "the inferior division in the midst of which I live. . . . As a citizen of a smaller society, I find that any kind of opposition to its now prevailing sentiments, immediately begets hatred: how easily do men pass from loving, to hating and cursing one another!"[122]

Under such circumstances, the principles over which the American Revolution was ostensibly being fought lost their pride of place. Instead, the frontiersman dismissed great leaders, noting, in Crevecouer's formulation, "were he situated where I am, were his house perpetually filled, as mine is, with miserable victims just escaped from the flames and the scalping knife, telling of barbarities and murders, that make human nature tremble; his situation would suspend every political reflection, and expel every abstract idea. My heart is full and involuntarily takes hold of any notion from whence it can receive ideal ease or relief."[123]

Joseph Doddridge echoed the sentiment. He grew up in the region and was one of the first to attempt collecting and recording oral histories and family stories from participants and their descendants. He described a similar loss of reason caused by years of unremitting warfare.

> The pressure of the Indian war along the whole of the western frontier, for several years preceding the event under consideration, had been dreadfully severe. From early in the spring until the commencement of winter, from day to day, murders were committed in every direction by the Indians. The people lived in forts which were in the highest degree uncomfortable. The men were harassed continually with the duties of going on scouts and campaigns. There was scarcely a family of the first settlers who did not, at some time or other, lose more or less of their number by the mer-

> ciless Indians. Their cattle were killed, their cabins burned and their horses carried off. These losses were severely felt by a people so poor as we were at that time. Thus circumstanced our people were exasperated to madness by the extent and severity of the war.[124]

Thus, by the summer of 1781, frontier settlers had managed to combine a sense of victimization with race hatred and demonstrated an inclination to "solve" their problem by destroying the source of their fear: the security problem that Continentals had been unable to address. It was a formula for disaster.

Four

Calamities

By the summer of 1781, the American Revolution had further isolated the Moravian mission communities. During the war's first years, British and American interest in not provoking the Delaware or, better yet, the hope of enlisting them as allies, had meant treating that nation with kid gloves. To the degree that the Moravians were helpful, they were off limits. So long as the community could maintain Delaware neutrality, it could hope to preserve the relatively "peaceful" state of affairs on the Muskingum. Tolerating the passing war parties and providing intelligence to the Americans were the price of safety. Several things undermined that strategy. First, Indian raids across the Ohio precluded true peace on the frontier for settlers. In the early years, the Delaware and other nations might proclaim neutrality and their leaders might disavow the actions of some warriors—which Continental authorities might be willing to accept—but the reality for frontier families was still violent. The raids only intensified as the war progressed. So, the peace that neutrality was meant to preserve never truly existed.

Second, unwittingly and against their will, the Moravian presence on the Muskingum was a factor that all sides had to consider. The British, western Indian nations, Delaware, and Americans had to take the Moravians into account, both as impediments and opportunities to achieving their strategic goals. The war parties passing through Moravian territory and being fed, the intelligence passed to Americans, and the potential pool of recruits among the Moravian Indians all represented variables beyond the control of either the British, the western Indians, Continental authorities, or the frontier militia. This guaranteed that the Moravian communities would remain the focus of attention from all sides, readily available scapegoats for plans that went awry. The Moravian missionaries and their Christian converts could not simply hope to sit out the war and be ignored.

Third, as the war progressed, Continental and state authorities realized they needed to undertake an offensive war against the British and western nations conducting the raids. When the Delaware split and a portion declared for Britain, American concerns about alienating the Delaware with an unsanctioned march evaporated. This meant that the Muskingum, which had been a no man's land between the lines, became a front line of battle, which Brodhead's campaign amply demonstrated.

Once Brodhead ended his campaign in April 1781, the dangers posed to the Moravians by the changed circumstances became all too clear. Initially, the threat did not come from the Americans but from the western tribes who were free to act once the Delaware blanket of security was withdrawn. A party of Indian warriors arrived on the Muskingum, captured two Moravian Indians, and then surrounded Gnadenhutten overnight. When morning broke, they demanded that the Moravians surrender Gelelemend, along with any other chiefs or counselors who followed him. Advised that the chief had gone to Pittsburgh with the Americans, the war party came into the town and searched it. Not finding Gelelemend, the Indians, led by a Delaware war captain named Pachgantschihilas, ordered the leaders of the three Moravian villages to assemble and then harangued them about the evils of the Americans. Pachgantschihilas reviewed the litany of bad behavior by frontier whites and even referenced the threat of the militia to attack the Moravian towns during Brodhead's campaign.[1] The Delaware leader invited the Moravians to join him in the west:

> Do not my friends, covet the land you now hold under cultivation. I will conduct you to a country equally good, where your fields shall yield you abundant crops; and where your cattle shall find sufficient pasture; where there is plenty of game; where your women and children, together with yourselves, will live in peace and safety; where no long knife shall ever molest you!—Nay, I will live between you and them, and not even suffer them to frighten you!—There, you can worship your God without fear! Here, where you are, you cannot do this![2]

The response was not up to the missionaries; they were not the audience. So, Moravian Indian leaders met and replied as a group. They thanked Pachgantschihilas for his concern but noted that the Americans had not mistreated them. In this, they appear to have had Continental officials in mind, although the militia had not committed overt acts against them as yet, having been restrained by Continental authorities and missionary diplomacy. The Moravian Indians went on to argue that they had not committed any hostile acts against the Americans and therefore had nothing to fear from them. Then, the Moravian Indians challenged Pachgantschihilas's promises, pointing out that the western nations had run their warpath through the Moravian towns with an eye toward inviting white retaliation. Thus, they turned Pachgantschihilas's argument back on him, painting the western nations as the cause of their insecurity.[3]

At that point, Pachgantschihilas let his mask slip: "When I first spoke to you, I did not intend to compel you, immediately to leave your settlements . . . but as the attachment for the place you now are living at, keeps your eyes closed against seeing the danger that is so near you; I will wave my first proposal, and introduce another which I ask of you to agree to. Let every one among you have his free will, either to go or stay!"[4] The Moravian Indians quickly agreed: living in the Moravian villages had never been compulsory. Yet, Pachgantschihilas had raised the issue of compulsion, a threat that would hang over the Moravian communities.

Thereafter, Pachgantschihilas and his warriors moved to Salem, where they were also welcomed. He ensured his warriors behaved and made it clear that they intended no harm. The chief met with Heckewelder, whom he had known since the missionary first ventured to the region. Pachgantschihilas promised not to molest the Moravian Indians and respect their Christian beliefs. He also revealed that he had been told the Moravian Indians were slaves to their missionary masters. He did not believe it, but the accusation confirmed the missionaries had enemies in the west, even if their congregations did not.[5] With that, Pachgantschihilas and his warriors left, promising to remain friendly to the Moravian Indians, missionaries included. Zeisberger suspected that the threat to use force to relocate the Moravian Indians would be made real at some point.[6]

In the following months, several of the white missionaries experienced suspicious activities, which Heckewelder interpreted as failed assassination attempts.[7] To him, at least, it was clear that the British and western Indian nations had set their sights on the missionaries as a problem. He blamed Hopocan and the American deserters who had passed through the area in 1778 for manipulating the western nations and British officers into holding the missionaries responsible for Delaware neutrality.[8] Heckewelder oversimplified the situation, but Pachgantschihilas's inability to entice the Moravian Indians sparked a new attempt to force the matter.

In mid-August the Moravian communities learned that Dunquat of the Wyandot was leading some warriors to the Moravian villages. The chief arrived with his own warriors and Captain Matthew Elliott, now of the British army. Elliott pitched his tent and raised the English flag in the center of Salem.[9] Glickhican visited the western Indians in their camp while Elliott entered Heckewelder's house. Elliott claimed that Dunquat had something to say to the Moravian Indians and had compelled the English to come along. Heckewelder invited Elliott and his flag bearer, Mr. McCormick, to evening tea, but the English captain deferred to Dunquat.[10] Elliott eventually left and Glickhican turned up to tell Heckewelder that Dunquat intended to address Moravian Indian leaders in front of the missionary. Face-to-face with Heckewelder and the Moravian Indian leaders, Dunquat assured them he meant no harm and asked for a place that everyone could meet. Gnadenhutten, which was larger and more centrally located, drew the short straw.

That evening, McCormick visited Heckewelder's house secretly to warn him that the visiting delegation had malicious intentions.[11] The missionary passed the word on to Zeisberger, who replied, "It then has the appearance as if Satan is again about to make himself merry by troubling and persecuting us!" He took it as a sign that their missions were succeeding, "he grows angry when he sees how many of his subjects he looses, by our preaching the gospel!"[12] Zeisberger might frame the issue as a conflict between God and Satan, but the real issue was a contest for the loyalty of the Moravian Indians.

Dunquat's group eventually set out for Gnadenhutten. Shortly thereafter, a smaller party of Munsee Delaware arrived with Hopocan and Wingenund, along with more Wyandot, Shawnee, Mahican, and Ottawa. The Moravian Indians fed them, and then they followed after Dunquat. At Gnadenhutten, the combined Indian force numbered about three hundred. It spent a week eating, drinking, and sleeping while Dunquat and other leaders sat in council.[13] On August 18, Zeisberger managed to send a letter to Brodhead, warning that Dunquat and his war parties were bound for the Ohio where they would wait to ambush any Americans crossing the river. He asked Brodhead to keep the letter secret, as always. Unfortunately, the colonel passed it up and down the frontier, warning all his forward posts. In the words of one Zeisberger biographer, "he might as well have published it in the Pittsburgh newspaper."[14] Finally, on August 20, Dunquat addressed the Moravian Indians:

> My cousins, ye believing Indians, in Gnadenhutten, Schonbrunn, and Salem, I am no little troubled about you, for I see you live in a dangerous place. Two powerful and mighty spirits or gods are standing and opening wide their jaws toward each other to swallow, and between the two angry spirits, who thus open their jaws,

> are you placed; you are in danger, from one or from the other, or even from both, of being bruised and mangled by their teeth; therefore it is not advisable for you to remain here longer, but bethink ye to keep alive your wives, and children and young people, for here must you all die. Therefore, I take you by the hand, raise you up and settle you there where I dwell, or at least near by me, where you will be safe and will live in quiet. Make not here your plantations and settlements, but arise and come with me, take with you also your teachers, and hold there, whither you shall come, your worship of God forever, as has been your wont. Ye will at once find food there, and will suffer no want, for on this account am I come to say this to you, and to bring you safety.[15]

It was the same offer Pachgantschihilas made that spring, with two critical differences. Dunquat brought a larger group of warriors, which would necessitate the Moravian departure by eating them out of house and home, and it could resort to force more quickly if Dunquat chose.

The Moravian Indians considered their response carefully and it is laden with Zeisberger's approach to diplomacy. They welcomed Dunquat's words and expressed continued friendship with the Wyandot and Delaware, going so far as to praise the Wyandot chief for his invitation. Zeisberger recorded the Moravians as saying they wished to take Dunquat up on his offer but that they needed time to ponder it and would reply sometime before next spring, that is, in 1782. Heckewelder remembered a stronger response, which included a denial of the danger Dunquat said they were in and insisting that they wished to remain where they were, and then requesting time to think the matter over.[16] Abandoning their crops so close to harvest season risked hunger over the winter. Of course, leaving during planting season in the spring was only slightly better. The timing and size of Dunquat's embassy were not happenstance. If his group consumed the bulk of the Moravian stores, they might have no choice but to go with him to the land of milk and honey he had promised. Certainly, his promise would appear more attractive. Possibly with that in mind, Dunquat and his councilors asked for time to consider the Moravian response. They took five days. Meanwhile, his warriors continued to eat while Elliott and Hopocan moved among the Moravian Indians, reinforcing Dunquat's message.

Dunquat's reply on August 25 was to declare the Moravian answer insufficient. They wanted too much time and he needed to show progress in his mission.[17] He alluded to the possibility that some of the Six Nations would not permit them to remain on the Muskingum—an old fear that opponents of a Delaware-American peace often raised—and that the Chippewa and Ottawa might attack. Failing that, he argued the Americans would.[18]

Meanwhile, Dunquat and his allies discovered two Moravian Indians were missing from their towns. Presuming they had gone to Pittsburgh for help, his scouts scoured the roads to intercept them. The two were eventually captured and searched but found with no messages. After a brief detention and hearing before his council, Dunquat dismissed both men to go about their lives.[19] In truth, they had carried verbal messages about their situation to Brodhead and Gibson, ostensibly to pass on to Moravian authorities in Bethlehem and determine whether the Continental officers could provide any assistance. The answer was no, both because the Americans had little to offer and an attempt to provide military relief might place the Moravians in greater danger.

Dunquat's August 25 speech put the onus of negotiations back on the Moravians, who still sought delay. The Moravian Indians shortened their horizon and announced it was impossible to agree to Dunquat's demands at that time, which would involve relocating without adequate provisions. They did not believe Dunquat's promise to provide resources and held out the possibility of moving after harvest time but also did not promise to relocate.[20]

While negotiations dragged on, the western warriors continued circulating amongst the Moravian Indians with an eye toward dividing them. Heckewelder recorded, "the most artful of their party were employed amongst the timid, and weaker class of them, and having first impressed their minds with the apprehension that, if they remained here longer, they would assuredly be murdered: they next gave them such an enchanting description of the country they intended to take them to, that they excited a desire in them to be there already."[21] Zeisberger also noted a growing split among the Moravian Indians, with some determined to stay on the Muskingum and others desirous of moving west to the Sandusky.[22]

With so many warriors on the Muskingum, it was impossible to restrain them. While Salem and Schoenbrunn remained relatively quiet, Dunquat turned Gnadenhutten into a forward operating base from which to conduct raids across the Ohio, often bringing captives through.[23] His warriors also hinted plainly enough that they might seize the missionaries and take them west, confident that the Moravian Indians would follow. Reportedly, his war captains went so far as to develop a plan to kill the white missionaries and their Indian assistants if necessary to bring off the Moravian Indians.[24]

Finally, on September 1, the missionaries were summoned to Gnadenhutten from all three mission towns. Rumors, veiled threats, and tension greeted them while the Wyandot and their allies grew undisciplined. According to Zeisberger, "When they first came here they were starving, and were glad to get something to eat, and herein we let them, suffer no want. After they were sated and become wanton, each one acted after the bent of his own wildness. They shot dead our cattle and swine, although we refused them nothing, and if they demanded swine or cattle for slaughter, gave them. This they did not only from hunger, but from caprice, for they left the swine lying dead round about in such number that the place stunk with them."[25] Heckewelder described the smell as "almost intolerable," likely worsened by the presence of three hundred warriors in a town with inadequate privies. The strategy had two parts. It made remaining on the Muskingum less attractive, but it also made it easier for Captain Elliott to buy out the herds.[26]

Dunquat and his chiefs spent September 2 in a secret council while their warriors waved spears at the missionaries and threatened them. After discussing their options, which still included murdering the white missionaries outright, Dunquat and his allies again brought the missionaries before them and asked whether the Moravians would move immediately to the Sandusky. Zeisberger offered the same answer: they could not move before the harvest. Of course, this was not a promise to move after the harvest, either.[27] The confrontation was tense. Heckewelder feared that any moment it would break out into firing all around between the Moravian Indians and the western nations.[28]

After the midday meal on September 3, Zeisberger, Heckewelder, and Gottlob Senseman were walking behind the Gnadenhutten gardens in the direction of the graveyard. While they were speaking with an Indian captain, three Wyandot ran up and seized the missionaries. The Wyandot initially stripped the missionaries, at least of their shirts, and started dragging them toward the Delaware camp, during which one Indian aimed several tomahawk blows at Senseman's head. The missionary dodged them, but then another Indian ran up and seized two of the missionaries by the hair, shaking them violently. Simultaneously, a separate band of Indians rushed the mission house, encountering a group of Moravian Indians armed only with tomahawks. The Moravian Indians gave way and a mixed group of Wyandot, Delaware, and others plundered the building.[29] Throughout the afternoon, parties of Indians cried out the "death cry," usually a prelude to execution by torture and no doubt calculated to exacerbate the terror of the moment.

Eventually, all three were brought to Captain Elliott's tent. There, Elliott announced that the missionaries were to be seized and carried away by force but that it should be done more gently. He provided some clothing; Heckewelder had to wear Anna Senseman's nightgown. Then, they were all confined to huts occupied by the Wyandot. In truth, the "huts" were simple structures of bark roofs set on poles and lacking walls. Scalping cries followed them the entire way from Elliott's tent to the huts. Zeisberger and Heckewelder were delivered to a Wyandot war chief from the lower Sandusky River, while Senseman was sent to a Wyandot war captain from the upper Sandusky River and confined in a set of stocks until promising not to escape.[30] An older missionary, Brother Edwards, had not been seized and eventually made his way to join Senseman. While Dunquat's party provided no amenities for the missionaries, women from the Moravian towns eventually turned up with blankets and a meal.

Meanwhile, other parties of Indians set out for Schoenbrunn and Salem to round up the missionaries and families who had remained there. Heckewelder was particularly concerned for his wife and new baby at Salem, as he could hear scalp cries carrying up and down the river valley. Heckewelder's anxiety grew as the party from Salem drew closer to Gnadenhutten.

All he could do was wait and worry.

> During a long and dreadful night, while we were lying upon the bare sod, with our eyes steadfastly fixed on the east, that we might catch the first glimpse of the morning light to revive our drooping spirits, the sound of the scalp yell was heard to the north, in the direction of Shonbrun, (though at a great distance,) it not only checked our prospects, but brought the whole body of savages into motion. That something had taken place at Shonbrun, was our first conclusion. There it was, that the wives of Zeisberger and Senseman, (now prisoners) were left, together with the missionary Youngman and his wife. The nearer the war party drew, the greater was the commotion throughout the warriors encampment; the scalp yell being sounded, and resounded from both sides, it seemed to indicate, that when we were all brought together, the scene would end in the massacre of the whole. That many of the savages expected this, we were not ignorant of, yet, under all these circumstances, and trials, we were wholly resigned to the will of the Lord.[31]

Eventually, Brother Michael Young arrived from Salem and told Heckewelder that his wife and baby were safe. On seeing his fellow missionaries, Young proclaimed, "good evening my brethren! our earthly career appears to be near its end, and we on the borders of eternity! Well, if they put us to death, we die in a good cause!"[32] Heckewelder later learned that Young had locked himself and Heckewelder's family inside the latter's home. The war party broke into it. Young was about to receive a hatchet blow when a war captain interceded, knocking it away. Moving Young and Heckewelder's family into the street, the party then proceeded to ransack his home.[33]

Things were little better at Schoenbrunn. Zeisberger's wife Susanna remembered, "In the night, I was dragged from my bed, and the terrible savages did not even allow me the time to dress myself. They took everything away, the bed was slashed, the feathers emptied by the door, and we were forced—bare of all covering—to run before them in rain and cold, and in constant fear of being cut down with an axe. With a terrible death-song, we were brought into the camp" at Gnadenhutten.[34]

All night long and the next day, the Moravian Indians did their best to provide what comfort they could to their ministers and teachers, offering blankets and food when Dunquat's polyglot army would allow it. Hopocan's Delaware had not participated in the looting. When the Moravian Indian women went to his nation and asked for help retrieving some items, he agreed, and the missionaries saw some of the goods taken by the Wyandot returned. Captain Elliott, however, played the role of trader and kept many of the goods he had managed to secure.[35]

On September 4, the scouting parties sent to the Ohio returned with a captive. Under questioning by Hopocan, he announced that the Christian/Moravian Indians were friendly to the United States and had passed intelligence of war parties raiding along the river. According to Heckewelder, Hopocan's Delaware loaded their weapons, as if preparing to shoot someone, most likely the missionaries. Hopocan restrained them, telling them that they had orders from the British commander at Detroit, Major De Peyster, to take the missionaries away from the Muskingum, not to destroy them. Then the hostile Delaware led the prisoner away.[36] Heckewelder believed he met the same man in Pittsburgh after the war and related that the former prisoner blamed the Moravian Indians for his imprisonment and rough treatment, which Heckewelder did not claim to witness.

On September 5, the hostile Delaware noticed a horse was missing. They initially suspected a missionary's wife of running off to Pittsburgh but eventually accepted it was a woman who felt guilty over the rough treatment of the missionaries on the 3rd.[37] Suspicion, however, fell on Glickhican, who was related to the missing Indian woman. So, a war party set out from Gnadenhutten to Salem, captured and bound him, then brought him back to Gnadenhutten.[38] Heckewelder and Zeisberger both describe a kind of trial in which

Glickhican was confronted and acquitted. Heckewelder, writing after the war, named Hopocan's Delaware as the chief prosecutors and Dunquat as his judge.

As the days passed, the initial shock dissipated, although the situation in Gnadenhutten remained far from peaceful. Heckewelder remembered:

> Our masters—(I mean those who had us under their custody)—had by this time become somewhat sociable, and showed some compassion for us. Indeed, it appeared as if they were sorry for what they had done, and no doubt some felt so. What incommoded us most was their custom of repeating the scalp yell so often, for each of their prisoners, during night as well as in the day time; but, this is a general custom with them, and is continued, until the prisoner is liberated or killed. Another very incommoding custom they have, is that of performing their war dances and songs, during the night, near their prisoners; all which we had to endure, exclusive of being thereby prevented from enjoying sleep. Other wise the addresses paid us by a jovial, and probably harmless Ottawa Indian, who, having obtained of the Wyandott warriors, sufficient of our clothes, to dress himself like a white man; and placing a white night cap on his head, being mounted on a horse, would ride through the camps, nodding to us every time he passed; caused much amusement through the camp, and in some measure, to us also.[39]

A Mahican baptized as Marcus worked to develop a friendly relationship with Hopocan and Wingenund and eventually arranged for the missionaries to appear before a war council on September 6. The discussion boiled down to three questions. Would the missionaries go with them to Sandusky? Would they encourage the Moravian Indians to go as well? Would they promise not to attempt to escape? The missionaries satisfied Dunquat and his allies on all three issues. With that, the missionaries were released from their confinement and free to move amongst their congregation.

The next day, Zeisberger, Heckewelder, the rest of the missionaries, their families, and many of the converted Indians set out for

Salem to prepare for departure to the west. Captain Elliott accompanied them, attempting to convince the missionaries that he was not responsible for the situation. Heckewelder disbelieved him but kept his thoughts to himself. At Salem, the English-born Moravian preacher was welcomed back to his village. He noticed that some Indians had continued working on their homes but that his garden had been trampled.[40] The change of circumstances came as a balm for Zeisberger. The congregation held services and celebrated the baptism of a new baby, Jonas, who was born the day the missionaries had been seized. "We were thankful to the Saviour. And it did us much good that we could be among our people, for it is a hellish life to be among murderers and robbers, and in their power."[41] Heckewelder remembered "a most extraordinary sensation of the presence of the Lord, comforted their hearts."[42] Uncharacteristically, Heckewelder highlighted that Hopocan's Delaware, who served as the guards, behaved and performed their function relatively kindly.[43] The peace not did last long. On September 10, one hundred warriors came down from Gnadenhutten and resumed their riotous behavior, throwing down fences, trampling gardens, looting houses, killing livestock, and so on. With them came the Indian congregation from Schoenbrunn and any others upstream who wished to stay with the missionaries.

On September 11, the Moravian communities all began their exodus to the Sandusky. They traveled in two groups, guarded by Hopocan's Delaware. One went by water with twenty canoes laden to the brim and the other overland with as many of the horses and cattle as they could manage. In addition to their homes, churches, and common buildings, plus many of their contents, they left behind cattle, roughly a hundred hogs, three acres of ripe corn, dried corn, and the contents of extensive gardens containing turnips, cabbage, potatoes, and the like, harvested and unharvested. They had already buried farming equipment in hopes of hiding it from the Wyandot when they first arrived: iron plows, harrow teeth, hoes, multiple types of saws, pewter and kitchen articles, etc.[44] Much of this was left behind as well. Typically, the Indians would dig a round hole about three feet deep, narrower at the top than the bottom. Then they would burn it out and line it with bark, giving it a degree of water resistance. It could then be filled with harvested corn or other materials and covered to store food and other materials in reasonable condition.[45] Zeisberger noted:

> we broke up, and thus turned our backs upon our homesteads and places where we had enjoyed so much that was good and blessed from the hands of the Saviour, and where he had really been among us and with us. Before us we saw indeed nothing wherein to rejoice, yes, we could imagine nothing but need, misery, and danger, and otherwise had we nothing to look forward to. We must possess our souls in patience, and go where certainly we were unwilling to go, for we saw no other result from our actions, but we went towards misery and hardship; thus also were our Indian brethren minded, but they must go against their will.[46]

The missionary speculated that some of the Moravian Indians might leave them on the trail, but Hopocan's Delaware and the Wyandot would permit no defections from the community. It was not to prevent their abandonment of Christianity but to prevent any from escaping to Pittsburgh and to ensure that the largest pool of potential recruits arrived on the Sandusky.

The forced migration plodded along on foot and by canoe, doing its best to hold services every night. They arrived at Goschgosching three days later, where Captain Elliott left them, bound for the Scioto. They now turned north and west, following the western branch of the Muskingum, known as the Walhonding, upstream. Heavy rains forced the Moravian captives away from the river, and they often had to wade or wait in knee-deep water. Dunquat and his warriors joined the march on September 19, bringing with them many of the things they had plundered from the mission towns, including two prisoners. The day after, one of the Indian prisoners gave birth under the difficult circumstances, an otherwise bright spot in a miserable trek.[47]

While the missionaries were largely passive, the Moravian Indians became more assertive. They started reclaiming property, including a pot and a horse.[48] The days blurred, whether on land or on river struggling against the current. Meanwhile, the Wyandot grew impatient. Finally, on September 23, Dunquat and his advisors met with the missionaries and urged them to leave some of the slower-moving captives behind. A gap developed between the missionaries and their congregations, causing some anxiety among the missionaries, whose safety remained tied in part to their congregations. At the close of September 28, a group of Delaware guards eager to reach home left the caravan entirely.[49]

On September 29, the Moravian procession finally emerged from the woods and on to a plain that dominates northwestern Ohio. Scraped relatively flat by glaciers, it was covered in grass that could rise as tall as a mounted rider. Things did not bode well. It was poor pasture land and there were no trees for fuel or construction in sight. The land drained poorly, dotting the land with bogs and morasses while ensuring moist soil ill-suited to Moravian farming techniques. Heckewelder wrote, "The prospect of this dreary and barren country, which had been described to us as a paradise, made those of our people ashamed who had listened to the favourable report that savages gave of it, while they were persuading them to leave their settlements on the Muskingum."[50]

By the beginning of October, the Moravians reached the Sandusky River. According to Zeisberger, "Here the Wyandots left us and went on ten miles towards their home, after they had abandoned us in the wilderness, where there was no food to be found and no game to hunt, and many among our brethren had nothing left to eat, but lived only upon what those, who yet had something, divided with them."[51]

Abandoned by their captors, the Moravian congregations began looking for a reasonable place to live as the days grew short and the nights long. They eventually settled on an abandoned Wyandot town site. It was along the river and there were a few stands of trees around, which would provide wood for shelters and fuel.[52] Having found a place to call home for the winter, the Moravians prepared it with a passion, throwing up rough houses as quickly as possible. Still, it was not a promising place. Poor pasturage led the milk cows to begin failing. Wild berry bushes had already given up their bounty.

Searches for edible roots generally failed due to frozen ground. Meanwhile, corn was generally unavailable for purchase, except at high prices exceeding the Moravians' ability to pay. The Wyandot and local Delaware had not planted enough and could barely feed themselves.[53] The missionaries continued to hold daily services, which some local Indians attended, largely to mock the faith the Moravian communities practiced.[54] Within days, the Moravian Indians resolved that small parties led by Schebosh (a.k.a. John Bull) should return to the Muskingum, gather what corn they could, and bring it back to the communities facing privation on the Sandusky.[55]

While the captives prepared for a difficult and dangerous winter, Dunquat and Hopocan revealed their real reasons for forcing the Muskingum communities to relocate. Dunquat and his advisors visited the brethren on October 3 and addressed all the gathered Christian Indians. Zeisberger recorded, "He said he was much rejoiced that we were now with them, and that all who had the same color, were together, a thing they had already long wished; we should now only look to him, guide ourselves by him, and if the Virginians should come, do as he would do."[56]

Heckewelder remembered that both Dunquat and Hopocan boasted that they now had the power "to compel the Christian Indians to go to war with them, whenever they chose to command them."[57] At the same time, Delaware living on the Sandusky moved among the Moravian congregations, encouraging their friends and relations to abandon the Christian communities and join them, even offering rewards to those Moravian Indians who would come to the Miami River to receive them. By undermining the cohesiveness of the "believing Indians" with a nativist message, they would strengthen their own nations. They had been at it for years but hoped for greater success now that the Moravian Indians were far from home and economically destitute.[58] In short, the western tribes wanted reinforcements for the war. Earlier promises to let them practice their faith, remain with their missionaries, or sit out the war were long forgotten. Instead, Dunquat and Hopocan insisted on racial unity at the expense of spiritual enlightenment and threatened to require Moravian participation in military operations. Worse for the missionaries, Dunquat clearly wanted to drive a wedge between the congregations and their missionaries. Success would remove the greatest protection from Indian attack that the missionaries possessed and make recruiting easier.

The British in Detroit had the same aim in mind. Rumors passed through the Native Americans along the Sandusky that the missionaries would be separated from their congregations and summoned to Detroit.[59] On October 25, Hopocan and Wingenund finally appeared at the new Moravian town with a message from the British.[60] It was addressed to the Wyandot and Hopocan's Delaware:

> [C]hildren! Your father on the other side of Lake Erie, is glad to hear that you have brought the believing Indians and their teachers, to Sandusky, for now all nations may be united, and all obstacles removed; and the little birds in the woods, cannot sing so many lies in your ears. Now the Virginians will sit in the dark, and hear nothing more about us, from which we expect to derive great advantages . . . he [De Peyster] requests that captain Pipe would conduct the teachers [Missionaries] and some of the chiefs of the believing Indians to him, as he wishes to see and speak to them himself. . . . I know better how to speak to them than you, for I know them, and can better provide for them having plenty of everything.[61]

The message also put the authority, and onus, of deciding how to provide for the Christian Indians on Dunquat.

The missionaries and their Indian leaders, men like Glickhican, had anticipated such an ultimatum and discussed their options. First, they were loath to separate from their congregations, knowing the intentions of the British and western tribes. Second, if they had to leave, they wanted to ensure the British had reasons to let them return. With that in mind, they began negotiating. Zeisberger, usually able to outsmart his opponents, agreed the missionaries should meet with De Peyster but that their families should remain behind, which would require leaving some of the missionaries with them. Hopocan gave in. Four missionaries (Brothers Edwards, Heckewelder, Zeisberger, and Senseman) and four senior Moravian Indian leaders (William, Isaac Eschicanahund, Tobias, and Joshua) would go to Detroit, leaving wives, babies, and the missionaries Jungmann and Jung behind.[62]

The small Moravian party made its way to Hopocan's town and eventually encountered a great number of prisoners taken from the American frontier, including some who appeared "half-starved."[63] They also caught up with a riotously drunk Hopocan surrounded by similarly inebriated Indians. Rather than risking an encounter, the Moravians made camp in the woods.[64] Heckewelder and one of the Moravian Indians tracked down Captain Elliott and asked whether they might proceed without Hopocan. He eventually agreed.

Arriving at Detroit on November 3, the missionaries met straight away with Major De Peyster. He conducted a short interview and was clearly perturbed that the missionaries had not brought their families. Zeisberger, ever the diplomat, blamed the Indians, indicating they had given the missionaries permission to leave some people behind. De Peyster asked about the number of Indians who had traveled to the Sandusky, how many males were in their number, their attitudes toward the war, and the missionaries' future intentions. He was clearly trying to understand whether the Moravian Indians were friend or foe, how many might be recruited to the British cause, and whether the missionaries would oppose it. Zeisberger gave the officer no cause for hope, telling him the Indians were neutral and that the missionaries planned to return to their congregations. De Peyster attributed their summons to the accusation that the Moravians were passing intelligence to the Americans, which they were. Zeisberger evaded a direct answer, only saying that he imagined De Peyster had been told a great number of things which he would find untrue upon further investigation. With the preliminaries out of the way, De Peyster dismissed the missionaries and boarded them with a local family.[65]

In Detroit, the missionaries were free to move about but not to leave, pending a final decision about their fates. While De Peyster waited for Hopocan to arrive, the missionaries became the object of idle curiosity and guarded suspicion by the town's authorities.[66] Finally, on November 9, De Peyster was able to assemble a grand council at Detroit. He summoned the missionaries to attend. The council began normally enough, with a leader from each tribe giving a speech and presenting scalps to De Peyster, which the officer accepted as a sign of the bond between the British and western tribes.[67] He then turned to the matter of the Moravian missionaries and Indians.

De Peyster framed the issue with Hopocan as the accuser and the missionaries as the accused, establishing for himself the responsibility of getting to the truth of the matter. In other words, the missionaries were being put on trial as a result of Hopocan's privately made accusations. The charges were simple: passing war-related information along to the Americans. The Moravians were guilty, of course, and everyone present knew it. However, this trial was not a fact-finding exercise to establish guilt and mete out justice in the middle of a war. Other interests were in play.

Removing the Moravians from the Muskingum had solved part of De Peyster's problem with them. They would no longer pass intelligence to the Americans. His next task was recruiting Indians to the British cause. The Moravian Indians were the largest pool of nonbelligerent Indians on the frontier. De Peyster needed to separate them from the missionaries who he rightly thought were keeping them out of the war.[68] Hopocan and other leaders from the western tribes shared that interest. Thus, De Peyster's frustration with Hopocan's failure to bring all the missionaries and their families from the Sandusky to Detroit is understandable. By giving in to the Moravians and leaving some missionaries on the Sandusky while announcing he was removing the missionaries at De Peyster's order, Hopocan revealed that the question of Moravian guilt was not on the table. Assigning responsibility for separating the missionaries from their congregations was. By attributing his orders to De Peyster on the Sandusky, Hopocan put the blame on the major's shoulders. By naming Hopocan as the chief accuser at Detroit, De Peyster put it back on Hopocan. He stated outright their separation was in response to Hopocan's accusations. De Peyster had done something similar by making Dunquat responsible for the care and feeding of the Moravian communities.

With the burden of making his case in public, Hopocan turned to his advisors and the other tribes gathered. Heckewelder remembered, "Pipe, standing at the time, now turned to his councellors, telling them to get upon their legs and speak; but finding them panic struck, he appeared to be at a loss how to act—once more turning to them, he endeavoured to make them sensible that this was the time to speak, and that the opportunity now granted them, for that purpose, would be lost for ever, if they spake not!"[69] When they kept their mouths shut, Hopocan was isolated and changed tactics. He declared the missionaries innocent of the charges. He also attributed any "wrong" acts to compulsion by the Americans, acknowledging that the Moravians had been compelled to provide the western tribes with assistance during their raids. That put the burden of trying to separate the Moravian Indians from their missionaries back on De Peyster's shoulders.

So, why was the blame game so important? For most of the war, the western tribes had wanted to enlist first the Delaware and then the Moravian Indians in their cause. To that end, the British and western tribes had spread stories that the Americans wished them harm and life would be better if only they would join the British. Even after the Delaware split, however, the Moravian Indian communities had largely resisted those efforts, due in part both to their missionaries and their own commitment to the new lives they had built as members of the church. By most metrics, those were successful lives. They had avoided the war's worst effects, built economically successful towns, started and raised families, and found a spiritual home that seemed to defy the nativism that frequently ran amok within the western tribes. Anyone who threatened that lifestyle, for instance, by removing the Moravians from their successful villages on the Muskingum to their miserable circumstances on the Sandusky or separating the missionaries from their congregations, risked the enmity of the entire community, possibly provoking a violent reaction. Thus, neither Hopocan nor De Peyster wanted to be seen by the Moravian Indians as responsible for doing it.

De Peyster tried to turn the tables on Hopocan by asking what the Delaware chief recommended he do with the missionaries. Having laid out his position publicly, Hopocan could do no less than recommend returning the missionaries to their congregations.[70] With that, De Peyster began questioning the missionaries in front of the council. His interview with Zeisberger, who did the talking for the Moravians, went much the same way the missionary's interrogation by New York authorities had gone in 1745. De Peyster sought to establish their loyalties and intentions. Satisfied that they desired to remain neutral in the war, De Peyster pronounced them innocent of the charges Hopocan had already repudiated and cautioned them against providing information to the Americans. They were free to go with the commandant's blessings and assistance. Zeisberger and his party finally left, marching over frozen ground and deep snow to return to the Sandusky on November 20.[71] In their absence, the western tribes had continued circulating among the Moravian Indians, telling stories and spreading lies about the missionaries, all with an eye toward encouraging the Moravian Indians to abandon their community.[72] About the same time, Schebosh's corn-gathering expedition back to the Muskingum returned with a small amount of provisions.[73] (Schebosh himself was captured during a militia raid and interned at Pittsburgh, then released.)[74]

Conditions on the Sandusky only worsened with the arrival of winter. Food had been the greatest challenge in the fall, but the cold weather was merciless. Thrown up quickly, the Moravian huts were small and had no wood floors. Their size limited the fires that could be built while the dirt floors constantly turned to mud. Cattle started dying from hunger and the ability to buy provisions locally only worsened. "Famine took place, and the calamity became general; many had now no other alternative but to live on the carcases of the starved cattle, and in a few instances, suckling babies perished for want of nourishment from their mothers' impoverished breasts. The missionaries had, at this time, reduced their daily allowance of provision for bread, to a pint of Indian corn, per man, per day."[75] Zeisberger noted they lived on wild potatoes dug up some distance away from the Sandusky villages.[76] They barely eked out an existence as the snows fell.

Dunquat, Hopocan, and the western tribes had broken their promises. But they were equally hungry and De Peyster could not adequately support them.[77] It led them to take what they could find from the Moravian communities at will. Heckewelder recalled one such incident: "The hungry Wyandots would often come in our huts, to see if there was any victuals cooking, or ready cooked. At one time, just as my wife had set down to what was intended for our dinner, the half king, Simon Girty, and another, a Wyandot, entered my cabin, and seeing the victuals ready, without ceremony began eating." An Indian Brethren passed through and upbraided the men, reminding them of what they had promised and accusing them of lies.[78] On a different occasion, another Moravian Indian berated the Wyandot leader in a similar fashion:

> When you came to Gnadenhutten with your men, we gave you not only enough to eat, of such provisions as the Indians generally make us of; but we supplied you with any thing you wished for, that we had; bread, pork, butter, milk, sugar, tea, chocolate, &c. You told us to rise and go with you, and not to stand looking at our cornfields, for we would find with you enough to live upon!—Now you have brought us hither, and never once offered us a single ear of corn! . . . Your conduct towards us, appears as if you had brought us here for the purposes of starving us![79]

The tension between the Moravian communities and their tribal jailors was palpable. Non-Christian Indians who refused to live by the rules of the Moravian communities moved in. They spread discord to undermine the influence of the missionaries, with some success. Zeisberger noted:

> Satan rages and it is if we were given over to devils to plague us utterly, to torment us and to make trial of fortune with us, while we are here, more than ever before, not only from without, but also from within. For in the church there were people who upheld them in their false disposition and applauded them, who wished to establish by force that wicked life of his and heathenism. If we oppose them they become angry and set on the wild Indians against us, and to bind our hands, so that we may do nothing to dispense the powers of darkness and root them out from among

> us. . . . Such a change has now come in the Indian church that the bad, wicked people can not be cast out, but they wish to be there and to cause harm in the church, for they in the wild towns have occasion enough therefor and no one would say any thing to them about their sinful life. If we discipline them, therefore, or only say it were better if they remained away from us, they go into the town and accuse us of sending people away, urge on the savages against us, who tell them they should not regard us, that we are prisoners, and that it is their business to command us.[80]

Hopocan reportedly boasted he had taken prisoners and slaves by relocating the Moravians.[81] He also continued whispering in De Peyster's ear that the missionaries were a problem. In the late winter, Girty and Dunquat joined in the campaign, insisting that the missionaries were still passing intelligence to the Americans and needed to be separated from their congregations.[82] Zeisberger recorded that "They went about, and when they saw so many cattle lying dead, they laughed and scoffed about it. The savages are pleased now that things go hard with us, that we suffer famine and anxiety, and our cattle all perish, and they say we have now become like them, we should be no better off than they, and so it was."[83] The reservation that Dunquat and his allies had set aside risked becoming a prison that finally destroyed the Moravian communities.

The Moravian Indians decided to take food matters into their own hands. The only place they could hope to find it was to recover crops left behind on the Muskingum. Small parties began returning in January and February, leaving an ever-shrinking population of Moravian Indians on the Sandusky.[84] Eventually, they needed to escalate their efforts and planned to send 150 men, women, and children east to the river, set their families outside of their old towns (Schoenbrunn, Gnadenhutten, and Salem) and then gather the corn that still lay in unharvested fields and underground stores. They would bury it in secure caches from which it could be recovered at will. Having developed a plan, the Moravian Indians presented it to the missionaries, who approved.[85] The Moravian Indians, who had been trickling back to the Muskingum for months, began leaving in larger numbers.

On March 1, the missionaries were summoned to Dunquat's town to receive a message. De Peyster had summoned the missionaries to Detroit.[86] On Sunday, March 8, they sent express riders to the Indian brethren with the Shawnee and on the Muskingum requesting help in making the journey.[87] After roughly six months in the hands of their enemies, the Moravian missionaries watched everything they had built, from those early days in eastern Pennsylvania before the French and Indian War, begin to fall apart. Things were actually worse than the missionaries feared.

Back at Fort Pitt, Colonel Brodhead endured civilian complaints about his management of the department and was engaged in a command dispute with Colonel John Gibson. Amidst that, he took command of a planned militia campaign to the Sandusky to cooperate with George Rogers Clark. He aborted it when word arrived of Dunquat's occupation of Gnadenhutten lest it provoke the western tribes to move more directly against the Moravian communities.[88] Within days, word reached Fort Pitt that Washington had relieved Brodhead.

In November 1781, the Pennsylvania militia again set out to do what Colonel Brodhead had prevented them from doing in the spring. Between seventy-five and a hundred Pennsylvania militia from Washington County under Lieutenant Colonel David Williamson arrived at the now-abandoned Moravian towns intent on either driving the Moravians farther from the Ohio River and American settlements, or making the entire lot prisoner and removing them to Fort Pitt.[89] So, it came as something of a surprise when they found the towns abandoned. Williamson rounded up the few Indians he could find in the area (including Schebosh, a.k.a. John Bull) and took them to Fort Pitt, from which they were eventually released. The result disappointed many settlers, who did not merely want a few Moravian Indians removed from the Muskingum but wanted their villages destroyed as the surest means of reducing raiding activity.[90]

Brigadier General William Irvine assumed command in November 1781.[91] A long-service veteran, Irvine arrived with the task of whipping his new command into shape. Congressional parsimony, war weariness among Continental officers and soldiers, command jealousies, and the sheer size of the department had rendered it chaotic. Irvine reported to Washington, "everything is in so wretched a state, that there is very little in my power. I never saw troops cut so truly a deplorable, and at the same time despicable, a figure. Indeed, when I arrived, no man would believe from their appearance that they were soldiers; nay, it would be difficult to determine whether they were white men."[92] His magazines were largely empty; Brodhead had issued much of its powder to the militia, who constituted most of the troops available to defend the frontier, and the defensive works were a shambles.

While groups of Moravian Indians were filtering back to the Muskingum, Irvine revealed the weakness of Continental power in his department. His front between Fort McIntosh and Wheeling stretched 110 miles. He only had 230 men available, 30 of whom were unfit for field duty. When repaired, Fort Pitt would require 450 men. Fort McIntosh needed another 150, Wheeling 25 to 30 more with the addition of soldiers for ranging parties to cover the ground between all the forts, at least 200 just to cover the ground between Fort Pitt and Laurel Hill.[93] Between Westmoreland and Washington County, he estimated there were 3,000 militia, but the inhabitants were threatening to leave in the spring, which would likely reduce their number. Nevertheless, the sheer disparity in numbers clearly indicates Irvine depended on the militia to defend the frontier, just as had Brodhead. To complicate matters further, Irvine did not spend the early months of his command in the saddle moving up and down the Ohio River, better acquainting himself with the frontier posts, militia forces, county leaders, or his own troops. Despite being ordered to assume command by Congress in September, Washington's order sending Irvine formally to Fort Pitt did not arrive until March. Much of Irvine's correspondence with Washington was carried on from his home in Carlisle, Pennsylvania, or even Philadelphia itself. In the interim, the chain of command was blurred, with Colonel John Gibson of the 7th Virginia exercising much of the day-to-day authority at Fort Pitt.[94]

Unfortunately, the same brief warming that had permitted the Moravian Indians to send foraging parties made it easier for the western tribes to send raiding parties toward the Ohio. One struck the Fink homestead at Fort Buchanan on February 8 and the Wallace farm a few days later, killing the wife and five children.[95] The Wallace family slayings drew considerable attention and were particularly brutal. According to one account, while the father, Robert, was away, a sizeable band of Indians attacked, seized his wife and children, including a baby, killed his livestock, and burned his cabin. The bodies of his wife and baby were later found near the Ohio River. She had been stripped and impaled while the infant was mutilated.[96] Heckewelder believed that this raiding party then passed near Gnadenhutten and told the Moravian Indians there what they had done to a woman and her baby. The raiders expected pursuit and advised the Moravian Indians to be on their guard and leave as soon as possible.[97] At about the same time, Indians captured John Carpenter near Buffalo Creek and then passed through the Moravian towns, now repopulated by the foraging teams who had returned to the Muskingum earlier in the winter. Of the six Indians who seized Carpenter and his horses, two claimed to be Moravian Indians and reportedly spoke German.[98] Carpenter, still a prisoner, also warned the Moravian Indians to leave before pursuing militia arrived.[99] Shortly thereafter, Carpenter escaped his captors and related his tale, making a direct connection between his captivity and the repopulated Moravian villages.[100]

Word of these attacks, so early in the season, traveled readily up and down the Ohio Valley. Animosity toward the Moravian Indians came as naturally to people on the frontier in 1782 as it had throughout the French and Indian War or Pontiac's War. Simply, the villages on the Muskingum were seen locally as either engaged in hostilities outright or as facilitators of violence against frontier settlements. Thus, it was a nearly universal sentiment that action had to be taken. Colonel Brodhead had foiled their desires in April 1781 and Williamson had come up empty when he marched on the villages in November 1781. The early outbreak of hostilities in 1782 prompted some to try again.

Frontier histories often frame this latest plan as a response to the spring raids, but that piece of conventional wisdom is misleading.[101] Zeisberger first reported a threat to destroy the towns in 1778. It reared its head quite publicly again in 1781, during both the Brodhead and Williamson campaigns. The germ of an idea for a more brutal attack may have been planted at a place called Vance's Fort in the summer of 1781, where some twenty-five to thirty families had gathered for protection during the summer raiding season. Williamson's excursion in November 1781 and his discovery that the villages had largely been abandoned preempted and seemingly eliminated the need for the attack.[102] Given the militia's behavior during Brodhead's campaign and Williamson's November march, 1781 is a more plausible time frame for the idea of a campaign to destroy the Moravian towns to have taken root. The raids in early 1782 and information that the villages had been reoccupied likely resurrected the idea. Settlers on the Ohio frontier were already primed for it and may have sought to take advantage of a break in the weather, just as the western tribes had.

There is also disagreement about the authority under which the campaign took place, whether the raiders were militia or a disorganized mob. Tradition lays it on the militia. Joseph Doddridge was a boy at the time and knew many of the raiders or their descendants and interviewed them. He was an early historian and concluded that the raid was an act by the militia. His interpretation dominated subsequent histories.[103] It was a reasonable conclusion. Lieutenant Colonel Williamson of the Washington County militia was again in charge and the number of raiders approximated the number in his battalion. At a minimum, many of the raiders had served, or were still serving, in the active militia. (Most should have been enrolled for service.) After word of the raid's outcome spread, Brigadier Irvine at Fort Pitt did nothing to punish the raiders, which would seem to validate their actions. In general, American attacks on Indians usually targeted villages in preemptive or preventative attempts to dislocate perceived sources of Indian power. With that in mind, it is not a great leap to lay responsibility for the raid and its outcome at the feet of the American and/or state government as the result of their intentional strategies for frontier warfare.[104]

However, if the Gnadenhutten campaign was launched as a formal action of the Pennsylvania militia, one would expect to find orders from the Washington County lieutenant James Marshel to Williamson directing it, official after-action reports, even in the form of simple correspondence, and perhaps a formal confirmation of it by General Irvine. One would also expect to find requests for pay or reimbursement for losses from participants. William Farrar studied the origins of the raid and found none of these. He concluded that it was undertaken outside the boundaries of any government authority.[105] Indeed, many of the raiders' identities are still unknown, although it is likely most had served in the militia during an active call-up. Most males did. Irvine did not refer to them as "militia," in his first report of the massacre but only as "country people."[106] Instead, we find careful directions from General Irvine to Colonel William Crawford that the next campaign against the Indians comply with proper standards of warfare, as if to avoid the kind of killings that took place at Gnadenhutten.[107] In that context, it becomes easier to characterize the Gnadenhutten raiders as a violent mob and the massacre as the happenstance collision of victims with an ad hoc force of whites pursuing Indian raiders. Such a binary choice between government-sanctioned violence and an angry mob, however, is unreasonable.

That leaves a third option: a sizeable number of settlers with militia experience decided to organize themselves and carry out the raid based on a bottom-up idea that had circulated on the frontier for months, if not years. (Indeed, when Irvine sought help relieving Fort Henry on the Ohio from Marshel, the militia officer's response made it clear that the locals were exercising their vaunted independence and coming up with all sorts of ideas of their own, outside of his formal authority. Marshel explained, "I can not comply with your requisition of engaging a number of men for the defense of Fort Wheeling, as I am heartily tired out with volunteer plans.")[108] Simply, settlers had concluded that the Moravian villages were a threat that needed to be eliminated, which earlier, state-sanctioned campaigns had failed to do. By attacking without the formal sanction of higher authorities, the settlers would be able to avoid the constraints that had prevented them from acting during the Brodhead and Williamson campaigns. It is also more consistent with well-established divisions between frontier settlers and formal authorities that they believed had let them down in the past. That the British, Wyandot, and other western tribes had already moved to destroy the permanent Moravian presence on the Muskingum was immaterial. The only remaining question was what the settlers' "solution" entailed.

Between 80 and 160 whites mustered at Mingo Bottom on the Ohio River by the evening of March 3 and elected David Williamson as their commander. (The higher estimate is more probable).[109] Williamson's force splashed across the Ohio on March 4 and rode for the Muskingum, moving on a direct line for Gnadenhutten. Back at Fort Pitt, Irvine was again absent. When his deputy, Colonel John Gibson, discovered the locals had turned out, he sent a warning to the villages. The messenger arrived too late.[110]

Specific reports of the expedition's undertakings suffer from confusing and inconsistent timelines, conflated events, repeated errors, bias, and the passage of time before they were imperfectly recorded. Early American historians tended to gloss over the details of the events themselves. Later historians have turned to Heckewelder and Zeisberger as offering the clearest material; both men had access to Indian witnesses shortly after the events. But firsthand accounts are often incomplete. Zeisberger's diary was written as close to the massacre as distances would allow, but he relied on rumors and reports passed on by two boys who survived and Indian observers who only witnessed bits and pieces. Heckewelder, writing well after the war, habitually beatified his congregations as victims and demonized the Americans, perhaps at the expense of accuracy. The raiders' perspective is largely missing, although some local historians recorded personal recollections and attitudes. The following account draws from both Moravian and American perspectives and lays out the story that seems most consistent.

While Williamson and his men made their way west from Mingo Bottom, the Moravian Indians decided to consider the warnings they had received from the western raiding parties and John Carpenter. Rather than camping in the woods during the cold nights, as planned, families had moved into their old homes. It made them more comfortable but also more vulnerable. So, they called a council of leaders from the three different foraging parties at Schoenbrunn, Gnadenhutten, and Salem. The group met at Salem and concluded they had nothing to fear from the Americans. At the same time, the council decided it had collected enough corn to get through the season and that it was time to pack up and leave.[111] Moving day would be March 7. They also dispatched a message to the brethren on the Sandusky that they would be leaving soon. It arrived on March 7.[112]

Williamson arrived about a mile outside Gnadenhutten on the evening of March 6. He held a council of officers which resolved to move into the town the next day.[113] The village of Gnadenhutten lay on the east bank of the Muskingum, but its cultivated fields were across the river. To prevent anyone from escaping, Williamson divided his force into two groups. One would cross the river and move through the fields then converge on the town from the west. It would cut off any Indians fleeing westward across the river. Of course, to enter town it would have to recross the Muskingum. The second group would divide into three parts and then approach Gnadenhutten from the north, south, and east.

The plan itself indicates a few notable things. First, Williamson did not expect armed resistance. Dividing his force made it vulnerable to defeat in detail, particularly if Indians from Schoenbrunn or Salem were alarmed and rode to Gnadenhutten's assistance. Indians determined to defend themselves could fall on each group separately. Taking time to cross the river also risked the element of surprise. Anyone might detect the crossing long before it was complete. In all likelihood, Williamson and his officers were comfortable running those risks because they did not anticipate resistance. He was not chasing Indian war parties after all. Second, if he had simply wanted to eliminate Gnadenhutten as a base of operations for raiding parties, the fastest way to do that was drive off the population and then loot and burn the villages and fields. Closing an escape route across the river suggests Williamson's first goal was to encircle and capture the population of Gnadenhutten. Thus, his men would approach the town under the guise of friendship.

When Williamson's first column reached the river intending to cross about a mile from town, it could find no canoes or rafts. Eventually, scouts spied what looked like a canoe on the western shore. So, a raider named Slaughter volunteered to swim the river and retrieve it, no doubt shivering the entire way. It was still winter, after all, and the brief warming in February had not lasted. Slaughter discovered it was merely a water trough, but he managed to return it to the eastern shore. Hardly sufficient to carry the entire group, the men stripped, piled their clothes, arms, and ammunition into the crude conveyance, and took turns swimming beside it to the west side of the Muskingum.[114] The first men over posted two pickets while the others crossed.

Before half the division was across the river, the two pickets spotted an Indian. One shot him from a distance, wounding him in the arm. As the man dropped, the other picket ran up and dispatched him with a tomahawk.[115] The Indian was a young man, Joseph Schebosh, who was out hunting a horse for the day's departure. He identified himself as a Christian with a white father (John Bull/Schebosh) and begged for his life, but it did not ward off the death blow or his eventual scalping.[116] Whether alerted by the gunshot or word sent from the group crossing the river, Williamson and his officers decided to advance on the town immediately. On the way, they passed Jacob Shabosh, young Joseph's brother-in-law, about thirty yards from the river and one hundred and fifty yards from the town. He was tying up corn sacks, also getting ready for departure. Jacob recognized some of the men moving toward the town. As the raiders moved between him and the river, he was about to yell to them, thinking that everyone was on friendly terms. But their attention was drawn to a different Indian, who was crossing the river in a canoe on his way to the cornfields on the west side of the Muskingum. They promptly shot that man, who dropped into his canoe. Jacob fled, not stopping until he was several miles away.[117]

Still, the Indians in town apparently remained unconcerned, perhaps not having heard the shots. The whites on the west side of the river moved toward Gnadenhutten's cornfields, where several Moravian Indians were working. Still believing that whites accepted their innocence of raids, the Indians greeted the Americans as friends and acquaintances, walking up to them and welcoming them, as had been the custom with all armed parties moving through the villages. The raiders reciprocated, announcing that they were there to take the Indians to Pittsburgh where they would be safe and fed. In the meantime, they announced everyone should gather at Gnadenhutten to make the trip easier.[118]

On the east side of the river, things did not go as smoothly for the Americans, where alarm had already spread among some of Gnadenhutten's inhabitants. Joseph Schebosh's wife was near the river's edge and hiding in bushes when they found her and promptly killed her. Other Indians made a run for the river thinking to escape to the western side, unaware that the Americans had already crossed over. Once arriving there, three were promptly killed by that western group of raiders.[119] Nevertheless, the bulk of the raiders made it into town, where they were also welcomed as friends and mingled freely with Gnadenhutten's populace, making the same promises of safety and wealth at Pittsburgh as a pretext for being there.[120] The warm welcome of armed men into town is suspect in the face of the shots being fired and individuals being killed as the raiders approached town, but that is how Zeisberger and Heckewelder portrayed events. If the behavior is factual, it might be explained as the result of confusion and misunderstanding on the part of the Indians (facilitated by American deception), blanket unawareness that the murders had occurred, or a desperate attempt by the Indians to reassure the Americans that they were no threat. Alternatively, Zeisberger, Heckewelder, or their sources might have embellished Indian behavior as a way of emphasizing the victims' innocence.

John Martin, a baptized Indian and national assistant was a leader in the church. He and his son spent the night of March 6-7 west of town in the woods where they had been moving corn from existing caches to new storage sites. They returned on the morning of March

7, after the Pennsylvanians had already moved through the cornfields and assembled the Gnadenhutten Indians in town. Coming into the fields, they noticed no one was working and identified multiple tracks of horses bearing shoes. It gave them pause, so Martin and his son found a slight rise on the west of the river from where they could observe events in town. At this point, the raiders and Indians still mixed under the guise of friendship, although it may have been a tense interaction upon closer inspection. Still, seeing no reason to fear, Martin sent his son across the river into town while he went to Salem to update the brethren there.[121]

It was a turn for the worse. Martin thought that the whites were there to remove them to Pittsburgh, where they might come away from the privation and misery of the Sandusky. He convinced Salem's leaders and they dispatched two brethren, Adam and Henry, to Gnadenhutten with Martin. If their beliefs were accurate, they planned to join the Americans and Gnadenhutten Indians and travel to safety in Pittsburgh.[122] Surely, the church and authorities in Bethlehem would help and dispatch new teachers while Zeisberger, Heckewelder, etc. rode out the war on the Sandusky or at Detroit. It was a reasonable hope. Continental authorities had made such offers throughout the war and Williamson had done just that in November. When Martin, Adam, and Henry spoke with the people at Gnadenhutten, they all encouraged Martin in his conclusions, suggesting that the population of Salem join them. The Americans then delegated several among their number to return to Salem and help the population there move to Gnadenhutten.[123]

Once the party for Salem departed, the American raiders began disarming the Indians in Gnadenhutten, removing anything that might be used for self-defense, such as firearms, axes, knives, and the like, explaining it would make transport easier. Everything would be returned at Pittsburgh.

Also on March 7, a messenger sent from the Sandusky arrived outside Schoenbrunn to hurry the Indians on the Muskingum along, as the missionaries and their families needed horses to comply with De Peyster's summons to Detroit. After listening to his words, the Indians at Schoenbrunn dispatched two messengers to Gnadenhutten to pass the message along. But, on the way, they came across Joseph Schebosh's scalped remains. Alarmed, they scouted the area and saw whites congregating in Gnadenhutten. They promptly returned to Schoenbrunn.[124] The Indians there at least had warning, swiftly packed up, and departed, leaving a canoe behind.

At Salem, the population was already packing to return to the Sandusky, so they turned out for Gnadenhutten relatively easily.[125] Behind them, the Americans began burning buildings, including the church. It may have set some Indians on edge, but the Americans continued to reassure them, likewise disarming them peacefully en route to Gnadenhutten with the same excuses used there. Later, the discovery of a wounded Indian and his bloody canoe on the way may have caused a panic. Heckewelder insisted that, even had they not been disarmed, the Indians would not have resorted to violence.[126]

While the Indians at Salem packed up, the Americans at Gnadenhutten turned ugly. They bound the population and separated the men from the women and children, eventually confining them to separate buildings. Throughout the day on March 7 after the Indians were secured, the American raiders flung accusations at their prisoners. As it was related to Zeisberger, the Indians from Salem had not arrived yet, so those at Gnadenhutten bore the burden entirely.[127] According to Heckewelder:

> They were further told: that the horses found with them, had been taken from white people, they being branded with letters, with which Indians were unacquainted; that the axes found with them, had the names of white people stamped upon them. Pewter basins and spoons were stolen property; the Indians making use of wooden bowls and spoons. Tea-kettles, pots, cups and saucers, was also declared stolen property. In short every thing they possessed, was said to have been taken from the white people whilst at war with them.[128]

Because "Indians" did not use such things, any "Indians" who possessed them must have taken them. It was tautological racism, pure and simple, and perhaps an attempt to justify looting the town and the murders to come. The Moravian Indians, of course, lived like white Americans and had been economically successful following the rules first laid down at Herrnhut. Indeed, in many cases, they were more successful than their white neighbors. Where Koquethaqechton had thought the Delaware needed to live like the whites, Indians who had joined the United Brethren already did, increasingly sharing their culture and even dressing like them. Heckewelder proclaimed, "the Christian Indians were well known by their dress, which was plain and decent, no sign of paint to be seen on their skin or clothes, they wore no feathers about their heads, neither did they shave and trim them as every Indian warrior does; but wore their hair as the Christians did."[129] Farrar indicates that the Indians were further accused of aiding the British by feeding war parties, which was true enough, and stealing horses from the Americans. The Indians could only insist on their own neutrality, the compulsory nature of their providing food for war parties, and their efforts to maintain Delaware neutrality for so many years. They also pointed out that they had supplied the Americans, particularly during Colonel Brodhead's campaign the prior year.[130] Alas, they were unaware of the intelligence that Zeisberger and Heckewelder had provided to the Americans, which remained hidden from them of necessity. It was all for naught.

One particularly controversial argument was that the Indians at the Moravian towns had participated in raids, including the recent spring raids on the frontier. Under pressure, the Moravian Indians allegedly admitted that ten Wyandot warriors had accompanied them to the Muskingum, four of whom were still in town.[131] It was a damning piece of evidence accepted by later historians but thinly sourced by an individual attempting to sort matters out after the fact for the Pennsylvania Assembly. Early historians of the period repeated it, but the suggestion was forgotten in later years.[132]

The taunting and accusations hurled at the Moravian Indians throughout March 7-8 have the stench of a mob trial in which the defenses offered by the Indians fell on ears uninterested in hearing the truth but only in working themselves into a frenzy of hatred and anger. At some point, the Moravian Indians gathered at Gnadenhutten, who had navigated frontier violence for so long, began to recognize that their time had come. Abraham, a Mohican convert who Zeisberger had worried was sliding away from his faith, sought salvation in Christianity in his last hours. According to the missionary, the penitent member of his congregation proclaimed, "Dear brethren, according to appearances we shall all very soon come to the Saviour, for as it seems they have so resolved about us. You know I am a bad man, that I have much troubled the Saviour and the brethren, and have not behaved as becomes a believer, yet to him I belong, bad as I am; he will forgive us all and not reject me; to the end I shall hold fast to him and not leave him."[133] After Abraham's repentance, the congregants began singing hymns and praying together, as they had done for years during daily services.[134] Heckewelder indicates they asked forgiveness and pardon from one another for any offenses, spent time in tears, and attempted to console one another—the actions of a condemned people.

Once the Indians were locked away, however, several events occurred among the whites. First, Williamson held an officer's council. He had been censured for his failure to eliminate the problem of the Muskingum Indians the previous November, even if the complaints were whispered by his neighbors and not offered by Continental or militia authorities. He did not want to bear sole responsibility for the next steps. Neither did his officers. Collectively, they decided to put the matter to a vote by the American raiders gathered in town.[135] It is not clear whether the Indians from Salem had arrived yet, but it seems likely that Williamson and his officers would have wanted everyone secured before bringing things to a head.

So, either late on March 7 or early on March 8, Williamson ordered the men into line and called upon those who favored mercy for the Indians to step forward. As presented, mercy would mean removing the Moravian Indians to Pittsburgh, as he had done in November. This clearly indicates the group had already decided on the question of guilt and found against the Moravian Indians. Between sixteen and eighteen men stepped forward, singling themselves out by standing up to the raider's mood.[136] The majority remained in place, signifying a death sentence. Had Williamson framed the vote the other way around and required those favoring death to step forward, he might have gotten a different answer, or at least closer results.

With the death sentence passed, the next issue the Americans faced was how to implement it. They could simply set fire to the buildings the Indians were in. Others wanted to take scalps as evidence of "victory." The Americans decided to do both. During the discussion, those opposing the death penalty either made themselves scarce or continued arguing that mercy was the more appropriate path, to no avail.[137] A group of those favoring mercy drifted to the river bank, out of view of the town. That group may have included Colonel Williamson.[138] With that, someone asked the bound Indians whether they were prepared to die, for their hour had come. Heckewelder, perhaps to insert some religious significance into the conduct of the Indians, wrote that the Indians replied they had consigned their souls to God, received assurance in their hearts that he would accept their souls, and were ready.[139] It was also the response of a pious community that had stayed together to pursue their new lives of faith in the face of horrifying violence and temptation.

With that, on March 8, some Indians suspected of participating in raids were led out of the buildings in which they had been kept and toward the river. There, they were killed with spears and tomahawks and then scalped, beginning with Abraham, whose long hair marked his scalp as desirable at the same time it confirmed his recent religious backsliding.[140] An early American historian of the war on the frontier recorded that one man attempted to get away while being led to his death. His two guards began arguing over who would own his scalp. Noticing their distraction, he drew a knife and cut his bindings, then attacked one of his would-be executioners. The executioner evaded the blow and the Indian ran for the woods, dodging a few bullets aimed his way. As he ran, an American mounted his horse and chased after the prisoner and tackled him by leaping from the saddle. As the American raised his tomahawk, another raider shot the Indian in the back.[141] A different account only relates that a bloodied Indian escaped from his captors and ran for the river, swam it, and then was shot while climbing the opposite bank.[142] One raider also saved an eight-year-old boy, Benjamin, and adopted him, taking him off to his own home.[143]

There are several versions of what happened next. Heckewelder reports that the men had been kept in the cooper's cabin and were killed there. Zeisberger agreed that Abraham was the first to fall, but his diary records Abraham as having been killed outside the cooper's house, perhaps as one of the first men led to the riverbank.[144] According to Heckewelder, one of the raiders picked up a cooper's mallet and began striking men in the head, cracking their skulls, until more than a dozen lay on the floor. He only stopped when his arm tired, proclaimed "I think I have done well," and then handed the mallet to another. The popular telling of the story ends there, suggesting an incident of cold-blooded or even gleeful race violence.[145] But research by Colonel J. T. Holmes, whose grand-uncle Obadiah Holmes, Jr., claimed to be on the raid and have voted for mercy, reported that afterward the man "sat down and cried because he found in it no satisfaction for his murdered wife and children."[146] Holmes was of two minds on how the rest of the men were dispatched, whether it was inside or outside the house in which they had been held. Other histories separate the places in which the Moravian Indians had been held from the place of their execution, reporting that Indians were dragged singly or in pairs to one of two "slaughter houses," where they were finally dispatched.[147] In the other house, the Americans began with aged widow Judith.[148] A different widow, Christina, a Mahican, had been with the Moravians since her youth at Bethlehem and reportedly threw herself at Williamson's feet, begging for her life in English. He only replied, "I cannot help you."[149] This, of course, would mean he had not loitered on the riverbank away from the murder sites but was nearby. The initial account Zeisberger pieced together was slightly different in that he believed the murders took place over two days. The Gnadenhutten residents were killed on March 7. After that, the raiders rode to Salem, brought the people there into Gnadenhutten, and killed them on March 8.[150]

After a time, the deed was largely finished. Their victims lay dead or dying, bleeding to death, mostly in the slaughter houses or perhaps down by the river. Robert Wallace, whose cabin had been raided and whose family was missing, but who did not yet know that his wife and infant had been brutally killed, reportedly sat down by the riverbank and burst into tears, proclaiming, "You know I couldn't help it!"[151] Now and then, one raider would return to the slaughter houses to make sure none had survived. In one, an Indian named Abel, already scalped and covered in blood, was still moving and attempted to rise, only to be beaten again until he moved no more.[152] From the floor, a scalped teenager named Thomas watched what happened to Abel and froze. After Abel had been beaten to stillness and his murderers left, Thomas crept over the dead bodies to reach the door. At dusk, he slipped out and hid again, keeping the slaughter house between himself and the raiders. When it was fully dark, he ran for the woods.[153] Another boy found a loose floorboard and managed to crawl down into the cellar. When the raiders set fire to the building, he slipped out of the cellar through an opening cut for a window. Another young survivor attempted to follow but got stuck and burned to death with the building.[154] Both boys eventually caught up with the Schoenbrunn Indians who were already fleeing toward the Sandusky River.

As the work of murder went on at Gnadenhutten, a party of raiders set out for Schoenbrunn, discovered that its inhabitants had left, and then looted what they could. Two Indians from the Schoenbrunn forage party, Samuel Nanticoke and Matthew, had returned to the town to recover their forgotten canoe. But about three hundred yards from town, they spotted mounted white men milling about in the village. The scouts waited for them to depart and then bolted back toward the foraging party, which had continued moving away from the Muskingum.[155] They eventually rejoined it, along with Jacob Shabosh, who had fled after the raiders passed him by. The two escaped boys, the messengers, and Jacob served as the primary sources for Zeisberger and Heckewelder, who were already on their way to Detroit.

After the Americans finished looting Salem, Gnadenhutten, and Schoenbrunn, they burned all three towns to the ground and set out for the Ohio, having enriched themselves with eighty Indian horses loaded down with plunder.[156] The possibility of securing loot had always motivated frontier settlers to participate in such raids. Behind them, they left three burned towns and over ninety bodies. Heckewelder believed ninety-six people had been killed; sixty-two adults of whom one third were women, and thirty-four children.[157] Five were national assistants, Native American leaders in the community who helped with services. These included John Martin, who had accidentally exposed the population of Salem to the Americans by inviting them to Gnadenhutten, and Isaac, formerly the Delaware war leader Glickhican, who had been instrumental in helping the Moravians navigate the war. A prisoner taken by the Wyandot and passing through the Sandusky reported that the "militia" had taken ninety-six scalps, which bewildered Zeisberger, for only eighty-six Moravian Indians were supposed to be at Salem and Gnadenhutten.[158] (The presence of Wyandot raiders among the Moravians might account for the discrepancy, but an exact count may be too much to expect absent extensive archeological work.) A monument erected by the local communities at Gnadenhutten in 1872 marked it as the site where ninety Christian Indians "triumphed in death."[159]

Once the raiders crossed the Ohio, they largely broke up and set out for their homes. But a core group was still resolved to wage war on Indians. Gelelemend's ever-declining faction of pro-American Delaware lived on an island in the Allegheny near Pittsburgh. On March 24, American raiders, reported to have participated in the Gnadenhutten massacre, attacked the Delaware on the island, some of whom, Gelelemend included, held commissions from the United States or had otherwise supported American military campaigns on the frontier. The great bulk of the Indians made it safely to Fort Pitt but not until several had been killed. The raiders pursued, outraged at their quarry's escape and the shelter Colonel Gibson offered the Delaware. They reportedly sent him a note announcing their intention to scalp him for his support of Indians should he fall into their hands.[160] Gibson's absent commander, Brigadier Irvine, returned the next day. He found:

> things were in a greater confusion than can well be conceived. The country people were, to all appearance, in a fit of frenzy. About three hundred had just returned from the Moravian towns, where they found about ninety men, women and children, all of whom they put to death, it is said, after cool deliberation and considering the matter for three days. The whole were collected into their church and tied when singing hymns. On their return, a party came and attacked a few Delaware Indians, who have yet remained with us, on a small island close by this garrison, killed two

> who had captains' commissions in our service, and several others. . . . There was an officer's guard on the island at the same time, but he either did not do his duty or his men connived at the thing. . . . A number of wrong-headed men had conceived an opinion that Colonel Gibson was a friend to Indians, and that he must be killed also.[161]

Irvine's own troops were in a disgruntled mood. The noncommissioned officers and enlisted men of the 7th Virginia posted at Fort Pitt greeted him with a petition complaining that they had not been paid for two years and three months, had been harassed and upbraided by the locals for passivity and ineffectiveness in the face of constant frontier raids—through no fault of their own—and highlighted rumors that both the Indians and soldiers of the Pennsylvania line had received some pay. Irvine had to resort to executions for desertion to maintain order.[162] Nevertheless, their complaints highlighted the weakness of Continental authority on the upper Ohio frontier, the kind of weakness that had long frustrated frontier settlers and led them to rely on themselves for security.

Since March 8, 1782, people have offered various interpretations of the Gnadenhutten massacre. At the time, many whites on the frontier welcomed it as justified. They had long viewed the Moravian Indians as either guilty or complicit in attacks on settlers, which often resulted in murder, captivity, and sometimes executions every bit as brutal as the massacre itself. Knowing that the Moravian Indians had been killed, their villages destroyed, that particular threat removed (as some whites saw it) proved highly gratifying.[163] Doddridge, who tried to capture frontier attitudes years later, concluded, "They were not miscreants or vagabonds; many of them were men of the first standing in the country. Many of them were men who had recently lost relations by the hand of the savages; several of the latter class found articles which had been plundered from their own houses, or those of their relations, in the houses of the Moravians."[164] Indeed, they were motivated to continue waging war on the Indians and soon launched a sanctioned campaign against the western tribes on the Sandusky, something the Continentals had only talked about. It ended in disaster for the Americans.

Of course, not everyone on the frontier looked at Gnadenhutten that way. Some began to realize that the raiders had murdered indiscriminately, resulting in the death of innocent people. Dorsey Pentecost, a member of the local county council, traveled to Pittsburgh to gather what information he could. He found it difficult, writing from Pittsburgh in May, "That affair is a subject of great speculation here—some condemning, other applauding the measure; but the accounts are so various that it is not only difficult, but almost, indeed, entirely impossible to ascertain the real truth. No person can give intelligence but those that were along; and notwithstanding there seems to have been some difference amongst themselves about that business, yet they will say nothing; but this far I believe may be depended on, that they killed rather deliberately the innocent with the guilty, and it is likely the majority was the former. I have heard it insinuated that about thirty or forty only of the party gave their consent or assisted in the catastrophe. It is said here, and I believe with truth, that sundry articles were found amongst the Indians that were taken from the inhabitants of Washington county."[165]

As people became more aware of the number of women and children killed, public opinion started to turn against the raiders. Colonel Edward Cook, lieutenant of Westmoreland County, wrote the executive council, "I am informed that you have it Reported that the Massacre of the Moravian Indians obtains the approbation of Every man on this side of the Mountains, which I assure your Excellency is false; that the better part of the community are of Opinion the Perpetrators of that wicked Deed ought to be brought to Condein [condign] Punishment; that without something is Done by Government in the Matter, it will disgrace the Annuls of the United States, and be an Everlasting Plea and cover for British cruelty."[166] Cook's letter was defensive, written after information about the number of women and children killed had begun to circulate. For his part, Pentecost recommended, "I think it is necessary that Council should take some Cognizance or notice of the matter, and in such a Time as may demonstrate their disapprobation of such parts of their conduct as are Censorable, otherwise it may be alleged that Govermt (Tacitly at least,) have Incouraged the killing of women and children, and in a proclamation of this kind it might be well, not only to recommend but to forbid that in future Excursions, that women, Children, and Infirm persons should not be killed, so Countrary to the Law of arms as well as Christianity."[167] Irvine took steps to make that clear in sanctioning the subsequent militia campaign to the Sandusky.

Far to the west, David Zeisberger, of all people, told the Moravian Indians gathered on the Sandusky that it was God's punishment for their turn away from Christianity and wicked behavior on the frontier. That, combined with his diary admissions that the missionaries were powerless to stop the spread of evil among those Indians baptized into the Moravian church, suggests that there may have been occasions during the Revolution in which the "Moravian Indians" had committed hostile acts against the Americans, as had likely been the case during the French and Indian War and Pontiac's War.

After the massacre, Samuel, one of the assistants from Schoenbrunn, shuttled back and forth between those Moravian Indians returning to the Sandusky and the missionaries making their way to Detroit. According to Zeisberger:

> we told him our thoughts and disposition in regard to their difficult and dangerous circumstances, and the great want in which our Indians now are; that all this hardship and their troubles have not come upon them without cause; they had sinned against the Lord, their God, had been disobedient to their teachers, had heaped sin upon sin, and if their teachers disciplined them therefor, and were strict with them, they had become wicked and scornful towards them, and when they got a chance, namely, when the warriors were strong enough in our towns, had as good as betrayed and sold their teachers, in order to show us we had no power to punish them for their sinful lives, as if they wished to show us that our life and position depended upon them; they wished to close our mouths that we might not bear witness against their wickedness and sinful ways; we had great compassion with those who

> remained true and upright, who had to suffer with the guilty; it grieved us to the heart that in all our need and perplexity there were yet ill-minded people among us, who were always heaping more sin upon themselves, and who, now that we are away, always lay the blame upon their teachers that they fare so ill, and indeed even say we were the cause of the death of the brethren in Gnadenhutten, and had well known it beforehand; we looked upon all the evil which has come upon them as a deserved punishment from the Saviour upon them, and to ask forgiveness from the Saviour, that he would again let them feel his mercy and pity; to this the assistant, Samuel, replied it was even so to him, and he had already long so thought.[168]

It was a heartless thing to say and surely reflected the frustration of a man who had been persecuted at every turn by every party on the frontier for most of his adult life and the pain of having lost so many people he trusted and cared for. But for Zeisberger, who could remain quite stoic in the face of all forms of turmoil, it also came as something of an admission of failure. Some of the Indians who had accepted his faith had then returned to older ways.

In Paris, Benjamin Franklin, who had visited the site of the first Gnadenhutten massacre on the Lehigh, dined with Moravian missionaries and attended services and then helped stop the Paxton Boys from marching into Philadelphia, wrote, "the abominable Murders committed by some of the frontier People on the poor Moravian Indians, has given me infinite Pain and Vexation. The Dispensations of Providence in this World puzzle my weak Reason. I cannot comprehend why cruel Men should have been permitted thus to destroy their Fellow Creatures." He then went on to lay the blame at King George's feet, "It is he who has furnished the Savages with Hatchets and Scalping Knives, and engages them to fall upon our defenceless Farmers, and murder them with their Wives and Children paying for their Scalps, of which the Account kept already amounts as I have heard, to near two Thousand. Perhaps the people of the Frontier exasperated by the Cruelties of the Indians have . . . been induced to kill all Indians that fall into their Hands, without Distinction, so that even these horrid Murders of our poor Moravians may be laid to his Charge."[169]

As much as he wanted to shift blame from the American killers, Franklin's argument points to a larger truth. Whether it was Iroquois surrogates raiding Gnadenhutten on the Lehigh in 1755, western Indians slaughtering British garrisons in 1763, the Paxton Boys murdering the Conestoga in 1763, or American raiders attacking Gnadenhutten on the Muskingum in 1782, frontier warfare had always been brutal and indiscriminate, no matter who waged it. Throughout, some communities tried to make their way in the chaos, living peacefully at the edge of two cultures, Native American and white, which were often in conflict. The Church of the United Brethren worked those cultural seams, offering a new way of life, whether in Moravia, Saxony, Pennsylvania, or Ohio. Living on the edge of two societies meant maintaining a foot in both, making Moravian communities suspect in both whenever conflict tested local loyalties. In the American Revolution, the Moravians maintained that position under the political shelter offered by the Delaware Indian nation, whom neither the Americans, the western tribes, or the British wanted to alienate. Still, even as the religious communities along the Muskingum flourished economically and spiritually, they were under constant threat as all parties sought influence among the Delaware. The Moravian response was to appease all parties in order to maintain neutrality for both the Delaware and themselves. Thus, they fed war parties passing through, making it easier for the British-allied Indian nations in the west to raid along the upper Ohio Valley. Their choices may have been limited—war parties took what they wanted otherwise—but for settlers being attacked, the Moravian choice was unacceptable. To make matters worse, Delaware warriors began participating in those raids without the sanction of their leaders. Those warriors had friends and family among the Moravian communities. Thus, Americans living on the frontier saw plenty of provocation to treat the Moravian communities as an enemy.

The Moravians also provided intelligence to Continental authorities at Fort Pitt, used their influence to support the Delaware peace faction, and supplied American forces in the field, but the former was kept secret from settlers along the frontier and the latter was difficult for the average homesteader to see. Sadly, the western tribes and the British knew it, giving them ample reason to want the missionaries ejected from Indian society.

The Moravian policy of appeasement had won no friends on the frontier, but it had exacerbated animosities from all belligerents in the war. When the Delaware eventually chose sides, the storms of war finally shredded the umbrella Netawatwees had opened to protect the Moravians. Add to that toxic mixture a healthy dose of nativism, race hatred, expansionist aspirations, distrust, and misunderstanding and you get ingredients for a disaster. The explosion of cold-blooded and brutal murders at Gnadenhutten on March 8, 1782, was the result.

NOTES

INTRODUCTION

1. Henry Loskiel, *History of the Mission of the United Brethren among the Indians in North America* (London: Brethren's Society for the Furtherance of the Gospel, 1794), Part II, Chapter XI, 157.
2. Edmund De Schweinitz, *The Life and Times of David Zeisberger: The Western Pioneer and Apostle of the Indians* (Philadelphia: J.B. Lippincott, 1871), 229-230.
3. Loskiel, *History of the Mission*, Part II, Chapter XII, 166; De Schweinitz, *The Life and Times of David Zeisberger*, 229, 231.
4. De Schweinitz, *The Life and Times of David Zeisberger*, 232, 236.
5. De Schweinitz, *The Life and Times of David Zeisberger*, 232.
6. Heckewelder, *Narrative*, 44-45; Loskiel, *History of the Mission*, Part II, Chapter XII, 166; Abraham Henry Senseman, *Historical Incidents in the Lives of Joachim and Anna Catharine Senseman, and his Son Gottlob Senseman, and His Wife* (Philadelphia: Senseman & Son, Printers, 1881), 34.
7. John Heckewelder, *A Narrative of the Mission of the United Brethren among the Delaware and Mohegan Indians, from its Commencement in the Year 1740 to the Close of the Year 1808* (Philadelphia: McCarty and Davis, 1820), 44-45.
8. De Schweinitz, *The Life and Times of David Zeisberger*, 233.
9. Loskiel, *History of the Mission*, Part II, Chapter XII, 166-167; Senseman, *Historical Incidents in the Lives of Joachim and Anna Catharine Senseman*, 34.
10. De Schweinitz, *The Life and Times of David Zeisberger*, 235.
11. Loskiel, *History of the Mission*, Part II, Chapter XII, 167; De Schweinitz, *The Life and Times of David Zeisberger*, 229.
12. Senseman, *Historical Incidents in the Lives of Joachim and Anna Catharine Senseman*, 11, 35.
13. De Schweinitz, *The Life and Times of David Zeisberger*, 234-235.
14. De Schweinitz, *The Life and Times of David Zeisberger*, 232, 236.
15. Loskiel, *History of the Mission*, Part II, Chapter XII, 167.
16. Loskiel, *History of the Mission*, Part II, Chapter XII, 168; Earl P. Olmstead, *David Zeisberger: A Life among the Indians* (Kent, OH: Kent State University Press, 1997), 90-91.
17. De Schweinitz, *The Life and Times of David Zeisberger*, 235.
18. Heckewelder, *Narrative of the Mission*, 46; Loskiel, *History of the Mission*, Part II, Chapter XII, 169-170.

19. Heckewelder, *Narrative of the Mission*, 46.
20. Colin G. Calloway, *The Indian World of George Washington* (Oxford: Oxford University Press, 2018), 5.
21. Richard White, *The Middle Ground: Indians, Empires, and Republics in the Great Lakes Region, 1650-1815* (Cambridge: Cambridge University Press, 2011).

CHAPTER ONE: MISSIONARIES AND MISSIONS

1. J.E. Hutton, *A History of the Moravian Church*, 2nd ed. (London: Moravian Publication Office, 1909), Part I, 159-160; Edmund De Schweinitz, *The Moravian Manual: Containing an Account of the Moravian Church, or Unitas Fratrum*, 2nd ed. (Bethlehem, PA; Moravian Publication Office, A.C. & H.T. Clauder, 1869), 15-16.
2. Hutton, *A History of the Moravian Church*, 2nd ed., 179; Edmund De Schweinitz, *A History of the Unitas Fratrum from 1627 to 1722* (Bethlehem, PA: Moravian Publication Office, 1877), 7.
3. Hutton, *A History of the Moravian Church*, 2nd ed., 179; De Schweinitz, *The Moravian Manual*, 18-19.
4. Hutton, *A History of the Moravian Church*, 2nd ed., 162.
5. De Schweinitz, *The Moravian Manual*, 29.
6. Hutton, *A History of the Moravian Church*, 2nd ed., 177-178.
7. De Schweinitz, *The Life and Times of David Zeisberger*, 14.
8. Hutton, *A History of the Moravian Church*, 2nd ed., 200.
9. Hutton, *A History of the Moravian Church*, 2nd ed., 195.
10. De Schweinitz, *The Moravian Manual*, 32-33.
11. Edmund De Schweinitz, *The Life and Times of David Zeisberger*, 13; Earl P. Olmstead, *David Zeisberger: A Life Among the Indians* (Kent, OH: Kent State University Press, 1997), 4.
12. De Schweinitz, *The Life and Times of David Zeisberger*, 13-14.
13. Olmstead, *David Zeisberger*, 7.
14. Hutton, *A History of the Moravian Church*, 2nd ed., 200-204; Rev. John Gill, after M. Felix Bovet, *The Banished Count; or, The Life of Nicholas Louis Zinzendorf* (London: James Nisbet, 1865), 89-90; De Schweinitz, *The Moravian Manual*`33-34; J. Taylor Hamilton, *A History of the Church Known as the Moravian Church, or The Unitas Fratrum, or The Unity of the Brethren, during the Eighteenth and Nineteenth Centuries* (Bethlehem, PA: Times Publishing Company, 1900), 35-36.
15. Hutton, *A History of the Moravian Church*, 2nd ed., 205-207.
16. Hutton, *A History of the Moravian Church*, 2nd ed., 209.
17. Hutton, *A History of the Moravian Church*, 2nd ed., 208-209.
18. Hutton, *A History of the Moravian Church*, 2nd ed., 212-214.
19. Hutton, *A History of the Moravian Church*, 2nd ed., 214-215.
20. Quoted in an unattributed translation of J.W. Verbeek, *A Concise History of the Unitas Fratrum, or Church of the Brethren Commonly Called Moravians* (London: Mallalieu, 1862), 48. The original by Verbeek was published in German in 1857.

21. Verbeek, *A Concise History of the Unitas Fratrum*, 62.
22. Hamilton, *A History of the Church Known as the Moravian Church*, 45; Verbeek, *A Concise History of the Unitas Fratrum*, 60-62.
23. Hamilton, *A History of the Church Known as the Moravian Church*, 47.
24. Hamilton, *A History of the Church Known as the Moravian Church*, 47.
25. Hamilton, *A History of the Church Known as the Moravian Church*, 45; Verbeek, *A Concise History of the Unitas Fratrum*, 69.
26. Hutton, *A History of the Moravian Church*, 2nd ed., 355.
27. Henry Rimius, *A Candid Narrative of the Rise and Progress of the Herrnhuters, Commonly Call'd Moravians, or, Unitas Fratrum* (London: A. Linde, Printer, 1753), 7-8.
28. Olmstead, *David Zeisberger*, 13; De Schweinitz, *The Life and Times of David Zeisberger*, 15-16.
29. Olmstead, *David Zeisberger*, 16.
30. Olmstead, *David Zeisberger*, 18; De Schweinitz, *The Life and Times of David Zeisberger*, 17-22.
31. De Schweinitz, *The Life and Times of David Zeisberger*, 22.
32. De Schweinitz, *The Life and Times of David Zeisberger*, 23.
33. John Hill Martin, *Historical Sketch of Bethlehem in Pennsylvania, with Some Account of the Moravian Church,* 2nd ed. (Philadelphia: Self-published, printed by John Pile, 1873), 6; De Schweinitz, *The Life and Times of David Zeisberger*, 23-24.
34. Heckewelder, *A Narrative of the Mission of the United Brethren*, 19.
35. Heckewelder, *A Narrative of the Mission of the United Brethren*, 20.
36. Loskiel, *History of the Mission*, Part II, Chapter 1, 10.
37. Loskiel, *History of the Mission*, Part II, Chapter I, 12.
38. Loskiel, *History of the Mission*, Part II, Chapter I, 10.
39. Loskiel, *History of the Mission*, Part II, Chapter I, 3, 21.
40. Heckewelder, *A Narrative of the Mission of the United Brethren*, 22-23.
41. Heckewelder, *A Narrative of the Mission of the United Brethren*, 29-30.
42. De Schweinitz, *The Life and Times of David Zeisberger*, 124.
43. Quoted in De Schweinitz, *The Life and Times of David Zeisberger*, 127-128.
44. Olmstead, *David Zeisberger*, 34-36; De Schweinitz, *The Life and Times of David Zeisberger*, 127-129.
45. Rev. Augustus Gottleib Spangenberg, Samuel Jackson, trans., *The Life of Nicholas Lewis Count Zinzendorf* (London: Samuel Holdsworth, Amen-Corner, 1838), 304-305; De Schweinitz, *The Life and Times of David Zeisberger*, 135.
46. Olmstead, *David Zeisberger*, 51-65; De Schweinitz, *The Life and Times of David Zeisberger*, 187.
47. Olmstead, *David Zeisberger*, 68.
48. Olmstead, *David Zeisberger*, 67, 71.
49. Olmstead, *David Zeisberger*, 71; Heckewelder, *A Narrative of the Mission of the United Brethren*, 40.
50. De Schweinitz, *The Life and Times of David Zeisberger*, 213-214, 226; Loskiel, *History of the Mission*, Part II, Chapter XI, 150-151.

51. Loskiel, *History of the Mission*, Part II, Chapter XI, 211; Heckewelder, *A Narrative of the Mission of the United Brethren,* 40-41. Loskiel reports that Teedyuscung and a Shawnee chief named Paxnous became the chief agitators and claimed to represent the Iroquois Council at Onondaga. Heckewelder is more inclined to attribute the threats to manipulation by Teedyuscung, but he also blamed the Iroquois for the overall pressure on the Gnadenhutten missions.
52. De Schweinitz, *The Life and Times of David Zeisberger*, 216.
53. Fred Anderson, *Crucible of War: The Seven Years' War and the Fate of Empire in British North America, 1754-1766* (New York: Alfred A. Knopf, 2000), 99; Thomas E. Crocker, *Braddock's March: How the Man Sent to Seize a Continent Changed American History* (Yardley, PA: Westholme, 2011), 204.
54. William A. Pencak, Christian B. Keller, and Barbara A. Gannon, *Pennsylvania: A Military History* (Yardley, PA: Westholme, 2016), 29.
55. Loskiel, *History of the Mission*, Part II, Chapter XI, 150, 159; Anthony F.C. Wallace, *King of the Delawares: Teedyuscung 1700-1763* (Syracuse, NY: Syracuse University Press, 1990), 80-82.
56. Loskiel, *History of the Mission*, Part II, Chapter XII, 165.
57. De Schweinitz, *The Life and Times of David Zeisberger*, 223; Heckewelder, *A Narrative of the Mission of the United Brethren,* 43.
58. Heckewelder, *A Narrative of the Mission of the United Brethren,* 43.
59. Joseph Mortimer Levering, *A History of Bethlehem Pennsylvania, 1741-1892* (Bethlehem, PA: Times Publishing Company, 1903), 301-302. Levering was a bishop in the Moravian Church.
60. Loskiel, *History of the Mission*, Part II, Chapter XIII, 182-184.
61. Loskiel, *History of the Mission*, Part II, Chapter XII, 172.
62. Loskiel, *History of the Mission*, Part II, Chapter XIII, 189.
63. Loskiel, *History of the Mission*, Part II, Chapter XIV, 193.
64. Loskiel, *History of the Mission*, Part II, Chapter XIV, 197.
65. Pencak, Keller, and Gannon, *Pennsylvania: A Military History*, 29.
66. De Schweinitz, *The Life and Times of David Zeisberger*, 242.
67. De Schweinitz, *The Life and Times of David Zeisberger*, 243-244.
68. *The History of Tuscarawas County, OH* (Chicago: Warner, Beers, 1884), 268; Kevin Kenny, *Peaceable Kingdom Lost: The Paxton Boys and the Destruction of William Penn's Holy Experiment* (Oxford: Oxford University Press, 2009), 100.
69. Rev. Edward Rondthaler, B.H. Coates, ed., *Life of John Heckewelder* (Philadelphia: Crissy and Markley, Printers, 1847), 35, note.
70. Christian Frederick Post, "Two Journals of Western Tours, by Christian Frederick Post: One, to the Neighborhood of Fort Duquesne (July-September, 1758); the Other, to the Ohio (October, 1758-January, 1759)," *Proud's History of Pennsylvania* (Philadelphia, 1798), ii, appendix, "Introduction." Post was not well educated; his spelling and grammar are atrocious. The citation here is from an introduction to a reprint of Post's journal, which was heavily edited. I use this reprint, which was originally published as an appendix to *An Enquiry into the Causes of the Alienation of the Delaware and Shawanese Indians from the British Interest* (London: Printed for J. Wilkie, 1759). *An Enquiry* was published

anonymously but was likely written by Charles Thomson and then made its way into *Proud's History of Pennsylvania*. This was reprinted in Philadelphia by John Campbell in 1867. Heckewelder, who served with Post later, claimed that he possessed the original, which was much more interesting than the version published in London. Heckewelder, *A Narrative of the Mission of the United Brethren,* 56.

71. Kevin Kenny, *Peaceable Kingdom Lost: The Paxton Boys and the Destruction of William Penn's Holy Experiment*, Kindle ed. (Oxford: Oxford University Press, 2009), 49. Shingas served as a war leader. Tamaqua was known by whites as King Beaver. The trio would figure prominently in bringing the Moravians to the Ohio Country. Pennsylvania also declined to recognize the trio's authority because Philadelphia preferred to deal with the Delaware through the Iroquois.

72. Richard Middleton, *Pontiac's War: Its Causes, Course, and Consequences* (New York: Routledge, 2007), 88.

73. Post, *Two Journals,* 189.

74. Post, *Two Journals,* 189-190.

75. Post, *Two Journals*, 200.

76. Post, *Two Journals*, 201-202.

77. Post, *Two Journals*, 210.

78. Post, *Two Journals*, 239-240.

79. Post, *Two Journals*, 257-259.

80. Post, *Two Journals*, 260.

81. Post, *Two Journals*, 273-276.

82. Post, *Two Journals*, 278.

83. Post, *Two Journals*, 280.

84. Rev. Edward Rondthaler, B.H. Coates, ed., *Life of John Heckewelder* (Philadelphia: Crissy and Markley, Printers, 1847), 31.

85. Rondthaler, *Life of John Heckewelder,* 33.

86. Rondthaler, *Life of John Heckewelder*, 33.

87. Heckewelder, *A Narrative of the Mission of the United Brethren,* 60.

88. Heckewelder, *A Narrative of the Mission of the United Brethren,* 62-63.

89. Heckewelder, *A Narrative of the Mission of the United Brethren,* 64; Rondthaler, *Life of John Heckewelder*, 46-48.

90. Heckewelder, *A Narrative of the Mission of the United Brethren,* 64.

91. Rondthaler, *Life of John Heckewelder*, 51.

92. Rondthaler, *Life of John Heckewelder*, 51.

93. Rondthaler, *Life of John Heckewelder*, 53.

94. Rondthaler, *Life of John Heckewelder*, 58; Larry L. Nelson, *A Man of Distinction among Them: Alexander McKee and the Ohio Country Frontier, 1754-1799,* Kindle ed. (Kent, OH: Kent State University Press, 1999), Loc. 807.

95. Rondthaler, *Life of John Heckewelder*, 58; Nelson, *A Man of Distinction among Them*, Loc. 807.

96. David Dixon, *Never Come to Peace Again: Pontiac's Uprising and the Fate of the British Empire in North America* (Norman: University of Oklahoma Press, 2005), 76-80.

97. Dixon, *Never Come to Peace Again*, 63.
98. Kenny, *Peaceable Kingdom Lost*, 115; Wallace, *Teedyuscung: King of the Delawares*, 254-258.
99. Wallace, *King of the Delawares*, 258-259.
100. Dixon, *Never Come to Peace Again*, 62.
101. Kenny, *Peaceable Kingdom Lost*, 125.
102. Heckewelder, *A Narrative of the Mission of the United Brethren*, 68; Loskiel, *History of the Mission*, Part II, Chapter XV, 207; Brady J. Crytzer, *Guyasuta and the Fall of Indian America*, Kindle ed. (Yardley, PA: Westholme, 2013), 122.
103. Loskiel, *History of the Mission*, Part II, Chapter XV, 207-208; Heckewelder, *A Narrative of the Mission of the United Brethren*, 68.
104. Loskiel, *History of the Mission*, Part II, Chapter XV, 207-208.
105. Loskiel, *History of the Mission*, Part II, Chapter XV, 209; Heckewelder, *A Narrative of the Mission of the United Brethren*, 68-70.
106. Loskiel, *History of the Mission*, Part II, Chapter XV, 210.
107. Olmstead, *David Zeisberger*, 118-119; Heckewelder, *A Narrative of the Mission of the United Brethren*, 74.
108. Kenny, *Peaceable Kingdom Lost*, 133.
109. Kenny, *Peaceable Kingdom Lost*, 128. Kenny argues that the abandoned campaign had been directed at Wyalusing, specifically targeting the Moravian Indians who lived there and later evacuated to Philadelphia. Kenny, *Peaceable Kingdom Lost*, 144.
110. Loskiel, *History of the Mission*, Part II, Chapter XV, 216.
111. Loskiel, *History of the Mission*, Part II, Chapter XV, 216.
112. Olmstead, *David Zeisberger*, 121-124.
113. Loskiel, *History of the Mission*, Part II, Chapter XVI, 219-220; Heckewelder, *A Narrative of the Mission of the United Brethren*, 81-83.
114. Kenny, *Peaceable Kingdom Lost*, 1, 140.
115. Kenny, *Peaceable Kingdom Lost*, 152-153.
116. "Diary of the Indian Gemeine in the Barracks in Philadelphia," February 4, 1764, Barracks in Philadelphia, Bethlehem Digital History Project. Available at: http://bdhp.moravian.edu/community_records/christianindians/diaires/barracks/1764/translation64.html.
117. Kenny, *Peaceable Kingdom Lost*, 160-162; Loskiel, *History of the Mission*, Part II, Chapter XVI, 224; Heckewelder, *A Narrative of the Mission of the United Brethren*, 86.
118. Heckewelder, *A Narrative of the Mission of the United Brethren*, 87-88; Loskiel, *History of the Mission*, Part II, Chapter XVI, 225-226.
119. Olmstead, *David Zeisberger*, 130.
120. Olmstead, *David Zeisberger*, 139-145; John Heckewelder, *An Account of the History, Manners, and Customs of the Indian Nations, Who Once Inhabited Pennsylvania and the Neighbouring States* (Philadelphia: Abraham Small, 1819), 83.

CHAPTER TWO: THE DELAWARE AT THE CROSSROADS

1. Russell Shorto, *The Island at the Center of the World* (New York: Doubleday, 2004), 54.
2. Robert S. Grumet, *The Lenapes* (New York: Chelsea House, 1989), 13.
3. C.A. Weslager, *The Delaware Indians: A History* (New Brunswick, NJ: Rutgers University Press, 1972), 31.
4. "Frequently Asked Questions about the Lenape or Delaware Tribe," Official Web Site of the Delaware Tribe of Indians, June 26, 2013. Available at: http://delawaretribe.org/blog/2013/06/26/faqs/. Accessed February 28, 2019.
5. Grumet, *The Lenapes*, 25, 31-32.
6. Grumet, *The Lenapes*, 13; Weslager, *The Delaware Indians*, 32.
7. Amy C. Schutt, *Peoples of the River Valleys: The Odyssey of the Delaware Indians* (Philadelphia: University of Pennsylvania Press, 2007), 26.
8. Grumet, *The Lenapes*, 22.
9. John Heckewelder, *History, Manners, and Customs of the Indian Nations Who Once Inhabited Pennsylvania and the Neighbouring States, New and Revised ed.* (Philadelphia: Publication of the Historical Society of Pennsylvania, 1881), 53; Grumet, *The Lenapes*, 15-16; A.G. Roeber, ed., *Ethnographies and Exchanges: Native Americans, Moravians, and Catholics in Early North America* (University Park: Pennsylvania State University Press, 2008).
10. Grumet, *The Lenape*, 36; Wallace, *King of the Delawares: Teedyuscung, 1700-1763*, 195.
11. Kenny, *Peaceable Kingdom Lost*, 16; Weslager, *The Delaware Indians*, 190-191.
12. Quoted in Wallace, *Teedyuscung: King of the Delawares*, 206. Teedyuscung's concerns about the English producing deeds signed by the deceased was a reference to the Walking Purchase. It should be recalled that Teedyuscung had led his followers to the Wyoming Valley from the Moravian mission at Gnadenhutten.
13. Kenny, *Peaceable Kingdom Lost*, 115.
14. Post, *Two Journals*, 196.
15. Post, *Two Journals*, 198.
16. Post, *Two Journals,* 199.
17. Post, *Two Journals*, 209-210.
18. Post, *Two* Journals, 210.
19. Post, *Two Journals*, 214.
20. Quotes in Anderson, *Crucible of War*, 95; McConnell, *A Country Between*, 119. Recent scholars have called this particular episode in Braddock's march into question, drawing attention to the story's heritage and its inconsistency with Braddock's orders. See, David L. Preston, *Braddock's Defeat: The Battle of Monongahela and the Road to Revolution*, Kindle ed. (Oxford: Oxford University Press, 2015), 113. Thomas E. Crocker, *Braddock's March* (Yardley, PA: Westholme, 2011). 137-139. In any event, Shingas and the Delaware did not join Braddock's campaign.
21. Post, *Two Journals*, 283-284.

22. Post, *Two Journals*, 285.
23. Post, *Two Journals*, 278.
24. *A Christian Indian of North America: or, John Papunhank* (Dublin: Thomas I. White, 1830), 21; Gregory Evans Dowd, *War Under Heaven: Pontiac, the Indian Nations, & the British Empire* (Baltimore: Johns Hopkins University Press, 2002), 194. Dowd reports Papanhunk was a Mohawk who lived among the Delaware and other people of the Susquehanna Valley.
25. Loskiel, *History of the Mission*, Part II, Chapter XIV, 191-192.
26. Loskiel, *History of the Mission*, Part II, Chapter XIV, 196.
27. Heckewelder, *A Narrative of the Mission of the United Brethren*, 91.
28. Richard White, *The Middle Ground: Indians, Empires, and Republics in the Great Lakes Region, 1650-1815*, Twentieth Anniversary ed. (Cambridge: Cambridge University Press, 2011), 279-280; Gregory Evans Dowd, *A Spirited Resistance: The North American Indian Struggle for Unity, 1745-1815* (Baltimore: Johns Hopkins University Press, 1993), 33-35.
29. Schott, *Peoples of the River Valleys*, 119-120; Daniel K. Richter, *Facing East from Indian Country: A Native American History of Early America* (Cambridge, MA: Harvard University Press, 2001), 193-199.
30. Dowd, *War Under Heaven*, 126.
31. William A. Pencak and Christian B. Keller, "Pennsylvania in the French and Indian Wars, 1748-1766," *Pennsylvania: A Military History*, 40-41; David Dixon, *Never Come to Peace Again: Pontiac's Uprising and the Fate of the British Empire in North America* (Norman: University of Oklahoma Press, 2005).
32. Pencak and Keller, "Pennsylvania in the French and Indian Wars, 1748-1766," *Pennsylvania: A Military History*, 41.
33. Richard Middleton, *Pontiac's War: Its Causes, Course and Consequences* (New York: Routledge, 2007), 84-85.
34. Rondthaler, *Life of John Heckewelder*, 57.
35. Middleton, *Pontiac's War*, 84.
36. Middleton, *Pontiac's War*, 86.
37. Middleton, *Pontiac's War*, 86.
38. Middleton, *Pontiac's War*, 88-89.
39. Pencak and Keller, "Pennsylvania in the French and Indian Wars, 1748-1766," *Pennsylvania: A Military History*, 42.
40. Pencak and Keller, "Pennsylvania in the French and Indian Wars, 1748-1766," *Pennsylvania: A Military History*, 43.
41. Pencak and Keller, "Pennsylvania in the French and Indian Wars, 1748-1766," *Pennsylvania: A Military History*, 48; Dixon, *Never Come to Peace Again*, 220-221.
42. Pencak and Keller, "Pennsylvania in the French and Indian Wars, 1748-1766," *Pennsylvania: A Military History*, 48.
43. Middleton, *Pontiac's War*, 172.
44. Col. James Smith, *An Account of the Remarkable Occurrences in the Life and Travels of Col. James Smith, During his Captivity with the Indians*, reprint (Cincinnati: Robert Clarke, 1870), 107-108.

45. Dowd, *War Under Heaven*, 165-166.
46. Middleton, *Pontiac's War*, 177-178. Seneca chiefs and representatives from the Shawnee also participated, but our focus is the Delaware. Netawatwees was known among whites as Newcomer and was a rival to Tamaqua for Delaware leadership, although they were both generally voices for peace.
47. William Smith, *An Historical Account of the Expedition Against the Ohio Indians, in the Year MDCCLXIV under the Command of Henry Bouquet, ESQ* (Philadelphia, 1766), 23. The original was published in London.
48. Middleton, *Pontiac's War*, 181.
49. Schutt, *Peoples of the River Valleys*, 141-143.
50. Charles Beatty, *The Journal of Two Months Tour; with a View of Promoting Religion among the Frontier Inhabitants of Pennsylvania, and of Introducing Christianity among the Indians to the Westward of the Alegh-geny Mountains* (London: Printed for William Davenill and George Pearch, 1768), 57-58.
51. McConnell, *A County Between*, 222; Olmstead, *David Zeisberger*, 149-150.
52. Edmund De Schweinitz, *The Life and Times of David Zeisberger: The Western Pioneer and Apostle of the Indians* (Philadelphia: J.B. Lippincott, 1871), 327.
53. Quotes in De Schweinitz, *The Life and Time of David Zeisberger*, 332-333; Loskiel, *History of the Mission*, Part III, Chapter II, 23-24. The missionaries referred to Wingenund as Wangomen, but more recent versions refer to him as Wingenund. See, for example, McConnell, *A Country Between*, 222-223; Weslager, *The Delaware Indians*, 284.
54. McConnell, *A Country Between*, 222-223.
55. Quoted in De Schweinitz, *The Life and Times of David Zeisberger*, 334.
56. De Schweinitz, *The Life and Times of David Zeisberger*, 347-348; Heckewelder, *A Narrative of the Mission of the United Brethren*, 103-104.
57. De Schweinitz, *The Life and Times of David Zeisberger*, 347-348.
58. De Schweinitz, *The Life and Times of David Zeisberger*, 349.
59. Weslager, *The Delaware Indians*, 284. Packanke had sought to move Zeisberger to the Beaver for some time, but the land he offered was not as desirable as Zeisberger hoped. Olmstead, *David Zeisberger*, 174-175.
60. McConnell, *A Country Between*, 226-227.
61. Schutt, *Peoples of the River Valleys*, 130; Downes, *Council Fires on the Upper Ohio*, 138-139; Heckewelder, *A Narrative of the Mission of the United Brethren, 99*.
62. Timothy J. Shannon, *Iroquois Diplomacy on the Early American Frontier* (New York: Viking, 2008), 167-169.
63. The Moravians believed that Pennsylvania's governor had assured them the Stanwix purchase would not affect their village, but whites made conflicting claims, which unsettled the Moravian Indians at Friedenshutten. Heckewelder, *A Narrative of the Mission of the United Brethren*, 107-108.
64. De Schweinitz, *The Life and Times of David Zeisberger*, 355.
65. Paul A.W. Wallace, ed., *The Travels of John Heckewelder in Frontier America* (Pittsburgh: University of Pittsburgh Press, 1958), 94.

66. De Schweinitz, *The Life and Times of David Zeisberger*, 355; Heckewelder, *A Narrative of the Mission of the United Brethren*, 109; Loskiel, *History of the Mission*, Part III, Chapter III, 46.
67. De Schweinitz, *The Life and Times of David Zeisberger*, 356-357; Heckewelder, *A Narrative of the Mission of the United Brethren*, 109-110.
68. De Schweinitz, *The Life and Times of David Zeisberger*, 359.
69. De Schweinitz, *The Life and Times of David Zeisberger*, 366. Gekelemukpechunk was really a complex of villages known collectively to whites as Newcomerstown, as whites called Netawatwees Chief Newcomer.
70. De Schweinitz, *The Life and Times of David Zeisberger*, 366.
71. De Schweinitz, *The Life and Times of David Zeisberger*, 367; Loskiel, *History of the Mission*, Part III, Chapter IV, 70-71.
72. Heckewelder, *A Narrative of the Mission of the United Brethren*, 112-113.
73. Heckewelder, *A Narrative of the Mission of the United Brethren*, 114.
74. Hermann Wellenreuther and Carola Wessel, eds., *The Moravian Mission Diaries of David Zeisberger, 1772-1781* (University Park: Pennsylvania State University Press, 2005), 94-95.
75. Schutt, *People of the River Valleys*, 136.
76. Heckewelder, *A Narrative of the Mission of the United Brethren*, 118-119.
77. Heckewelder, *A Narrative of the Mission of the United Brethren*, 124-125.
78. Heckewelder, *A Narrative of the Mission of the United Brethren*, 128.
79. Loskiel, *History of the Mission*, Part III, Chapter IV, 82.
80. Wallace, ed., *The Travels of John Heckewelder in Frontier America*, 98.
81. Reverend David Jones, *A Journal of Two Visits Made to Some Nations of Indians on the West Side of the River Ohio, in the Years 1772 and 1773*, reprint (New York: Joseph Sabin, 1865), vii-viii.
82. Jones, *A Journal of Two Visits*, 89.
83. Jones, *A Journal of Two Visits*, 92-97.
84. Jones, *A Journal of Two Visits*, 97.
85. Bemino was likely referring to the 1766 visit of Reverend Charles Beatty. While Netawatwees put the Presbyterians off then, Beatty's account indicates a general curiosity about different Christian sects among the Delaware. Beatty, *The Journal of Two Months Tour*, 45-49.
86. Jones, *A Journal of Two Visits*, 98-99.
87. Jones, *A Journal of Two Visits*, 99.
88. Wellenreuther and Wessel, eds., *The Moravian Mission Diaries of David Zeisberger, 1772-1781*, 174.
89. Glenn F. Williams, *Dunmore's War: The Last Conflict of America's Colonial Era* (Yardley, PA: Westholme, 2017).
90. Schutt, *Peoples of the River Valleys*, 145.
91. Schutt, *Peoples of the River Valleys*, 147.
92. Wellenreuther and Wessel, eds., *The Moravian Mission Diaries of David Zeisberger, 1772-1781*, 204-205.
93. Wellenreuther and Wessel, eds., *The Moravian Mission Diaries of David Zeisberger, 1772-1781*, 204-205.

94. Heckewelder, *A Narrative of the Mission of the United Brethren,* 135; De Schweinitz, *The Life and Times of David Zeisberger*, 413-415.
95. Wellenreuther and Wessel, eds., *The Moravian Mission Diaries of David Zeisberger, 1772-1781*, 260.
96. Reuben Gold Thwaites and Louise Phelps Kellogg, eds., "Affairs at Fort Pitt," *The Revolution on the Upper Ohio, 1775-1777*, Draper Series, Volume II (Madison: Wisconsin Historical Society, 1908), 19-20; Wellenreuther and Wessel, eds., *The Moravian Mission Diaries of David Zeisberger, 1772-1781*, 260.
97. Thwaites and Kellogg, eds., *Revolution on the Upper Ohio*, 34.
98. "Journal of James Wood," Thwaites and Kellogg, eds., *Revolution on the Upper Ohio*, 36-37.
99. Hermann Wellenreuther, "The Succession of Head Chiefs and the Delaware Culture of Consent: The Delaware Nation, David Zeisberger, and Modern Ethnography;" A.G. Roeber, ed., *Ethnographies and Exchanges: Native Americans, Moravians, and Catholics in Early North America* (University Park: Pennsylvania State University Press, 2008) contains an insightful discussion of the relationship among Delaware leaders and the Moravians after Netawatwees's "retirement."
100. "Journal of James Wood," Thwaites and Kellogg, eds., *Revolution on the Upper Ohio*, 39-40.
101. Thwaites and Kellogg, eds., *Revolution on the Upper Ohio*, 109. The quote was addressed to the Wyandot nation and is taken from American notes on a council meeting between Ohio Indians and Virginia Indian commissioners at Fort Pitt.
102. Thwaites and Kellogg, eds., *Revolution on the Upper Ohio*, 84-85.
103. Thwaites and Kellogg, eds., *Revolution on the Upper Ohio*, 85-88.
104. Thwaites and Kellogg, eds., *Revolution on the Upper Ohio*, 86.
105. Heckewelder, *A Narrative of the Mission of the United Brethren,* 141.
106. Calloway, *The Indian World of George Washington*, 263.
107. Library of Congress, *Journals of the Continental Congress, 1774-1789, Volume 4, January 1-June 4, 1776* (Washington, DC: Government Printing Office, 1906), 208. Congressional representatives appear to have received Koquethaqechton's proposal on March 2. *Journals of the Continental Congress*, 4: 269.
108. *Journals of the Continental Congress*, 4: 269.
109. *Journals of the Continental Congress*, 4: 269-270.
110. Gregory Schaaf, *Wampum Belts and Peace Trees: George Morgan, Native Americans and Revolutionary Diplomacy* (Golden, CO: Fulcrum Publishing, 1990), 4-5; Lewis S. Shimmell, *Border Warfare in Pennsylvania During the Revolution* (Harrisburg, PA: R.L. Myers, 1901), 60-61.
111. Schaaf, *Wampum Belts and Peace Trees*, 21-22.
112. Wellenreuther and Wessel, eds., *The Moravian Mission Diaries of David Zeisberger, 1772-1781*, 309-311.
113. Quotes in Schaaf, *Wampum Belts and Peace Trees*, 47.
114. Heckewelder, *A Narrative of the Mission of the United Brethren,* 142.

115. Heckewelder, *A Narrative of the Mission of the United Brethren*, 143.
116. Schaaf, *Wampum Belts and Peace Trees*, 32-33; "Report from Niagara: Neutrality to be Maintained," Thwaites and Kellogg, eds., *The Revolution on the Upper Ohio*, 171-172.
117. Wellenreuther and Wessel, eds., *The Moravian Mission Diaries of David Zeisberger, 1772-1781*, 316-319.
118. Wellenreuther and Wessel, eds., *The Moravian Mission Diaries of David Zeisberger, 1772-1781*, 324, 325.
119. Wellenreuther and Wessel, eds., *The Moravian Mission Diaries of David Zeisberger, 1772-1781*, 321. One of the brothers on the stroll was Isaac, Glickhican's baptismal name.
120. *Journals of the Continental Congress*, 4: 270.
121. Wellenreuther and Wessel, eds., *The Moravian Mission Diaries of David Zeisberger, 1772-1781*, 335.
122. Wellenreuther and Wessel, eds., *The Moravian Mission Diaries of David Zeisberger, 1772-1781*, 335; Heckewelder, *A Narrative of the Mission of the United Brethren*, 146.
123. Wellenreuther and Wessel, eds., *The Moravian Mission Diaries of David Zeisberger, 1772-1781*, 335-337; Schaaf, *Wampum Belts and Peace Trees*, 161-163.
124. Schaaf, *Wampum Belts and Peace Trees*, 167.
125. Wellenreuther and Wessel, eds., *The Moravian Mission Diaries of David Zeisberger, 1772-1781*, 335-337.
126. Wellenreuther and Wessel, eds., *The Moravian Mission Diaries of David Zeisberger, 1772-1781*, 339. This may have been a reference to a reported attack at Fish Creek earlier in the month. Later reports reduced the number killed to two women and a single boy kidnapped. Schaaf, *Wampum Belts and Peace Trees*, 170.
127. Wellenreuther and Wessel, eds., *The Moravian Mission Diaries of David Zeisberger, 1772-1781*, 340.
128. Wellenreuther and Wessel, eds., *The Moravian Mission Diaries of David Zeisberger, 1772-1781*, 341; Heckewelder, *A Narrative of the Mission of the United Brethren*, 148-149.
129. Schaaf, *Wampum Belts and Peace Trees*, 177-180.
130. Schaaf, *Wampum Belts and Peace Trees*, 182.
131. Schaaf, *Wampum Belts and Peace Trees*, 192-196.
132. Heckewelder, *A Narrative of the Mission of the United Brethren*, 154.
133. Wellenreuther and Wessel, eds., *The Moravian Mission Diaries of David Zeisberger, 1772-1781*, 358-359.
134. Wellenreuther and Wessel, eds., *The Moravian Mission Diaries of David Zeisberger, 1772-1781*, 446.
135. Wellenreuther and Wessel, eds., *The Moravian Mission Diaries of David Zeisberger, 1772-1781*, 360-361.
136. Schaaf, *Wampum Belts and Peace Trees*, 197.
137. Quoted in John D. Barnhart, ed., *Henry Hamilton and George Rogers*

Clark in the American Revolution with the Unpublished Journal of Lieut. Gov. Henry Hamilton (Crawfordsville, IN: R.E. Banta, 1951), 29.
138. Henry Hamilton, "Council at Detroit, June 17, 1777," Reuben Gold Thwaites and Louise Phelps Kellogg, eds., *Frontier Defense on the Upper Ohio, 1777-1778*, Draper Series, Vol. III (Madison: Wisconsin Historical Society, 1912), 7-13.
139. "Hamilton's Proclamation" in Thwaites and Kellogg, eds., *Frontier Defense on the Upper Ohio*, 14.
140. Wellenreuther and Wessel, eds., *The Moravian Mission Diaries of David Zeisberger, 1772-1781*, 382.
141. Wellenreuther and Wessel, eds., *The Moravian Mission Diaries of David Zeisberger, 1772-1781*, 390.
142. Wellenreuther and Wessel, eds., *The Moravian Mission Diaries of David Zeisberger, 1772-1781*, 391.
143. "David Zeisberger to Gen. Edward Hand, July 29th, 1777," Thwaites and Kellogg, eds., *Frontier Defense on the Upper Ohio*, 27-28.
144. "Col. John Gibson to Gen. Hand, July 31, 1777," Thwaites and Kellogg, eds., *Frontier Defense on the Upper Ohio*, 35.
145. Edgar Hassler, *Old Westmoreland: A History of Western Pennsylvania During the Revolution* (Pittsburgh: J.R. Weldin, 1900), chapter VI, Available from PA-Roots.com.
146. "The Murder of Cornstalk: Narrative of Capt. John Stuart," Thwaites and Kellogg, eds., *Frontier Defense on the Upper Ohio*, 160; "Deposition on the murder," November 10, 1777, Thwaites and Kellogg, eds., *Frontier Defense on the Upper Ohio*, 162.
147. "Gen. Edward Hand to Gov. Patrick Henry, December 9th, 1777," and "Gen. Edward Hand to Jasper Yeates, December 24th, 1777," Thwaites and Kellogg, eds., *Frontier Defense on the Upper Ohio*, 175-177, 188; "Gov. Patrick Henry to Col. William Fleming, March 14th, 1778," Thwaites and Kellogg, eds., *Frontier Defense on the Upper Ohio*, 225-226; "Gov. Patrick Henry to Col. William Preston and Col. William Fleming, March 27th, 1778," Thwaites and Kellogg, eds., *Frontier Defense on the Upper Ohio*," 240-241; De Hass, *History of the Early Settlement and Indian Wars of Western Virginia*, 173.
148. "Rev. David Zeisberger to General Hand, November 16, 1777," Thwaites and Kellogg, eds., *Frontier Defense on the Upper Ohio*, 164-165.
149. "General Edward Hand to a committee of Congress, 21st Decr. 1777," Thwaites and Kellogg, eds., *Frontier Defense on the Upper Ohio*, 184-185.
150. Larry L. Nelson, *A Man of Distinction among Them: Alexander McKee and the Ohio Country Frontier, 1754-1799*, Kindle ed. (Kent, OH: The Kent State University Press, 2000), Loc 1746-1755.
151. Nelson, *A Man of Distinction among Them*, Loc 1888-1903.
152. Phillip W. Hoffman, *Simon Girty: Turncoat Hero* (Franklin, TN: Flying Camp Press, 2008), 17-18.
153. Hoffman, *Simon Girty*, 82-83.
154. Butterfield, *History of the Girtys*, 38-41.

155. Reuben Gold Thwaites, ed., Alexander Scott Withers, *Chronicles of Border Warfare* (Glendale, CA: Arthur H. Clark, 1895), 210, note 1. The original work by Withers appeared in 1831. Withers was a local historian who collected oral histories from descendants of frontier families, some of which had already been printed locally. His work suffers from all the weaknesses attendant in his methodology. Another historian fascinated with the period, Lyman Draper, saved Withers's work for future generations, annotated it in places, and collected supplemental material, much of which was later published by the Wisconsin Historical Society. Thwaites came along late in the nineteenth century and further annotated the material. The reference here is to the first printing of the Thwaites edition. Because Thwaites was so prolific, this source will be cited as Withers, *Chronicles of Border Warfare*. Butterfield, *History of the Girtys*, 48-49.
156. "Edward Hand to Jasper Ewing, March 7th, 1778" Thwaites, ed., *Frontier Defense on the Upper Ohio*, 215.
157. "Recollections of Samuel Murphy," in Thwaites, ed., *Frontier Defense on the Upper Ohio*, 219.
158. Heckewelder, *A Narrative of the Mission of the United Brethren*, 170-171. This is likely a summary of the main points McKee made as told to Heckewelder.
159. Nelson, *A Man of Distinction among Them*, Kindle ed., loc 2034.
160. Wellenreuther and Wessel, eds., *The Moravian Mission Diaries of David Zeisberger, 1772-1781*, 440-441.
161. Wellenreuther and Wessel, eds., *The Moravian Mission Diaries of David Zeisberger, 1772-1781*, 441.
162. Wellenreuther and Wessel, eds., *The Moravian Mission Diaries of David Zeisberger, 1772-1781*, 441.
163. George Rogers Clark's Illinois campaign was still several months in the future.
164. Heckewelder, *A Narrative of the Mission of the United Brethren*, 172.
165. Heckewelder, *A Narrative of the Mission of the United Brethren*, 175-176.
166. Heckewelder, *A Narrative of the Mission of the United Brethren*, 177.
167. Heckewelder, *A Narrative of the Mission of the United Brethren*, 179-180.
168. Heckewelder, *A Narrative of the Mission of the United Brethren*, 182.
169. Wellenreuther and Wessel, eds., *The Moravian Mission Diaries of David Zeisberger, 1772-1781*, 448.
170. Wellenreuther and Wessel, eds., *The Moravian Mission Diaries of David Zeisberger, 1772-1781*, 460.
171. Wellenreuther and Wessel, eds., *The Moravian Mission Diaries of David Zeisberger, 1772-1781*, 462.
172. Wellenreuther and Wessel, eds., *The Moravian Mission Diaries of David Zeisberger, 1772-1781*, 469.
173. "Article II, Treaty With the Delawares, 1778." Available at: http://avalon.law.yale.edu/18th_century/del1778.asp. Accessed June 4, 2019. All Treaty citations are from this Yale Law School database.
174. Morgan quoted in Downes, *Council Fires on the Upper Ohio*, 216; Killbuck quoted in Weslager, *The Delaware Indians*, 305.

175. Downes, *Council Fires on the Upper Ohio*, 216-217; "Capt John Killbuck's Message to Colo Morgan, January 20th, 1779," Kellogg, *Frontier Advance on the Upper Ohio, 1778-1779*, 202. Killbuck made his accusation after a Delaware council meeting in 1779, when the Delaware were concerned that the Americans had built Fort Laurens too far north to protect them from warlike western Indians. His letter to Morgan may have been an attempt to distance himself from the treaty, since circumstances had changed, and to protect his political interests vis-à-vis other Delaware asserting leadership over the tribe.
176. "Speech of the Delawares to Washington and Congress, May 10th, 1779," Kellogg, *Frontier Advance on the Upper Ohio*, 317-319.
177. Wellenreuther and Wessel, eds., *The Moravian Mission Diaries of David Zeisberger, 1772-1781*, 474-475.
178. Wellenreuther and Wessel, eds., *The Moravian Mission Diaries of David Zeisberger, 1772-1781*, 475.
179. Wellenreuther and Wessel, eds., *The Moravian Mission Diaries of David Zeisberger, 1772-1781*, 475-476.
180. Weslager, *The Delaware Indians*, 306.

CHAPTER THREE: FRONTIER SETTLERS

1. Kevin Kenny, *Peaceable Kingdom Lost: The Paxton Boys and the Destruction of William Penn's Holy Experiment*, Kindle ed. (Oxford: Oxford University Press, 2009), 162.
2. *A Declaration and Remonstrance of the Distressed and Bleeding Frontier Inhabitants of the Province of Pennsylvania, Presented by them to the Honourable Governor and Assembly of the Province, Shewing the Causes of their late Discontent and Uneasiness and the Grievances Under which they have labored, and which they humbly pray to have redress'd*, 1764. Hereafter, *Declaration and Remonstrance*. The document was prepared as a single broadside with no listed printer but was reprinted widely. It has two parts, the *Declaration* and then a separate, more refined, *Remonstrance* to which Matthew Smith and John Gibson attached their names. Kenny found evidence that the two had assistance in composing the Remonstrance. Kenny, *Peaceable Kingdom Lost*, 164-165.
3. *Declaration and Remonstrance*, 3-4.
4. *Declaration and Remonstrance*, 8.
5. *Declaration and Remonstrance*, 12-13.
6. *Declaration and Remonstrance*, 4-7.
7. *Declaration and Remonstrance*, 13-14.
8. *The Conduct of the Paxton-Men, Impartially represented* (Philadelphia: A. Steuart, printer, John Creaig, bookseller, 1764), 8-9. As published, this pamphlet did not list an author, but he is generally known to be an Anglican minister, Thomas Barton, who had long experience on the frontier and had organized a volunteer militia unit around Carlisle while the Pennsylvania Assembly dithered over a militia bill. Kenny, *Peaceable Kingdom Lost*, 76.
9. *The Conduct of the Paxton-Men*, 29.
10. Benjamin Franklin, *A Narrative of the Late Massacres, in Lancaster County, of a Number of Indians, Friends of this Province, By Persons Unknown* (1764),

24-25. The original pamphlet appeared without attribution, either to an author or printer. Also available online at the Library of Congress: https://founders.archives.gov/?q=Paxton%20Boys&s=1111311111&r=2. Accessed March 21, 2019.

11. Patrick Spero, *Frontier Country: The Politics of War in Early Pennsylvania*, Kindle ed. (Philadelphia: University of Pennsylvania Press, 2016), Chapter 1.

12. Spero, *Frontier Country*, 34.

13. Bernard Bailyn, *Voyagers to the West* (New York: Vintage Books, 1988), 14.

14. Spero, *Frontier Country*, 40.

15. Kenny, *Peaceable Kingdom Lost*, Chapter 2.

16. See Samuel J. Newland, *The Pennsylvania Militia: Defending the Commonwealth and the Nation, 1669-1879* (Annville, PA: Commonwealth of Pennsylvania, 2002); William A. Pencak and Christian B. Keller, "Pennsylvania in the French and Indian Wars, 1748-1766," in William A. Pencak, Christian B. Keller, and Barbara A. Gannon, eds., *Pennsylvania: A Military History* (Yardley, PA: Westholme, 2016).

17. Joseph Seymour, *The Pennsylvania Associators, 1747-1777*, Kindle ed. (Yardley, PA: Westholme, 2012), 27-28.

18. Seymour, *The Pennsylvania Associators*, 133-137.

19. Thomas Verenna, "The Darker Side of the Militia," *Journal of the American Revolution*, February 26, 2014. Available at: https://allthingsliberty.com/2014/02/the-darker-side-of-the-militia/. Accessed September 24, 2019; Dennis Ness, "York County Pennsylvania Militia 1777," *Journal of the American Revolution*, September 21, 2016. Available at: https://allthingsliberty.com/2016/09/york-county-pennsylvania-militia-1777/. Accessed September 24, 2019.

20. Reverend David Jones, *A Journal of Two Visits Made to Some Nations of Indians on the West Side of the River Ohio, in the Years 1772 and 1773*, reprint (New York: Joseph Sabin, 1865), 52.

21. Jones, *A Journal of Two Visits*, 71.

22. J. Hector St. John Crevecoeur, *Letters from an American Farmer* reprint (New York: Fox, Duffield, 1904), 294.

23. David Zeisberger, Archer Butler Hulbert, and William Nathaniel Schwarze, eds., *David Zeisberger's History of the Northern American Indians* (Ohio State Archeological and Historical Society, 1910), 18. Hulbert and Schwarze report that the volume is based on a manuscript Zeisberger composed in 1779-1780 in German.

24. Zeisberger, *History of the North American Indians*, 18-19.

25. Zeisberger, *History of the North American Indians*, 19.

26. Darren Reid, "Anti-Indian Radicalization in the Early American West, 1774-1795," *Journal of the American Revolution*, June 19, 2017. Available at: https://allthingsliberty.com/2017/06/anti-indian-radicalisation-early-american-west-1774-1795/. Accessed September 24, 2019.

27. Spero, *Frontier Country*, 146.

28. Post, *Two Journals of Western Tours*, 214.

29. Jones, *A Journal of Two Visits*, 71-72.

30. John Heckewelder, *History, Manners and Customs of the Indian Nations who once Inhabited Pennsylvania and the Neighbouring States*, new and revised ed. (Philadelphia: Publication Fund of the Historical Society of Pennsylvania, 1881), 187. The original was published in 1818. The Wyandot held similar views: Rev. James B. Finley, *History of the Wyandott Mission at Upper Sandusky, Ohio under the Direction of the Methodist Episcopal Church* (Cincinnati: J.F. Wright and L. Swormstedt, 1840), 28.
31. Crevecoeur, *Letters from an American Farmer*, xiii-xiv. From the introduction by Ludwig Lewisohn. Crevecoeur's letters were originally published in London in 1782, reprinted and published in Philadelphia in 1783, and then Paris in 1784. The French draft was republished in 1787 and then the English version was reprinted in Philadelphia in 1793, all signifying its popularity in bridging the understanding between America and Europe in the late eighteenth century. Patrick Spero reintroduced twenty-first century readers to this volume in Patrick Spero, *Frontier Country: The Politics of War in Early Pennsylvania* (Philadelphia: University of Pennsylvania Press, 2016).
32. Crevecoeur, *Letters from an American Farmer*, 283-286.
33. Paul A.W. Wallace, *Indians in Pennsylvania* (Harrisburg: Pennsylvania Historical and Museum Commission, 1961), 146.
34. Ruth Ann Denaci, "The Penn's Creek Massacre and the Captivity of Marie Le Roy and Barbara Leininger," *Pennsylvania History: A Journal of Mid-Atlantic Studies*, Vol. 72. No. 4, 2007.
35. Anderson, *Crucible of War*, 162.
36. William A. Pencak, Christian B. Keller, "Pennsylvania in the French and Indian Wars, 1748-1766," William A. Pencak, Christian B. Keller, and Barbara A. Gannon, *Pennsylvania: A Military History* (Yardley, PA: Westholme, 2016), 29.
37. Quoted in Consul Willshire Butterfield, *History of the Girtys* (Cincinnati: Robert Clarke, 1890), 14-15.
38. "Account of the Sufferings of Massy Herbeson and her Family, who were taken Prisoners by a Party of Indians," Archibald Loudon, *A Selection, of some of the Most Interesting Narratives, of Outrages, Committed by the Indians in Their Wars with the White People*, Vol. I (Carlisle: A. Loudon, 1803), 86-87.
39. Middleton, *Pontiac's War*, 88; Dixon, *Never Come to Peace Again*, 163-164. John Papanhunk was the source of intelligence identifying Shamokin Daniel as the raid leader. Dowd, *War Under Heaven*, 194.
40. Dixon, *Never Come to Peace Again*, 164.
41. Pencak and Keller, "Pennsylvania in the French and Indian Wars, 1748-1766," in *Pennsylvania: A Military History*, 48; Dixon, *Never Come to Peace Again*, 223.
42. Wellenreuther and Wessel, eds., *The Moravian Mission Diaries of David Zeisberger, 1772-1781*, 340, 342, 344, 348.
43. Wellenreuther and Wessel, eds., *The Moravian Mission Diaries of David Zeisberger, 1772-1781*, 353.
44. Wellenreuther and Wessel, eds., *The Moravian Mission Diaries of David Zeisberger, 1772-1781*, 372.

45. Wellenreuther and Wessel, eds., *The Moravian Mission Diaries of David Zeisberger, 1772-1781*, 376, 379, 381.
46. Wellenreuther and Wessel, eds., *The Moravian Mission Diaries of David Zeisberger, 1772-1781*, 383.
47. Wellenreuther and Wessel, eds., *The Moravian Mission Diaries of David Zeisberger, 1772-1781*, 386, 389.
48. Wellenreuther and Wessel, eds., *The Moravian Mission Diaries of David Zeisberger, 1772-1781*, 396-403.
49. Wellenreuther and Wessel, eds., *The Moravian Mission Diaries of David Zeisberger, 1772-1781*, 401.
50. Wellenreuther and Wessel, eds., *The Moravian Mission Diaries of David Zeisberger, 1772-1781*, 399.
51. Wills De Hass, *History of the Early Settlement and Indian Wars of Western Virginia* (Wheeling, VA: H. Hoblitzell, 1851), 221.
52. Col. John Gibson to Gen. Edward Hand, July 31st, 1777, Thwaites, ed., *Frontier Defense on the Upper Ohio*, 33-35. The family was taken to Detroit, treated reasonably well, and eventually returned to the frontier.
53. "Col. William Crawford to President of Congress, April 22, 1777," Reuben Gold Thwaites and Louise Phelps Kellogg, eds., *The Revolution on the Ohio, 1775-1777*, Draper Series, Vol. III (Madison: Wisconsin Historical Society, 1908), 249-251.
54. De Hass, *History of the Early Settlement and Indian Wars of Western Virginia*, 235-236.
55. "Col. Archibald Lochry to Gen. Edward Hand, 6th July 1778," Louise Phelps Kellogg, ed., *Frontier Advance on the Upper Ohio, 1778-1779*, Collections, Volume XXIII, Draper Series, Volume IV (Madison: Wisconsin Historical Society, 1916), 102.
56. *Journals of the Continental Congress, 1774-1789, Volume IX, 1777*, October 3-December 31, 944.
57. See Thomas I. Pieper & James N. Gidney, *Fort Laurens, 1778-1779* (Kent, OH: Kent State University Press, 1976).
58. Heckewelder, *A Narrative of the Mission of the United Brethren,* 195.
59. "David Zeisberger to Col. George Morgan, July 19th 1778," Kellogg, *Frontier Advance on the Upper Ohio*, 119.
60. "Capt. White Eyes to Col. George Morgan," July 19th 1778," Kellogg, *Frontier Advance on the Upper Ohio,* 118. Italics added.
61. "Gov. Patrick to Col. William Fleming, Novr 20th 1778," Kellogg, *Frontier Advance on the Upper Ohio*, 177.
62. "Gen. Lachlan McIntosh to Vice-President George Bryan, 29th December, 1778," Kellogg, *Frontier Advance on the Upper Ohio*, 189.
63. Pieper and Gidney, *Fort Laurens*, 38-39.
64. "Delawares Council with McIntosh," Kellogg, *Frontier Advance on the Upper Ohio*, 178-179.
65. "Col. John Gibson to Gen. Lachlan McIntosh, Jany 1st 1779," Kellogg, *Frontier Advance on the Upper Ohio*, 190.

66. Wellenreuther and Wessel, eds., *The Moravian Mission Diaries of David Zeisberger, 1772-1781*, 481-482.
67. "Col. John Gibson to Gen. Lachlan McIntosh, Decr 21st 1778," Kellogg, *Frontier Advance on the Upper Ohio*, 186. Gelelemend again warned Gibson that hostile Delaware were moving about the Muskingum towns in January. "Capt. John Killbuck to Col. John Gibson," Kellogg, *Frontier Advance on the Upper Ohio*, 212.
68. "Indians Well Disposed, Information Received by Capt John KillBuck from Capt Pipe and the Wiandot Half King, Decr 21st, 1778," Kellogg, *Frontier Advance on the Upper Ohio*, 187.
69. Pieper and Gidney, *Fort Laurens*, 49-50.
70. Wellenreuther and Wessel, eds., *The Moravian Mission Diaries of David Zeisberger, 1772-1781*, 490; "David Zeisberger to Col. George Morgan, January 20th, 1779," Kellogg, *Frontier Advance on the Upper Ohio*, 201.
71. Pieper and Gidney, *Fort Laurens*, 51-52. The commander of the supply party reported they were Mingoes led by Simon Girty. "Gen. Lachlan McIntosh to Col. Archibald Lochry," Jan. 29, 1779," Kellogg, *Frontier Advance on the Upper Ohio*, 210.
72. Pieper and Gidney, *Fort Laurens*, 54.
73. Pieper and Gidney, *Fort Laurens*, 58-59.
74. "Capt. John Killbuck to Col. John Gibson, 29th January 1779," Kellogg, *Frontier Advance on the Upper Ohio*, 212-214; Wellenreuther and Wessel, eds., *The Moravian Mission Diaries of David Zeisberger, 1772-1781*, 498; Pieper and Gidney, *Fort Laurens*, 59.
75. "Gen. Lachlan McIntosh to Gen. George Washington, March 12th 1779," Kellogg, *Frontier Advance on the Upper Ohio*, 240-241.
76. "John Heckewelder to Col. Daniel Brodhead, April 9th 1779," Kellogg, *Frontier Advance on the Upper Ohio*, 282-283.
77. "Summary of an anonymous letter, Fort Pitt, April 20, 1779 in Almon's Rememberancer, VIII, 274" and "Summary of extract of a letter, Washington County, Maryland Journal, April 27, 1779," Kellogg, *Frontier Advance on the Upper Ohio*, 292-293.
78. "Col. Archibald Lochry to Col. Daniel Brodhead, 1st May 1779," Kellogg, *Frontier Advance on the Upper Ohio*, 299.
79. "Extract of a letter from Col. Daniel Brodhead to Gen. George Washington, May 3d, 1779," Kellogg, *Frontier Advance on the Upper Ohio*, 307.
80. "Extract of a letter from Pres. Joseph Reed to Col. Daniel Brodhead, July 8, 1779," Kellogg, *Frontier Advance on the Upper Ohio*, 384-385.
81. John B.B. Trussell, Jr., "The Sullivan and Brodhead Expeditions: Historic Pennsylvania Leaflet No. 41" (Harrisburg, PA: Pennsylvania Historical and Museum Commission, 1976); Brady J. Crytzer, "Allegheny Burning: George Washington, Daniel Brodhead, and the Battle of Thompson's Island," *Journal of the American Revolution*, May 12, 2015. Available at: https://allthingsliberty.com/2015/05/allegheny-burning-george-washington-daniel-brodhead-and-the-battle-of-thompsons-island/. Accessed August 30, 2019.

82. Trussell, "The Sullivan and Broadhead Expeditions," 2, 4.
83. "Capt. John Killbuck to Gen. Lachlan McIntosh, March 15th 1779," Kellogg, *Frontier Advance on the Upper Ohio,* 254. The original was in Heckewelder's handwriting.
84. "Col. Daniel Brodhead to Gen. George Washington, March 21st 1779," Kellogg, *Frontier Advance on the Upper Ohio*, 262.
85. Pieper and Gidney, *Fort Laurens*, chapter 6.
86. "Summary of a letter of Col. Daniel Brodhead, Oct. 26, 1779 to John Jay," Louise Phelps Kellogg, *Frontier Retreat on the Upper Ohio, 1779-1781*, Collections, Volume XXIV Draper Series, Volume V (Madison: State Historical Society of Wisconsin, 1917), 107.
87. "Col. Daniel Brodhead to Col. David Shepherd, Octr 10th 1779," Kellogg, *Frontier Retreat on the Upper Ohio*, 96.
88. "Col. Daniel Brodhead to the Delaware chiefs, Octr 11th 1779," Kellogg, *Frontier Retreat on the Upper Ohio,* 97.
89. Wellenreuther and Wessel, eds., *The Moravian Mission Diaries of David Zeisberger, 1772-1781*, 493-494. The question of moving closer to the fort had been an issue among the Delaware for some time. Several Delaware leaders wanted to move the missionaries to Pittsburgh in order to better protect them from hostile Indians, but Zeisberger remained firmly opposed.
90. "Rev. David Zeisberger to Col. Daniel Brodhead, April 2nd 1780," Kellogg, *Frontier Retreat on the Upper Ohio*, 161.
91. "Summary of a letter of Col. Daniel Brodhead, Mar. 18, 1780," Kellogg, *Frontier Retreat on the Upper Ohio*, 151, and "Summary of a letter of Col. Daniel Brodhead to Rev. David Zeisberger, Mar. 22, 1780," Kellogg, *Frontier Retreat on the Upper Ohio*, 156.
92. "Delawares to Col. Daniel Brodhead, March ye 30th 1780," Kellogg, *Frontier Retreat on the Upper Ohio*, 157.
93. "Extract of a letter of Rev. John Heckewelder to Col. Daniel Brodhead, March 30th 1780," Kellogg, *Frontier Retreat on the Upper Ohio*, 159.
94. "Summary of a letter of Col. Daniel Brodhead to Gen. George Washington, April 24, 1780," Kellogg, *Frontier Retreat on the Upper Ohio*, 173.
95. Brady Crytzer, *Fort Pitt: A Frontier History* (Charleston, SC: History Press, 2012), 167; "Col. Daniel Brodhead to Col. David Shepherd, April 13th 1780," Kellogg, *Frontier Retreat on the Upper Ohio*, 169.
96. "Bounty for Scouts," Kellogg, *Frontier Retreat on the Upper Ohio*, 183-184.
97. "The Delaware chiefs to Col. Daniel Brodhead and Captain Killbuck, April 23d 1780," Kellogg, *Frontier Retreat on the Upper Ohio*, 172.
98. "Summary of a letter of Col. Daniel Brodhead to Pres. Joseph Reed, Nov. 2, 1780," Kellogg, *Frontier Retreat on the Upper Ohio*, 290-291.
99. "Summary of a letter of Col. Daniel Brodhead to Capt. Uriah Springer, Oct. 20, 1780," Kellogg, *Frontier Retreat on the Upper Ohio*, 285-286.
100. "Col. Daniel Brodhead to Samuel Irvin, Feby 2d 1781," Kellogg, *Frontier Retreat on the Upper Ohio*, 327-328.

101. "Col. Daniel Brodhead to Richard Peters, Decr 7th 1780," Kellogg, *Frontier Retreat on the Upper Ohio*, 301-302.
102. "Col. Daniel Brodhead to Rev. David Zeisberger, Jany 21st 1781," Kellogg, *Frontier Retreat on the Upper Ohio*, 320.
103. Wellenreuther and Wessel, eds., *The Moravian Mission Diaries of David Zeisberger, 1772-1781*, 537, 540.
104. "Delaware chiefs to Col. Daniel Brodhead, Janry ye 13th 1781," Kellogg, *Frontier Retreat on the Upper Ohio*, 315.
105. "Captain Killbuck to Col. Daniel Brodhead, Janry ye 15th 1781," Kellogg, *Frontier Retreat on the Upper Ohio*, 316-317.
106. Col. Daniel Brodhead to Rev. John Heckewelder, Jany 21st 1781," Kellogg, *Frontier Retreat on the Upper Ohio*, 321.
107. Wellenreuther and Wessel, eds., *The Moravian Mission Diaries of David Zeisberger, 1772-1781*, 549.
108. "Captain Killbuck to Col. Daniel Brodhead, February 26, 1781," Kellogg, *Frontier Retreat on the Upper Ohio*, 339-340.
109. "Rev. John Heckewelder to Col. Daniel Brodhead, February 26th 1781," Kellogg, *Frontier Retreat on the Upper Ohio*, 337-338.
110. "Col. Daniel Brodhead to Col. David Shepherd, March 8, 1781," Kellogg, *Frontier Retreat on the Upper Ohio*, 339-340.
111. "Summary of a letter of Pres. Joseph Reed to Col. Archibald Lochry, Mar. 26, 1781," Kellogg, *Frontier Retreat on the Upper Ohio*, 352.
112. "Expedition against Delawares," Kellogg, *Frontier Retreat on the Upper Ohio*, 376.
113. Heckewelder, *A Narrative of the Mission of the United Brethren*, 214.
114. Heckewelder, *A Narrative of the Mission of the United Brethren*, 214; Wills De Hass, *History of the Early Settlement and Indian Wars of Western Virginia* (Wheeling, VA: H. Hoblitzell, 1851), 179-180; Joseph Doddridge, *Notes on the Settlement and Indian Wars of the Western Parts of Virginia and Pennsylvania from 1763 to 1783* (Pittsburgh: John S. Ritenour and Wm. T. Lindsey, 1912), 224. This is the third printing of a collection of articles printed initially in the *Wellsburg* (VA) *Gazette* in 1824.
115. Doddridge, *Notes on the Settlement and Indian Wars of the Western Parts of Virginia and Pennsylvania*, 224-225; Alexander Scott Whithers, *Chronicles of Border Warfare, or a History of the Settlement by the Whites, of North-Western Virginia, and of the Indian Wars and Massacres in that section of the State*, New Ed., 7th Printing (Glendale, CA: Arthur H. Clark, 1920), 301-302; De Hass, *History of the Early Settlement and Indian Wars of Western Virginia*, 180-181.
116. "Expedition against the Delawares," Kellogg, *Frontier Retreat on the Upper Ohio*, 378-379; "Summary of letter of Col. Daniel Brodhead to Pres. Joseph Reed," Kellogg, *Frontier Retreat on the Upper Ohio*, 399. Brodhead reported to Reed that goods plundered from the Delaware villages sold for $80,000 at Fort Henry.
117. Doddridge, *Notes on the Settlement and Indian Wars of the Western Parts of Virginia and Pennsylvania*, 224-225; "Expedition against the Delawares,"

Kellogg, *Frontier Retreat on the Upper Ohio*, 378-379; Whithers, *Chronicles of Border Warfare*, 302-303.

118. Whithers, *Chronicles of Border Warfare*, 303-304; "Expedition against the Delawares," Kellogg, *Frontier Retreat on the Upper Ohio,* 379; De Hass, *History of the Early Settlement and Indian Wars of Western Virginia*, 181; Doddridge, *Notes on the Settlement and Indian Wars of the Western Parts of Virginia and Pennsylvania*, 226.

119. "Expedition against the Delawares," Kellogg, *Frontier Retreat on the Upper Ohio*, 378-379.

120. Crevecoeur, *Letters from an American Farmer*, 283.

121. Crevecoeur, *Letters from an American Farmer*, 288-289.

122. Crevecoeur, *Letters from an American Farmer*, 287. It is worth noting that Crevecouer continued by discounting "the great moving principles" of the war as being "much hid from vulgar eyes like mine."

123. Crevecoeur, *Letters from an American Farmer*, 292-293.

124. Doddridge, *Notes on the Settlement and Indian Wars of the Western Parts of Virginia and Pennsylvania*, 198.

CHAPTER FOUR: CALAMITIES

1. Heckewelder, *A Narrative of the Mission of the United Brethren,* 217-218.
2. Heckewelder, *A Narrative of the Mission of the United Brethren,* 219.
3. Heckewelder, *A Narrative of the Mission of the United Brethren,* 220.
4. Heckewelder, *A Narrative of the Mission of the United Brethren,* 221.
5. Heckewelder, *A Narrative of the Mission of the United Brethren,* 226.
6. Eugene Bliss, translator and editor, *Diary of David Zeisberger: A Moravian Missionary Among the Indians of Ohio*, Volume I (Cincinnati: Robert Clarke & Co. for the Historical Society of Ohio, 1885,) 3.
7. Heckewelder, *A Narrative of the Mission of the United Brethren,* 226-228.
8. Heckewelder, *A Narrative of the Mission of the United Brethren,* 231.
9. Bliss, ed., *Diary of David Zeisberger*, 3. Heckewelder, *A Narrative of the Mission of the United Brethren,* 232.
10. Heckewelder, *A Narrative of the Mission of the United Brethren,* 232-233.
11. Heckewelder, *A Narrative of the Mission of the United Brethren,* 234.
12. Heckewelder, *A Narrative of the Mission of the United Brethren,* 235.
13. Heckewelder, *A Narrative of the Mission of the United Brethren,* 236.
14. Earl P. Olmstead, *David Zeisberger: A Life among the Indians* (Kent, OH: Kent State University Press, 1997), 313.
15. Bliss, ed., *Diary of David Zeisberger*, 4.
16. Bliss, ed., *Diary of David Zeisberger*, 5; Heckewelder, *A Narrative of the Mission of the United Brethren,* 238.
17. Bliss, ed., *Diary of David Zeisberger*, 5; Heckewelder, *A Narrative of the Mission of the United Brethren,* 238.
18. Heckewelder, *A Narrative of the Mission of the United Brethren,* 240.
19. Heckewelder, *A Narrative of the Mission of the United Brethren,* 239.
20. Bliss, ed., *Diary of David Zeisberger*, 6.
21. Heckewelder, *A Narrative of the Mission of the United Brethren,* 242.

22. Bliss, ed., *Diary of David Zeisberger*, 6-7.
23. Bliss, ed., *Diary of David Zeisberger*, 8.
24. Bliss, ed., *Diary of David Zeisberger*, 9; Heckewelder, *A Narrative of the Mission of the United Brethren*, 243.
25. Bliss, ed., *Diary of David Zeisberger*, 9.
26. Heckewelder, *A Narrative of the Mission of the United Brethren*, 244-245.
27. Bliss, ed., *Diary of David Zeisberger*, 9-10.
28. Heckewelder, *A Narrative of the Mission of the United Brethren*, 252.
29. Abraham Henry Senseman, *Historical Incidents in the lives of Joachim and Anna Catharine Senseman* (Philadelphia: Senseman & Son, Printers, 1881), 37; Bliss, ed., *Diary of David Zeisberger*, 10-11; Heckewelder, *A Narrative of the Mission of the United Brethren*, 252.
30. Bliss, ed., *Diary of David Zeisberger*, 11-12; Heckewelder, *A Narrative of the Mission of the United Brethren*, 253-254.
31. Heckewelder, *A Narrative of the Mission of the United Brethren*, 259.
32. Heckewelder, *A Narrative of the Mission of the United Brethren*, 257.
33. Heckewelder, *A Narrative of the Mission of the United Brethren*, 258.
34. "Susanna Zeisberger Narrative," Translated by Katherine E. Carte, *Bethlehem Digital History Project*, http://bdhp.moravian.edu/personal_papers/memoirs/zeisberger/zeisberger.html. Accessed August 18, 2019.
35. Heckewelder, *A Narrative of the Mission of the United Brethren*, 262; Bliss, ed., *Diary of David Zeisberger*, 13-14. Zeisberger recorded that the Moravian Indians simply took some of the stolen items.
36. Heckewelder, *A Narrative of the Mission of the United Brethren*, 264.
37. Heckewelder, *A Narrative of the Mission of the United Brethren*, 267-269; Bliss, ed., *Diary of David Zeisberger*, 14-15.
38. Heckewelder, *A Narrative of the Mission of the United Brethren*, 269-270; Bliss, ed., *Diary of David Zeisberger*, 14.
39. Heckewelder, *A Narrative of the Mission of the United Brethren*, 272.
40. Heckewelder, *A Narrative of the Mission of the United Brethren*, 274; Bliss, ed., *Diary of David Zeisberger*, 15-16.
41. Bliss, ed., *Diary of David Zeisberger*, 16.
42. Heckewelder, *A Narrative of the Mission of the United Brethren*, 275.
43. Heckewelder, *A Narrative of the Mission of the United Brethren*, 275-276. Heckewelder did not look kindly on Hopocan and eventually blamed the Delaware for much of the Moravian community's difficulties.
44. Heckewelder, *A Narrative of the Mission of the United Brethren*, 275-276.
45. Heckewelder, *A Narrative of the Mission of the United Brethren*, 302, footnote.
46. Bliss, ed., *Diary of David Zeisberger*, 16-17.
47. Bliss, ed., *Diary of David Zeisberger*, 17.
48. Bliss, ed., *Diary of David Zeisberger*, 18; Heckewelder, *A Narrative of the Mission of the United Brethren*, 279-280.
49. Bliss, ed., *Diary of David Zeisberger*, 18-19; Heckewelder, *A Narrative of the Mission of the United Brethren*, 280-281.

50. Heckewelder, *A Narrative of the Mission of the United Brethren,* 282.
51. Bliss, ed., *Diary of David Zeisberger*, 20.
52. Bliss, ed., *Diary of David Zeisberger*, 21.
53. Bliss, ed., *Diary of David Zeisberger*, 24.
54. Bliss, ed., *Diary of David Zeisberger*, 21-22; Heckewelder, *A Narrative of the Mission of the United Brethren,* 282-283.
55. Bliss, ed., *Diary of David Zeisberger*, 22-23; Heckewelder, *A Narrative of the Mission of the United Brethren,* 287.
56. Bliss, ed., *Diary of David Zeisberger*, 20.
57. Heckewelder, *A Narrative of the Mission of the United Brethren,* 283.
58. Bliss, ed., *Diary of David Zeisberger*, 27-28.
59. Larry L. Nelson, *A Man of Distinction among Them: Alexander McKee and the Ohio Country Frontier, 1754-1799*, Kindle ed. (Kent, OH: Kent State University Press, 1999), Loc. 2335.
60. Bliss, ed., *Diary of David Zeisberger*, 29; Heckewelder, *A Narrative of the Mission of the United Brethren,* 283-284.
61. Heckewelder, *A Narrative of the Mission of the United Brethren,* 283-284.
62. Bliss, ed., *Diary of David Zeisberger*, 24, 29.
63. Bliss, ed., *Diary of David Zeisberger*, 30.
64. Heckewelder, *A Narrative of the Mission of the United Brethren,* 285.
65. Bliss, ed., *Diary of David Zeisberger*, 34. See also, Eric Sterner, "A Curious 'Trial' on the Frontier: Zeisberger, Heckewelder, et. al. vs. Great Britain," *Journal of the American Revolution*, June 5, 2018. Available at: https://allthingsliberty.com/2018/06/a-curious-trial-on-the-frontier-zeisberger-heckewelder-et-al-vs-great-britain/
66. Bliss, ed., *Diary of David Zeisberger*, 35-36; Heckewelder, *A Narrative of the Mission of the United Brethren,* 289-290.
67. Bliss, ed., *Diary of David Zeisberger*, 37; Heckewelder, *A Narrative of the Mission of the United Brethren,* 291-292.
68. This, of course, means De Peyster viewed the Moravian Indian conversions as weak and denies them a degree of agency in both their spiritual and political choices. Sadly, one often detects the same patronizing attitude from Zeisberger and Heckewelder. The attitude colors later histories of the Ohio frontier and downplays the role of men like Koquethaqechton and Glickhican, not to mention women, in determining their own future.
69. Heckewelder, *A Narrative of the Mission of the United Brethren,* 293.
70. Heckewelder, *A Narrative of the Mission of the United Brethren,* 294.
71. Heckewelder, *A Narrative of the Mission of the United Brethren,* 298.
72. Bliss, ed., *Diary of David Zeisberger*, 46.
73. Bliss, ed., *Diary of David Zeisberger*, 47.
74. Harper, *Unsettling the West*, 134.
75. Heckewelder, *A Narrative of the Mission of the United Brethren,* 300.
76. Bliss, ed., *Diary of David Zeisberger*, 54.
77. Alan Fitzpatrick, *Wilderness War on the Ohio*, 2nd ed. (Benwood, WV: Fort Henry Publications, 2005), 445-446.

78. Heckewelder, *A Narrative of the Mission of the United Brethren,* 300.
79. Heckewelder, *A Narrative of the Mission of the United Brethren,* 300-301. Heckewelder does not name the Indian, but Zeisberger claimed it was Isaac, the baptized name of Glickhican. Bliss, ed., *Diary of David Zeisberger*, 65.
80. Bliss, ed., *Diary of David Zeisberger*, 56-57.
81. Bliss, ed., *Diary of David Zeisberger*, 52.
82. Fitzpatrick, *Wilderness War on the Ohio*, 450-451; Heckewelder, *A Narrative of the Mission of the United Brethren,* 303.
83. Bliss, ed., *Diary of David Zeisberger*, 66-67.
84. Bliss, ed., *Diary of David Zeisberger*, 61, 65-66.
85. Heckewelder, *A Narrative of the Mission of the United Brethren,* 302.
86. Bliss, ed., *Diary of David Zeisberger*, 68.
87. Bliss, ed., *Diary of David Zeisberger*, 69.
88. C.W. Butterfield, "Introduction," in *Washington-Irvine Correspondence: The Official Letters Which Passed between Washington and Brig.-Gen. William Irvine and Between Irvine and Others Concerning Military Affairs in the West from 1781 to 1783* (Madison, WI: David Atwood, 1882), 58.
89. C.W Butterfield, *An Historical Account of the Expedition against Sandusky under Col. William Crawford in 1782* (Cincinnati: Robert Clarke, 1873), 37; Joseph Doddridge, *Notes on the Settlement and Indian Wars of the Western Parts of Virginia and Pennsylvania from 1763 to 1783* (Pittsburgh: John S. Ritenour and Wm. T. Lindsey, 1912), 199. This is the third printing of a collection of articles printed initially in the *Wellsburg* (VA) *Gazette* in 1824; Whithers, *Chronicles of Border Warfare*, 313-314. Williamson, of Washington County, PA. was Lieutenant Colonel, 3rd Battalion, Pennsylvania Militia, raised in the area around Donegal Township. Item 13, Militia Officers Index Cards, 1775-1800, Pennsylvania State Archives, Archives Records Information Access System (ARIAS). Available at: http://www.digitalarchives.state.pa.us/archive.asp. Accessed January 13, 2018. C.H. Mitchener, *Ohio Annals: Historic Events in the Tuscarawas and Muskingum Valleys and in other Portions of the State of Ohio* (Dayton, OH: Thomas W. Odell, 1876), 99; Boyd Crumrine, *History of Washington County, Pennsylvania, with Biographical Sketches of Many of its Pioneers and Prominent Men* (Philadelphia: L.H. Everts, 1882), 102. Mitchener believed the campaign was conducted by Captain Biggs out of Wheeling, but he followed Heckewelder. Doddridge and Whithers make a better case that Williamson conducted the mission.
90. Doddridge, *Notes on the Settlement and Indian Wars of the Western Parts of Virginia and Pennsylvania from 1763 to 1783*, 199.
91. In September, Congress instructed him to take command at Fort Pitt, but Irvine was then in Philadelphia and required time to settle his affairs and travel west. Washington's formal orders did not come until March.
92. "Irvine to Washington, December 2, 1781," in *Washington-Irvine Correspondence*, 75.
93. "Irvine to Washington, February 7, 1781," in *Washington-Irvine Correspondence*, 89-90.

94. Gibson had commanded the 13th Virginia when the Treaty of Fort Pitt was signed in 1778. Subsequent reorganizations had eventually redesignated the unit as the 7th Virginia.
95. Reuben Gold Thwaites, ed., *Chronicles of Border Warfare, or A History of the Settlement by the Whites, of North Western Virginia, and of the Indian Wars and Massacres in that section of the State with Reflections, Anecdotes, &c* (Cincinnati: Stewart & Kidd, 1912), 318-319. The original version of this book under the same title, by Alexander Scott Whithers, was originally published in Clarksburg, VA, by Joseph Israel in 1831. The work will hereafter be cited as Whithers, *Chronicles of Border Warfare*, but the pagination is from the 1912 edition annotated by Thwaites. Note 2, *Washington-Irvine Correspondence*, 99-100.
96. Some sources name the family as that of David or William Wallace, understandable as they were all related. Doddridge, *Notes on the Settlement and Indian Wars of the Western Parts of Virginia and Pennsylvania from 1763 to 1783*, 188. Doddridge settles on Robert. Doddridge, 200. Sources conflict about whether the militia found Mrs. Wallace's body, but Doddridge believes they did not and dismisses the brutal slaying of Wallace's family as a cause of the subsequent massacre. A family history indicates the Wyandot attacked Robert Wallace's family while he was away, capturing his wife and three children, then later impaling her on a stake while killing and mutilating one infant child. See, F.S. Reader, *Some Pioneers of Washington County, PA: A Family History* (New Brighton, PA: F.S. Reader & Son, 1902), 40-41. It was popular for nearly a hundred years after to claim that the bodies of Mrs. Wallace and her baby were quickly found, which enraged frontier settlers. But most historians now accept that she and her baby were not discovered for several years, meaning their deaths were unknown at the time of the Gnadenhutten massacre. William M. Farrar, "The Moravian Massacre," *Ohio Archeological and Historical Publications, Volume III* (Columbus: Ohio Archeological and Historical Society, n.d.), 289-290.
97. Heckewelder, *A Narrative of the Mission of the United Brethren,* 312.
98. C.W. Butterfield, *An Historical Account of the Expedition against Sandusky under Col. William Crawford in 1782* (Cincinnati: Robert Clarke), 34-35.
99. *The History of Tuscarawas County, Ohio* (Chicago: Warner, Beers, 1884), 296; Note 2, *Washington-Irvine Correspondence*, 101. This mention of Carpenter comes from the first draft of a Congressionally ordered investigation into the Gnadenhutten affair, which is reprinted within the note.
100. Bliss, ed., *Diary of David Zeisberger*, 82.
101. Edgar W. Hassler, *Old Westmoreland: A History of Western Pennsylvania During the Revolution* (Cleveland: Arthur H. Clark, 1900), 154-156.
102. Doddridge, *Notes on the Settlement and Indian Wars*, 203. Oral history recorded at the beginning of the century by the descendant of someone claiming to have been on the raid indicated the germ of the idea in 1782 took root again in February or March 1782 at Carpenter's block house. Doddridge, *Notes on the Settlement and Indian Wars of the Western Parts of Virginia and Pennsylvania*, Note 1, 202. But that was late given the need for the men to depart Mingo

Bottom by March 4. Farrar, "The Moravian Massacre," *Ohio Archeological and Historical Publications, Volume III*, 292.

103. Doddridge, *Notes on the Settlement and Indian Wars*, 199. For example, Don Glickstein, *After Yorktown* (Yardley, PA: Westholme, 2015), 150-155; Calloway, *The Indian World of George Washington*, 274-275; Leonard Sadosky, "Rethinking the Gnadenhutten Massacre;" David Curtis Skaggs & Larry L. Nelson, eds, *The Sixty Years' War for the Great Lakes, 1754-1814* (East Lansing: Michigan State University Press, 2001).

104. Rob Harper, *Unsettling the West*, 122; Calloway, *The Indian World of George Washington*, 274-275.

105. Farrar, "The Moravian Massacre," 276-281.

106. "Irvine to Washington, April 20, 1782," C.W. Butterfield, ed., *Washington-Irvine Correspondence*, 100.

107. Irvine's orders to the expedition commander, who was as yet to be determined when he wrote them, are contained in Irvine's instructions, May 14, 1782, *Washington-Irvine Correspondence,* 118-119, note 1. Indeed, Irvine likely arranged Crawford's election as commander of the expedition to preempt Williamson from leading it.

108. Quoted in Butterfield, *The Expedition against Sandusky*, 24.

109. Whithers, *Chronicles of Border Warfare*, 320. Crumrine, *History of Washington County, Pennsylvania, with Biographical Sketches of Many of its Pioneers and Prominent Men*, 104. The higher estimate of militia involved tends to be most widely accepted. (It was also the first number reported contemporaneously by the *Pennsylvania Packet.* See Butterfield, *Washington-Irvine Correspondence*, note 2, 99-103.) Crumrine, *History of Washington County, Pennsylvania, with Biographical Sketches of Many of its Pioneers and Prominent Men*, Note 1, 104 offers the best review of varying estimates and arrives at 160, which would be typical for a campaign call-up. For example, in the summer of 1782, when preparing for an expedition to the Sandusky, Williamson's 3rd Battalion counted 140 men and 53 horses on its roster. Note 1, *Washington-Irvine Correspondence*, 308.

110. *The History of Tuscarawas County, Ohio*, 296.

111. Heckewelder, *A Narrative of the Mission of the United Brethren,* 312.

112. Bliss, ed., *Diary of David Zeisberger*, 72.

113. Whithers, *Chronicles of Border Warfare*, 321.

114. Whithers, *Chronicles of Border Warfare*, 321.

115. Whithers, *Chronicles of Border Warfare*, 322.

116. Heckewelder, *A Narrative of the Mission of the United Brethren,* 313; Bliss, ed., *Diary of David Zeisberger*, 79. Joseph was John Bull's son. Bull went by the Indian name Schebosh.

117. Heckewelder, *A Narrative of the Mission of the United Brethren,* 313.

118. Whithers, *Chronicles of Border Warfare*, 322; Heckewelder, *A Narrative of the Mission of the United Brethren,* 314; Bliss, ed., *Diary of David Zeisberger*, 79.

119. Whithers, *Chronicles of Border Warfare*, 322.

120. Heckewelder, *A Narrative of the Mission of the United Brethren,* 314-315.

121. Heckewelder, *A Narrative of the Mission of the United Brethren,* 314-315; Bliss, ed., *Diary of David Zeisberger*, 80.
122. Heckewelder, *A Narrative of the Mission of the United Brethren,* 315.
123. Heckewelder, *A Narrative of the Mission of the United Brethren,* 315.
124. Bliss, ed., *Diary of David Zeisberger*, 81; Willett, *Scenes in the Wilderness: Authentic Narrative of the Labours and Sufferings of the Moravian Missionaries among the North American Indians* (New York: G. Lane & P.P. Sandford, 1842), 190.
125. Some writers assert that the initial attack on Gnadenhutten, the capture of its population, the dispatch of a force to Salem and its return, the "trial" and the "vote" condemning the Indians to death were all conducted on March 7. Crumrine, *History of Washington County, Pennsylvania, with Biographical Sketches of Many of its Pioneers and Prominent Men*, 106.
126. Heckewelder, *A Narrative of the Mission of the United Brethren,* 316. This is inconsistent with missionary fears that the Moravian Indians would violently resist Dunquat's war party in September 1781, perhaps signifying a bit of spin on the missionary's part.
127. Bliss, ed., *Diary of David Zeisberger*, 79-80; Heckewelder, *A Narrative of the Mission of the United Brethren,* 320.
128. Heckewelder, *A Narrative of the Mission of the United Brethren,* 317.
129. Heckewelder, *A Narrative of the Mission of the United Brethren,* 318. Nineteenth-century illustrations of the massacre failed to capture this nuance, usually portraying the Moravian Indians shirtless, dressed in buckskin, and often wearing a top-knot adorned with feathers more common among the Lenape.
130. Farrar, "The Moravian Massacre," 300.
131. "Dorsey Pentecost to President Moore, May 8th, 1782," *Pennsylvania Archives Commencing 1781, Vol. IX*, Samuel Hazard ed. (Philadelphia: Joseph Severns & Co., Printers, 1854), 540.
132. Lewis S. Shimmell, *Border Warfare in Pennsylvania During the Revolution* (Harrisburg, PA: R.L. Myers, 1901), 133; Edgar W. Hassler, *Old Westmoreland*, 156.
133. Bliss, ed., *Diary of David Zeisberger*, 79.
134. Bliss, ed., *Diary of David Zeisberger*, 79-80; Heckewelder, *A Narrative of the Mission of the United Brethren,* 318-319.
135. Whithers, *Chronicles of Border Warfare*, 323; Farrar, "The Moravian Massacre," 300.
136. Whithers, *Chronicles of Border Warfare*, 323.
137. Farrar, "The Moravian Massacre," 300; Heckewelder, *A Narrative of the Mission of the United Brethren,* 319.
138. Farrar, "The Moravian Massacre," 294; Williamson's location is not known and different accounts place him both in town and closer to the riverbank.
139. Heckewelder, *A Narrative of the Mission of the United Brethren,* 319-320; *The History of Tuscarawas County, Ohio,* 301.
140. Whithers, *Chronicles of Border Warfare*, 324-325; *A True History of the Massacre of Ninety-Six Christian Indians at Gnadenhutten, Ohio, March 8th,*

1782 (New Philadelphia, OH: Gnadenhutten Monument Society, 1847), 10; De Schweinitz, *Life of Zeisberger*, 549.
141. Whithers, *Chronicles of Border Warfare*, 325-326.
142. Farrar, "The Moravian Massacre," 294-295.
143. Heckewelder, *A Narrative of the Mission of the United Brethren,* 324.
144. Bliss, ed., *Diary of David Zeisberger*, 79.
145. Heckewelder, *A Narrative of the Mission of the United Brethren,* 320. Most histories follow Heckewelder's telling, which he drew from a boy who survived and escaped.
146. Doddridge, *Notes on the Settlement and Indian Wars of the Western Parts of Virginia and Pennsylvania*, 203. Holmes's research did not make it into many of the early prints of Doddridge's account of the frontier war. Doddridge was, after all, long deceased. Indeed, Doddridge glosses over the facts of the massacre itself, focusing more on the settler perspective, while still condemning their acts.
147. Crumrine, *History of Washington County, Pennsylvania, with Biographical Sketches of Many of its Pioneers and Prominent Men*, 106-108; De Schweinitz, *Life of Zeisberger*, 549. Crumrine draws his account from third- or fourth-hand information provided to the Church of the United Brethren and forwarded to Congress.
148. Heckewelder, *A Narrative of the Mission of the United Brethren,* 320.
149. Bliss, ed., *Diary of David Zeisberger*, 80; De Schweinitz, *Life of Zeisberger*, 549.
150. Bliss, ed., *Diary of David Zeisberger*, 80.
151. Farrar, "The Moravian Massacre," 295.
152. Heckewelder, *A Narrative of the Mission of the United Brethren,* 320.
153. Willett, *Scenes in the Wilderness*, 188-189; Heckewelder, *A Narrative of the Mission of the United Brethren,* 322; Bliss, ed., *Diary of David Zeisberger*, 81.
154. Willett, *Scenes in the Wilderness*, 189; Mitchener, ed., *Ohio Annals*, 163; Heckewelder, *A Narrative of the Mission of the United Brethren,* 324.
155. Willett, *Scenes in the Wilderness*, 190; Whithers, *Chronicles of Border Warfare*, 326; Bliss, ed., *Diary of David Zeisberger*, 83.
156. Crumrine, *History of Washington County, Pennsylvania, with Biographical Sketches of Many of its Pioneers and Prominent Men*, 106-108.
157. Heckewelder, *A Narrative of the Mission of the United Brethren,* 320-321.
158. Bliss, ed., *Diary of David Zeisberger*, 85. Heckewelder remembered that 150 had departed the Sandusky for all three towns. Heckewelder, *A Narrative of the Mission of the United Brethren,* 302.
159. Author notes from a site visit in July 2018.
160. Crumrine, *History of Washington County, Pennsylvania, with Biographical Sketches of Many of its Pioneers and Prominent Men*, 108.
161. "Irvine to Washington, April 20, 1782," *Washington-Irvine Correspondence*, 99-103.
162. "Irvine to Washington, May 2, 1782," *Washington-Irvine Correspondence*, 111-112.

163. Whithers, *Chronicles of Border Warfare*, 325-327.
164. Doddridge, *Notes on the Settlement and Indian Wars of the Western Parts of Virginia and Pennsylvania*, 200.
165. Quoted in Farrar, "The Moravian Massacre," 283-284.
166. Quoted in Farrar, "The Moravian Massacre," 284-285.
167. "Dorsey Pentecost to Pres. Moore, May 9th, 1782," in *Pennsylvania Archives, Vol. IX*, 541.
168. Bliss, ed., *Diary of David Zeisberger*, 84.
169. "From Benjamin Franklin to James Hutton, 7 July 1782," in *Founders Online*. Available at: https://founders.archives.gov/?q=Moravian%20Author%3A%22Franklin%2C%20Benjamin%22&s=1111311111&r=30&sr=. Accessed July 18, 2019.

BIBLIOGRAPHY

PRIMARY SOURCES

American Philosophical Society, *Transactions of the Historical & Literary Committee, Vol. I, No. II, A Correspondence Between the Rev. John Heckewelder, of Bethlehem and Peter S. Duponceau, Respecting the Languages of the American Indians* (Philadelphia: Abraham Small, 1819).

Beatty, Charles, *The Journal of Two Months Tour; with a View of Promoting Religion among the Frontier Inhabitants of Pennsylvania, and of Introducing Christianity among the Indians to the Westward of the Alegh-geny Mountains* (London: Printed for William Davenill and George Pearch, 1768).

Bliss, Eugene, translator and editor, *Diary of David Zeisberger: A Moravian Missionary among the Indians of Ohio, Volume I* (Cincinnati: Robert Clarke, 1885).

Butterfield, C.W., ed., *Washington-Irvine Correspondence: The Official Letters Which Passed Between Washington and Brig.-Gen. William Irvine and Between Irvine and Others Concerning Military Affairs in the West from 1781 to 1783* (Madison, WI: David Atwood, 1882).

Declaration and Remonstrance of the Distressed and Bleeding Frontier Inhabitants of the Province of Pennsylvania, Presented by them to the Honourable Governor and Assembly of the Province, 1764.

De Peyster, Arent Schuyler, J. Watts De Peyster, ed., *Miscellanies by an Officer* (Dumfries, Scotland: C. Munro, Printer, 1888).

"Diary of the Indian Gemeine in the Barracks in Philadelphia," Bethlehem Digital History Project.

Dodge, John, *Narrative of Mr. John Dodge During his Captivity at Detroit*, reprint (Cedar Rapids, IA: Torch Press, 1909).

Fitzpatrick, Alan, *In Their Own Words: Native-American Voices from the American Revolution* (Benwood, WV: Fort Henry Publications, 2009).

Hazard, Samuel, ed., *Pennsylvania Archives: Commencing 1781, Vol. IX* (Philadelphia: Joseph Severns & Co., Printers, 1854).

Heckewelder, John, *History, Manners, and Customs of The Indian Nations Who Once Inhabited Pennsylvania and the Neighbouring States*, new and revised ed. (Philadelphia: The Historical Society of Pennsylvania, 1881).

Heckewelder, John, *Map and Description of Northeastern Ohio* (Cleveland: William W. Williams, 1884). Reprinted from the *Magazine of Western History*.

Heckewelder, John, *A Narrative of the Mission of the United Brethren among the Delaware and Mohegan Indians from its Commencement, in the Year 1740, to the Close of the Year 1808* (Philadelphia: M'Carty & Davis, 1820).

Jones, David, *A Journal of Two Visits Made to Some Nations of Indians on the West Side of the River Ohio in the Years 1772 and 1773* (Burlington: Isaac Collins, 1774).

Journals of the Continental Congress, 1774-1789, Library of Congress.

Kellogg, Louise Phelps, ed., *Frontier Advance on the Upper Ohio, 1778-1779*, Draper Series, Vol. IV (Madison: Wisconsin Historical Society, 1916).

Kellogg, Louise Phelps, ed., *Frontier Retreat on the Upper Ohio, 1779-1781*, Draper Series, Vol. V (Madison: State Historical Society of Wisconsin, 1917).

Narratives of a Late Expedition against the Indians; With An Account of the Barbarous Execution of Col. Crawford; and The Wonderful Escape of Dr. Knight and John Slover from Captivity, in 1782 (Philadelphia: Francis Bailey, 1783).

Post, Christian Frederick, "Two Journals of Western Tours, by Christian Frederick Post: One, to the Neighborhood of Fort Duquesne (July-September, 1758); the Other, to the Ohio (October, 1758-January, 1759)," *Proud's History of Pennsylvania* (Philadelphia, 1798).

Smith, Col. James, *An Account of the Remarkable Occurrences in the Life and Travels of Col. James Smith, During his Captivity with the Indians*, reprint (Cincinnati: Robert Clarke, 1870).

Thwaites, Reuben Gold, ed., *Frontier Defense on the Upper Ohio, 1777-1778*, Draper Series, Vol. III (Madison: Wisconsin Historical Society, 1912).

Thwaites, Reuben Gold and Louise Phelps Kellogg, eds., *The Revolution on the Upper Ohio, 1775-1777*, Draper Series, Vol. II (Madison: Wisconsin Historical Society, 1908).

Treaty with the Delaware, 1778, Yale Law School.

Wallace, Paul A.W., ed., *The Travels of John Heckewelder in Frontier America* (Pittsburgh: University of Pittsburgh Press, 1985).

Wellenreuther, Hermann and Carola Wessel, eds., *The Moravian Mission Diaries of David Zeisberger, 1772-1781* (University Park: Pennsylvania State University Press, 2005).

Zeisberger, David, *History of the North American Indians*, edited by Archer Hulbert and William Schwarze (Ohio State Archeological and Historical Society, 1910).

SECONDARY SOURCES

Allen, Robert S., *His Majesty's Indian Allies: British Indian Policy in the Defence of Canada, 1774-1815* (Toronto: Dundurn Press, 1992).

Anderson, Fred, *Crucible of War: The Seven Years' War and the Fate of Empire in North America, 1754-1766* (New York: Alfred A. Knopf, 2000).

Butterfield, Consul Willshire, *History of the Girtys* (Cincinnati: Robert Clarke, 1890).

Butts, Edward, *Simon Girty: Wilderness Warrior* (Toronto: Dundurn, 2011).

Calloway, Colin G., *The American Revolution in Indian Country* (Cambridge: Cambridge University Press, 1995).

Calloway, Colin G., *The Indian World of George Washington* (Oxford: Oxford University Press, 2018).

Calloway, Colin G., *The Scratch of a Pen: 1763 and the Transformation of North America*, Kindle ed. (Oxford: Oxford University Press, 2006).

Calloway, Colin G., *The Shawnees and the War for America* (New York: Viking, 2007).

A Christian Indian of North America: or, John Papunhank (Dublin: Thomas I. White, 1830).

The Conduct of the Paxton-Men, Impartially represented (Philadelphia: A. Steuart, printer, John Creaig, bookseller, 1764).

Crevecoeur, J. Hector St. John, *Letters from an American Farmer*, reprint (New York: Fox, Duffield, & Company, 1904).

Crocker, Thomas E., *Braddock's March* (Yardley, PA: Westholme, 2009).

Crumrine, Boyd, *History of Washington County, Pennsylvania with Biographical Sketches of Many of Its Pioneers and Prominent Men* (Philadelphia: L.H. Everts, 1882).

Crytzer, Brady J., *Fort Pitt: A Frontier History*, Kindle ed. (Charleston, SC: History Press, 2012).

Crytzer, Brady J., *Guyatusa and the Fall of Indian America* (Yardley, PA: Westholme, 2013).

De Hass, Wills, *History of the Early Settlement and Indian Wars of Western Virginia* (Wheeling, WV: H.H. Hoblitzell, 1851).

De Schweinitz, Edmund, *The Life and Times of David Zeisberger: The Western Pioneer and Apostle of the Indians* (Philadelphia: J.B. Lippincott, 1871).

De Schweinitz, Edmund, *A History of the Unitas Fratrum from 1627 to 1722* (Bethlehem, PA: Moravian Publication Office, 1877).

De Schweinitz, Edmund, *History of the Church Known as the Unitas Fratrum or The Unity of the Brethren* (Bethlehem, PA: Moravian Publication Office, 1885).

De Schweinitz, Edmund, *The Moravian Manual: Containing an Account of the Moravian Church or Unitas Fratrum* (Bethlehem, PA: Moravian Publication Office, 1869).

Dixon, David, *Never Come to Peace Again: Pontiac's Uprising and the Fate of the British Empire in North America* (Norman: University of Oklahoma Press, 2005).

Doddridge, Joseph, *Notes on the Settlement and Indian Wars of the Western Parts of Virginia and Pennsylvania from 1763 to 1783* (Pittsburgh: John S. Ritenour and Wm. T. Lindsey, 1912).

Dowd, Gregory Evans, *A Spirited Resistance: The North American Indian Struggle for Unity, 1745-1815* (Baltimore: Johns Hopkins University Press, 1992).

Dowd, Gregory Evans, *War Under Heaven: Pontiac, the Indian Nations, & the British Empire* (Baltimore: Johns Hopkins University Press, 2002).

Downes, Randolph C., *Council Fires on the Upper Ohio* (Pittsburgh: University of Pittsburgh Press, 1969).

Farmer, Silas, *The History of Detroit and Michigan or The Metropolis Illustrated: A Chronological Cyclopedia of the Past and Present* (Detroit: Silas Farmer, 1884).

Farrar, William S., "The Moravian Massacre," *Ohio Archeological and Historical Publications, Volume III* (Columbus: Ohio Archeological and Historical Society, n.d.).

Finley, Rev. James B., *History of the Wyandott Mission at Upper Sandusky, Ohio under the Direction of the Methodist Episcopal Church* (Cincinnati: J.F. Wright and L. Swormstedt, 1840).

Fitzpatrick, Alan, *Wilderness War on the Ohio* (Benwood, WV: Fort Henry Publications, 2003).

Gill, John, *The Banished Count: or The life of Nicholas Louis Zinzendorf from the French by M. Felix Bovet* (London: James Nisbet, 1865).

Glickstein, Don, *After Yorktown: The Final Struggle for American Independence* (Yardley, PA: Westholme, 2015).

Grenier, John, *The First Way of War: American War Making on the Frontier, 1607-1814* (Cambridge: Cambridge University Press, 2005).

Grumet, Robert S., *The Lenapes* (New York: Chelsea House, 1989).

Hamilton, J. Taylor, *A History of the Church Known as the Moravian Church, or The Unitas Fratrum, or The Unity of the Brethren, during the Eighteenth and Nineteenth Centuries* (Bethlehem, PA: Times Publishing Company, 1900).

Harper, Rob, *Unsettling the West: Violence and State Building in the Ohio Valley* (Philadelphia: University of Pennsylvania Press, 2018).

Hassler, Edgar W., *Old Westmoreland: A History of Western Pennsylvania During the Revolution* (Cleveland: Arthur H. Clark, 1900).

Hildreth, Samuel P., *Contributions to the Early History of the North-West Including the Moravian Missions in Ohio* (Cincinnati: Poe and Hitchcock, 1864).

Hintzen, William, *Border Wars of the Upper Ohio Valley, 1769-1794* (Ashland, KY: Jesse Stuart Foundation, 2011).

The History of Tuscarawas County Ohio (Chicago: Warner, Beers, 1884).

Hoffman, Phillip W., *Simon Girty: Turncoat Hero* (Franklin, TN: American History Press, 2008).

Huebner, Francis C., *The Moravian Missions in Ohio* (Washington, DC: Simms & Lewis, Printers, 1898).

Hurt, R. Douglas, *The Ohio Frontier: Crucible of the Old Northwest, 1720-1830* (Bloomington: Indiana University Press, 1996).

Hutton, J.E., *A History of the Moravian Church*, 2nd ed. (London: Moravian Publication Office, 1909).

Jeffries, Ewel, ed., *A Short Biography of John Leeth, Giving a Brief Account of his Travels and Sufferings among the Indians for Eighteen Years* (Lancaster, OH: Printed at The Gazette Office, 1831).

Kenny, Kevin, *Peaceable Kingdom Lost: The Paxton Boys and the Destruction of William Penn's Holy Experiment*, Kindle ed. (Oxford: Oxford University Press, 2009).

Levering, John Mortimer, *A History of Bethlehem Pennsylvania, 1741-1892* (Bethlehem, PA: Times Publishing Company, 1903).

Loskiel, George Henry, Christian Ignatius La Trobe, trans., *History of the Mission of the United Brethren among the Indians in North America* (London: Brethren's Society for the Furtherance of the Gospel, 1794).

Mangus, Michael, *Ohio: A Military History*, Westholme State Military History Series, 17 (Yardley, PA: Westholme, 2016).

Martin, John Hill, *Historical Sketch of Bethlehem in Pennsylvania with Some Accounts of the Moravian Church*, 2nd ed. (Philadelphia: John Pile, Printer, Self-Published, 1873).

McConnell, Michael N., *A Country Between: The Upper Ohio Valley and Its Peoples, 1724-1774* (Lincoln: University of Nebraska Press, 1992).

McMechen, James II, *Legends of the Ohio Valley or Thrilling Incidents of Indian Warfare* (Wheeling, WV: West Virginia Printing Company, 1887).

Middleton, Richard, *Pontiac's War: Its Causes, Course and Consequences* (London: Routledge, 2007).

Mitchener, C.C., ed., *Ohio Annals: Historical Events in the Tuscarawas and Muskingum Valleys, and in Other Portions of the State of Ohio* (Dayton, OH: Thomas W. Odell, 1876).

Nelson, Larry L., *A Man of Distinction Among Them: Alexander McKee and the Ohio Country Frontier, 1754-1799* (Kent, OH: Kent State University Press, 1999).

Newland, Samuel J., *The Pennsylvania Militia: Defending the Commonwealth and the Nation, 1669-1870* (Annville, PA: Commonwealth of Pennsylvania, Department of Military and Veterans Affairs, 2002).

Olmstead, Earl P., *David Zeisberger: A Life among the Indians* (Kent, OH: The Kent State University Press, 1997).

Pencak, William A., Christian B. Keller, and Barbara A. Gannon, *Pennsylvania: A Military History*, Westholme State Military History Series, 2 (Yardley, PA: Westholme, 2016).

Perkins, Elizabeth, *Border Life: Experience and Memory in the Revolutionary Ohio Valley* (Chapel Hill: University of North Carolina Press, 1998).

Pieper, Thomas I. and James B. Gidney, *Fort Laurens, 1778-1779: The Revolutionary War in Ohio* (Kent, OH: Kent State University Press, 1976).

Preston, David L., *Braddock's Defeat: The Battle of the Monongahela and the Road to Revolution* (Oxford: Oxford University Press, 2015).

Reader, F.S., *Some Pioneers of Washington County, PA: A Family History* (New Brighton, PA: F.S. Reader & Son, 1902).

Richter, Daniel, *Facing East from Indian Country: A Native American History of Early America* (Cambridge, MA: Harvard University Press, 2001).

Rimius, Henry, *A Candid Narrative of the Rise and Progress of the Herrnhuters, Commonly Called Moravians, or Unitas Fratrum*, 2nd ed. (London: A. Linde, Printer, 1753).

Roeber, A.G., ed., *Ethnographies and Exchanges: Native Americans, Moravians, and Catholics in Early North America* (University Park: Pennsylvania State University Press, 2008).

Rondthaler, Rev. Edward, B.H. Coates, MD, ed., *Life of John Heckewelder* (Philadelphia: Crissy & Markley, Printers, 1847).

Schaaf, Gregory, *Wampum Belts & Peace Trees: George Morgan, Native Americans and Revolutionary Diplomacy* (Golden, CO: Fulcrum Publishing, 1990).

Schmidt, Ethan A., *Native Americans in the American Revolution* (Santa Barbara, CA: Praeger, 2014).

Schutt, Amy C., *Peoples of the River Valleys: The Odyssey of the Delaware Indians* (Philadelphia: University of Pennsylvania Press, 2007).

Senseman, Abraham Henry, *Historical Incidents in the Lives of Joachim and Anna Catharine Senseman, and his son Gottlob Senseman, and his wife, Who were Missionaries among the North American Indians* (Philadelphia: Senseman & Son, Printers, 1881).

Seymour, Joseph, *The Pennsylvania Associators, 1747-1777* (Yardley, PA: Westholme, 2012).

Shannon, Timothy J., *Iroquois Diplomacy on the Early American Frontier* (New York: Viking, 2008).

Shimmell, Lewis S., *Border Warfare in Pennsylvania During the Revolution* (Harrisburg, PA: R.L. Myers, 1901).

Shorto, Russell, *The Island at the Center of the World* (New York: Doubleday, 2004).

Silver, Peter, *Our Savage Neighbors: How Indian War Transformed Early America* (New York: W.W. Norton, 2008).

Skaggs, David Curtis and Larry L. Nelson, eds., *The Sixty Years' War for the Great Lakes, 1754-1814* (East Lansing: Michigan State University Press, 2001).

Smith, William, *An Historical Account of the Expedition Against the Ohio Indians, in the Year MDCCLXIV under the Command of Henry Bouquet, ESQ* (Philadelphia: 1766).

Spangenberg, August Gottlieb, *The Life of Nicholas Lewis Count Zinzendorf* (London: Samuel Holdsworth, 1838).

Spero, Patrick, *Frontier Country: The Politics of War in Early Pennsylvania* (Philadelphia: University of Pennsylvania Press, 2016).

Spero, Patrick, *Frontier Rebels: The Fight for Independence in the American West, 1765-1776* (New York: W.W. Norton, 2018).

Sterner, Eric, "A Curious Trial on the Frontier: Zeisberger, Heckewelder, et al. vs. Great Britain," *Journal of the American Revolution*, June 5, 2018.

Sugden, John, *Blue Jacket: Warrior of the Shawnees* (Lincoln: University of Nebraska Press, 2000).

Taylor, James W., *History of the State of Ohio: First Period, 1650-1787* (Cincinnati: W. Derby, 1854).

Teachers and Friends of the Salem Home Sunday School, *A Brief History of the Moravian Church* (Winston-Salem, NC: Edwards & Broughton, 1909).

Thompson, Robert N., *Disaster on the Sandusky: The Life of Colonel William Crawford* (Staunton, VA: American History Press, 2017).

Thwaites, Reuben Gold, ed., Alexander Scott Withers, *Chronicles of Border Warfare* (Glendale, CA: Arthur H. Clark, 1895).

A True History of the Massacre of Ninety-six Christian Indians, at Gnadenhutten, Ohio, March 8th, 1782 (New Philadelphia, OH: Gnadenhutten Monument Society, 1870).

Trussell, John B. Jr., "The Sullivan and Brodhead Expeditions: Historic Pennsylvania Leaflet No. 41" (Harrisburg: Pennsylvania Historical and Museum Commission, 1976).

Van Every, Dale, *A Company of Heroes: The American Frontier, 1775-1783* (Endeavour Media, 2018).

Verbeek, J.W., *A Concise History of the Unitas Fratrum, or Church of the Brethren Commonly Called Moravians* (London: Mallalieu, 1862).

Wallace, Anthony F.C., *Teedyuscung: King of the Delawares 1700-1763*, reprint (Syracuse, NY: Syracuse University Press, 1990).

Wallace, Paul A.W., *Indians in Pennsylvania* (Harrisburg: Pennsylvania Historical and Museum Commission, 1961).

Weslager C.A., *The Delaware Indians: A History* (New Brunswick, NJ: Rutgers University Press, 1972).

White, Richard, *The Middle Ground: Indians, Empires, and Republics in the Great Lakes Region, 1650-1815* (Cambridge: Cambridge University Press, 2011).

Willett, William M., *Scenes in the Wilderness: Authentic Narrative of the Labours and Sufferings of the Moravian Missionaries among the North American Indians* (New York: G. Lane & P.P. Sandford, 1842).
Williams, Glenn F., *Dunmore's War: The Last Conflict of America's Colonial Era* (Yardley, PA: Westholme, 2017).
Wimer, James, *Events in Indian History* (Lancaster: G. Hills, 1841).
Winslow, Miron, *A Sketch of Missions; Or History of the Principal Attempts to Propogate Christianity Among the Heathen* (Andover: Flagu and Gould, 1819).

ACKNOWLEDGMENTS

Acknowledging someone else's contribution to your writing project always seems insufficient. I don't just want to acknowledge them but thank them and express my appreciation for the time and effort they took to make this book possible.

Don N. Hagist gave me a writing home at the *Journal of the American Revolution* and has always supported and encouraged various articles and projects I wanted to pursue. He thought Gnadenhutten would make a good book, which was enough for me to dig deeper before I worked up the courage to pitch it to the publisher. At Westholme, I owe thanks to Bruce H. Franklin, who liked the idea and patiently answered my questions throughout the process, even in the midst of a pandemic. Without the two of them, this book would never have seen the light of day. Nate Best did a great job copy editing the manuscript, as did Trudi Gershenov with the book jacket.

I also benefitted from the advice and assistance of several historians. Brady J. Crytzer has been leading the charge to rediscover the American Revolution on the Upper Ohio River and across the American frontier. In addition to his own work teaching, writing, and hosting the journal's podcast, Brady took some time to read a draft and offer advice. A few years ago, Rob Orrison and Phil Greenwalt invited me to join them and a cadre of historians building out the Emerging Revolutionary War blog. History has become my second career and it's been a lot of fun working with a younger crowd, from whom I always learn something. Rob and Phil also tackled early drafts and helped out with comments and suggestions. Thomas McCullough at the Moravian Archives was very helpful finding suitable images of David Zeisberger and John Heckewelder. Thanks to all. As ever, the remaining mistakes are mine.

In the summer of 2018, I had a chance to visit Gnadenhutten, Ohio, taking my mom, Reverend Connie Sterner, and daughter, Nicole, to see the village and the gravesites of some of the people in this book in nearby Goshen—most memorably David Zeisberger and the Delaware leader Gelelemend. Thanks mom and Nicole for letting me bend your ears for several hours in the car. Gnadenhutten has a small museum dedicated to the area's history, particularly the story of the Moravian missions and the massacre, but it's only open intermittently. While we were there on a beautiful summer day, one of the museum's staff interrupted his afternoon to open it for us and share his own knowledge of local history and the story of the mission. I foolishly forgot to ask his name, but in his honor I want to thank the people of Gnadenhutten who maintain the site and keep that museum functioning. It's important work.

Last, I need to thank my family. My daughters, Abigail and Nicole, give my wife and me a million reasons every day to be proud of them. They each have developed their own interests but don't roll their eyes too much when dad starts going off on tangents about his own history research and writing. Finally, and most importantly, I want to thank my wife, Suzy. On top of her busy and successful career, she is a wonderful wife and mother who keeps us all on track. Suzy made it possible for me to take a new path and was always there with support when I hit a roadblock. Thanks for saying yes all those years ago!

INDEX